This work is dedicated to those who want to love their Father back with all that is in them, and to my beautiful friend and companion.

For a fuller treatment of individual topics or issues the commentary notes address, please see www.thepeacefulrevolution.info

The Light of
the World

The life, words, teachings and true story of Jesus of Nazareth, the Freedom Giver and the Sure Way Home

The four 'gospels' books with commentary by a student of the Light, not by a 'bible scholar', ancient language expert, or popular religious leader.

By Tim Spiess

Revision 1.9
Re-Published June 2022

Table of Contents:

Page #

Description

Introduction: The Purpose of this Book 6

Introductory Concept: Every Person's Basic Need . 8

Recovering that which has been Lost 15

Human Beings Fundamental Problem: A Nature of 23
Self-Pride, Fear and Selfishness . . . .

Principles of Understanding what Jesus/Joshua 31
Says . . . .

The Re-Ordering of the Traditional Sequence of the 35
Four Books . . . .

Intro to the Gospel of John 36

The Gospel of John 39

Intro to the Gospel of Luke 110

The Gospel of Luke 114

Intro to the Gospel of Mark 194

The Gospel of Mark 197

Intro to the Gospel of Matthew 256

The Gospel of Matthew 259

Summary of Joshua's Truths 346

Two Basic and Clear Options 348

Suggested Test 350

Answers to Test 354

Falsehood, Lies and Destiny 361

Finding Eternal Life Amidst the Darkness 365

Primary Manifestations of Self-Pride and Fear and 369
Selfishness for the Average Christian . . . .

Two Enlightening Conversations 370

Religious Fear and Pride: An Impenetrable Wall . . . 378

The Great Religious Delusion 383

Perhaps Life's Most Important Question: 385
Am I Part of the Problem or Part of the Solution? . .

The Purpose of this Book

The purpose of this presentation of the first four books of the New Testament is to try to assist in recovering something extremely valuable that has been lost.

What extremely valuable thing has been lost?

Before we investigate what extremely valuable thing has been lost, let us first take a small but important digression. Most people are familiar with the expression, "you should not throw the baby out with the bathwater". It is an effective saying to teach the principle of not dismissing a true or valuable or important thing (the baby) that might be surrounded by, or associated with, false or valueless or unimportant things (the dirty bath water). I would ask the reader to please apply this principle to the person of Jesus (or Joshua) of Nazareth. In other words, before you throw the baby (Jesus of Nazareth) away with the bathwater (bible-christian-messianic beliefs and religion in his name), you ought to take a careful look at the baby. After all, what do you have to lose by reading Joshua's words, teaching and life story? It won't take you long to read, and you will be one of an increasingly few number of people on the earth who actually read his words and teachings.

This author would suggest that it is unfair to throw away 'the whole jesus religious thing' as irrelevant to your life or as 'a bunch of silly or hypocritical rubbish' without first giving his words and teachings a honest and fair read. It is also irrational to deny that the person known as "jesus christ" has had a very significant impact on both human history as well as countless millions of individuals. You should be curious as to **why**, and as a person that might be seeking truth, it would be unreasonable to avoid his own words in order to understand the very important 'why' question. Even if you are a skeptic or critic, if you don't read Jesus' own teachings, then at best you are a lazy and poor quality skeptic or critic who doesn't bother to go to the source of the object of your skepticism or criticism. Please, be a diligent skeptic or critic and search Jesus' teachings

6

YOURSELF for the faults and errors in his person or teachings that you assume account for the mess that covers much of the planet and is known as 'christianity' or bible based religious groups call 'the church'.

OK, let's end the first digression. So, what extremely valuable thing has been lost? Please allow me digress again before answering that question in order to briefly address those reading who have not seriously looked into the life and teachings of Jesus (or Joshua) of Nazareth. (This author will use "Joshua" instead of the popular "Jesus" in order to refer to the person who is the subject of the first four books of what is referred to as the "new testament". I do this because Joshua is a better translation of his name, and because of all the religious junk associated with the name "Jesus" or "Jesus Christ" or "Christ".)

Every Person's Basic Need

Every living person has hope in something because it has been proven time and time again that a person without any hope (some self-perceived purpose for their life-existence) will seek to destroy themselves through suicide or other destructive behavior in order to try and end the inner emptiness of life-level hopelessness. The reader should ask why that is. Why is it that human's alone (not animals) need a future reason for living (known as hope or purpose) or else they seek to dull or to end their existence?

What is your hope in dear reader?

Some 'better' material tomorrow…a better house, car, or vacation…a more 'successful' career? Is your hope in a better education and thus more opportunity to accumulate wealth or influence over other people? Is your hope in some better form of pleasing yourself or entertainment? Is it in the next movie or the newest electronic device that you believe is somehow going to make your life more meaningful? Is it in sporting events, challenges, vacations, hobbies or activities yet to come? Do you find your purpose in life through the primary work that you do? Is your hope in a person, like yourself, or a spouse, friend or partner? Is your hope in your family or children? Is your hope in religious beliefs or practices?

Has having your hope in any of these things ever satisfied your soul in a deeply meaningful and permanent way? Or does the pleasure of the pursuit or aurora of the lesser-hope fade as it passes, and you find yourself dissatisfied or somewhat empty until the next time? When you largely accomplish your goals associated with your hope or purpose, what happens then? Do you just pick up a new temporary one without thought to the fact that it too will end? Do you ever take the time to just sit back and ask the import questions of life like why am I here? What is the purpose of my life? What does my existence mean? If you don't, why do you think that is so? Are those not really important matters that deserve attention?

Looking at this important topic from another perspective, have you come to the sad place of believing you are nothing more than a random accumulation of molecules with no soul and little or no meaningful purpose? Or do you realize something fundamental is missing from your life? Have you come to the place of acknowledging that your own efforts to run your life are not working well? Have you come to the place of understanding that what is most important in life is relationships with other people? That whatever pain or stress or anxiety or conflict or frustration or failure you are experiencing normally has to do with how you are relating to other people or even how you are relating to yourself? Is there a right way and a wrong way to relate to people, and if so, where can I find that way or standard? Can I be rightly related to all the people that I know and thus be a nearly perfect person and have a justifiably clear conscience? Wouldn't that be wonderful?

Everyone has beliefs about what the purpose of their life is, including atheists (those who believe there is no God) and agnostics (those who believe one cannot know if God exists). Many atheists and agnostics are physicalists, meaning they believe a person's self-expression (or personality) can be accounted for by physics-chemical reactions alone – this author believes that is an un-reasonable belief. By definition, however, a physicalists purpose for their life must end when their life ends, and thus their hope can only be in temporary things listed previously which will undeniably end. They (and we) will die. Their body will decay and return to dust. In their belief, all the events, emotions, friendships, relationships, expressions of love and good in their life, all the special experiences they had and all the good things they accomplished – all will be gone forever, and perish with their death and the death of those who knew them...there will be nothing but the black, dark, void of existential destruction...for to lose something valuable is just like having it destroyed. This is hopelessness – a meaningless-ness to life that is typically denied

9

and buried under daily busyness, noise, entertainment and a denial of most things important – never peering over the edge of the approaching and undeniable event called death.

Most physicalists are relativists, meaning they believe there is no absolute truth. They say each person makes up their own reality. Is that true? No, because the relativist's clearest statement, like, "No absolute truth exists" is a self-defeating statement. That means that the laws of logic demonstrate that statement to be false. Can you see it? For if the relativist makes the statement, "no absolute truth exists", one only need ask them, 'is that statement absolutely true'? If they answer, 'yes', then at least one absolute truth exists and thus their statement is false. And if they answer, 'no', then they acknowledge the statement to be false. **It is undeniable that absolute truths exist, and it is reasonable to deduce that someone (a master Programmer?) created reason and logic to be based on absolute truth**.

The fact that it is undeniable that absolute truth exists - that everything is not relative according to a person's (or even a collective culture's) perspective or experiences - has a very significant implication. That implication is that it is possible (even reasonable) that a Creator of that absolute truth has an absolute standard of truth which human's will be held accountable to...or from another perspective, will set their after-death destiny by. For if we do have a metaphysical part (beyond being able to sense with our five senses) to our person (often referred to as a soul, spirit or personality), and that part does survive physical death, then what becomes of us? Dear reader, if you lost both your arms and legs and had your face badly disfigured, would that change who you really are? With medical sciences advancing, it is reasonably conceivable that if all that was left of you was your head, you could be kept alive. Would that change who you are? The reasonable answer is no, it would not. This is yet another proof that humans are more than just our physical bodies.

Is religion the place where I will find answers to these things, or can I find those answers somewhere else? What is the truth regarding these matters? To ignore those critical life questions and not seek answers is to live less than a full life...it is to refuse to take life's most important journey.

And this brings us to a person, **not a religion**, who said, "I am the Truth". No matter what you think about that claim, it is a very important claim that warrants investigation. While anyone (and many have) can make that claim, the same one who said that also defeated death, at least according to the four accounts of his life, and that makes his claim worthy of sincere investigation. No one else in human history defeated death in as genuine, authentic and validated way.

Religion in a general sense is human's attempt to understand the purpose of their existence – the why's of life. More specifically, religion is often people's attempt to be accepted by their God or god(s) so that when they die, their existence will continue typically in a more favorable manner than their existence has been on the earth.

From the student of Joshua's viewpoint, **religion is the things that people believe and do** in order to answer the why questions of life or to be accepted by their god(s), by means *other* than what Joshua has taught. Please re-read that carefully.

There are many religions and many people who hold to their religion's beliefs and practices. But there is only one person who – in a genuine, authentic way - defeated death to prove all he said and did is true, and he is not a religion! While this person has been wrongfully used to create religion, he not only does not support that religion, but he rebukes it and its practices time and time again in his teachings. **No, he doesn't rebuke bible-based christian religion's failures, hypocrisies, faults and abuses, but rather he rebukes the very essence, beliefs and practices which the religious leaders of the bible-based religious**

system build their kingdoms (or denominations or churches) on. If this is true, this should impact the reader.

You have no doubt heard of the person of Jesus of Nazareth (Joshua is a more accurate translation of his name than "Jesus"), the person that the christian religions claim as their figure head. But of all the hundreds of millions of people claiming to be some type of 'christian' or somehow claiming that 'Jesus Christ' is important to them, probably less than two percent have taken seriously the reading of his life and teachings, let alone trying to understand him or do what he says. If this is true, this should also peak your curiosity, for it certainly doesn't make sense. And perhaps this is one of the reasons for the obvious failures and powerlessness of bible or christian or church religion to change people towards the Standard of perfection that God has given mankind – the person of Joshua of Nazareth?

So, in your hands you have the Words of Joshua of Nazareth, the one who said, **"I am the Way (Home to your Father), I am the (absolute) Truth (that eternally matters), and I am Life (Everlasting)"**. He not only said that (for anyone can *say* that), but he performed many miracles, including defeating death, **to prove** that all he said and did was true, including what was just quoted.

No one else in history has done that.

Joshua addresses the most important questions of life, directly, head on, and gives clear answers. Can I have a Hope that will last? What is the purpose to my life? If I have a soul and it survives death, what becomes of me? What is true love, and can I experience that and live that out? Can I have proper relationships with all the people in my life? Can I have inner peace and joy in my life on the earth? Where can I get the power to change myself to be the way I know I ought to be? Is there a superior form of love, and if so, how can I experience it? Joshua answers all these questions and point's people to the source of power to change.

12

This author can testify to this truth. I was once chasing the American dream and all it entails, and to a large measure, I had attained it. However, that pursuit and it's 'success' only left me more empty, selfish and hopeless. People viewing my life from the outside would say how successful I was, but I knew the truth. One beautiful day, however, as my life was spiraling downward (even while people said I was climbing the ladder of success), I met the Person Joshua of Nazareth. I testify that he has changed my life in a way I could never have done myself, for I had not the wisdom nor the power to fix my broken and hopeless life. Empty and circular psychological beliefs or legally prescribed emotion controlling drugs are not the answer to your problems. Alcohol, drugs, busyness, materialism, entertainment-ism or other means to try and dull or hide the hopelessness are not the answer either.

So, dear reader, please don't be afraid to read and seek to understand Joshua of Nazareth's...he is NOT a religion, but rather a person like no other. And the chances are very good that the real Joshua of Nazareth is nothing like you have experienced through most christian or bible religious people...he is not the "Jesus Christ" of the christians/biblians or church people. He is not someone handing out free passes to 'heaven' to those who believe certain facts about him. Nor is he the God of wrath eager to punish the imperfect. Rather, he has the solution to your deepest need and is eager to provide it to you...he can clean your soul and bring your spirit alive!

Does YOUR life need fixing? What have you got to lose, and perhaps, you've got everything to gain?

Do you want true freedom? You can have it, but it does cost something. To gain the Life which you really need, you must be willing to forsake the temporary and that which this world (and yourself) considers valuable.

13

"He who loves his life loses it, and he who hates his life in this world will keep it to life eternal."

"If you continue in <u>*my word*</u>, then you are truly disciples of mine; and you will know the truth, and the truth will set you free."

May the Words of the Rescuer, the Freedom and Life Giver in the pages to come do their beautiful work in your life!

Recovering That Which Has Been Lost...

To those who think they know "Jesus Christ", the following illustrations will help you understand that which has been lost.

Imagine you were kidnapped and put in a horrible place, and other than the kidnapper, there was only one person on the planet who knew where you were. Fortunately, this person cared about you and although they were half way around the planet, they knew someone near you who could rescue you. So, they wrote a message to the prospective rescuer, telling him exactly where you were and how you could be rescued. They then mailed the message to the prospective rescuer. The message arrived safely at the remote post office, however the post office employee only delivered mail to the rescuer occasionally. So, he took the letter and placed it in a large envelope with many other letters to the rescuer, and on the outside of that envelope was written, "Important Messages". By the time the rescue letter was delivered to the rescuer, it was just one note among many hundreds in the large envelope labeled, "Important Messages". Therefore, your note was 'drowned' is a sea of other people's notes, and thus you had little hope of being free from your bondage any time soon if at all.

Here is another illustration to help you understand what has been lost.

Imagine you are stranded on a remote island with only one piece of paper, pen and bottle. So you write a note to tell those who find the bottle where you are and your situation and you throw the bottle into the ocean. The bottle finds a current which carries the bottle towards land, but there are thousands of other bottles in that current as well. It seems there were many people who, while not desperately needing to be rescued like yourself, never-the-less greatly enjoyed putting messages in bottles and throwing them in the ocean. Unfortunately for you, all those other bottles found their way to the same current which carried your bottle, and thus your bottle arrives at the beach with thousands of other like bottles containing 'urgent' (but pretend) messages. Thus, you have little hope of your message being found anytime soon, and little hope as well of getting free from the island.

Perhaps the most accurate illustration of that which has been lost, would be as follows. Let us say you wandered into a large and dangerous city and got yourself lost in a maze of streets, and you desperately need directions out of the city. Let us say that a person who knows the way out of the dangerous city has clearly and concisely written the directions down in two sentences on a page of paper. That person makes those clear directions available to any who request them and many groups and organizations of people take the directions and use them for their own purposes. In your case, the person you request the directions from is a member of one of those organizations, and they feel they need to add to the directions, even though they don't know for certain the way out of the city because they have never been out of the city. So they write, on a copy of the correct directions, *their* beliefs on how to get out of the city. And so, when you are handed the one page document, the two sentences containing the way to freedom are surrounded by many sentences which contain errors and which at best confuse you and at worst, hide the truth in the two sentences of the way out of the dangerous city. Thus, you don't find your way out of the dangerous city because in your sincere efforts to read the directions, you get more and more lost due to the errors surrounding the fact.

To continue that illustration, let us say that many people regularly get lost in the large and dangerous city, and so there is a regular need for clear directions out of the city. However, the main authority of the city benefits economically from having more people in their city, even if some are lost and don't want to be there. The paper with the two sentences of clear directions becomes well known amongst the city dwellers, as well as the one page that contains both the two sentences of clear directions surrounded by the erroneous opinions of others. The city authority wants to give to those people lost in their city, the confused one full page of 'directions' instead of the two clear sentences out, since they gain city members and make more money that way. So that authority formally makes a diligent practice of telling the people that the one page document is one-hundred percent truth and they ought to believe all that is written on that page. They also tell the people that the page with the two clear sentences of correct directions is 'inadequate and incomplete' and people should not rely solely on that document or its instructions. Now, if a person looking to escape the city respects that authority-person more than wanting to know truth (correct directions), then what will happen to their ability to find their way out of the city? Will it not be compromised at best, or destroyed at worst? If disagreeing with the authority will have uncomfortable consequences, or even cost the person something they value, won't they be in even a worse situation to find the truth buried in that one page?

One final step to complete the illustration...

In the same way, what if there is a book which contains sixty-six chapters, and only four of the sixty-six chapters contain what you need to be set free. And what if an authority that many people respect including yourself, and who claims to know the book better than you, tells you that all sixty-six chapters contain the truth that you need to be set free. And what if they tell you that the four chapters which contain what you need to be set free are "inadequate and insufficient" in-and-of themselves? If you respect the authority more than wanting to know the truth, then what will happen to your ability to find the actual truth in the four chapters? Will it not be compromised at best, or destroyed at worst? And what if the cost of rejecting the authority's beliefs about the book will mean you will be rejected by friends and family? Perhaps you will pretend the dangerous city is not so bad after all? Or perhaps you will believe that the dangerous city or places just like it, is all that is available on the earth? Or perhaps you actually like some aspects of the dangerous city and thus you are not looking to be set free since you see no need to be?

This brings us to that which is most valuable and has been lost.

What if there was a man who said...

> "*__I am__* the Way, **the Truth** and the Life, and no one gets to the Father except through me."

...and...

> "If you continue in *__My word__*, then you are truly disciples of mine; and you will know the truth, and **the truth** will *__set you free__*."

...and he performed many miracles including defeating death to prove what he said was true...

...but other's come along after he leaves and place his Words in a big book with many other people's words and say, 'this whole book is truth', not just the person who says, "I am the truth"...

...and the religious authorities who like having authority over others say, 'you need more than the red letters, you need the whole counsel of God's Word, and you need us to understand it'...

...and as years, decades and centuries pass, the book is handed down from generation to generation, each generation before it saying that the whole book is the truth that people need. And if a person can't understand the book due to the errors and contradictions, the people's religious leaders say, "well, you need us or christian leader so-and-so or bible scholar so-and-so to properly understand the book"...

...and the religious leaders, whose authority the people respect, point people to the book as well as many other voices, both dead and living, in addition to the one who says, "I am the truth", and they say, "the book and all these other voices which quote the book are "the truth" you need to be set free, not just the one who says, "I am the Truth" ... not just the one who says, "If the Son sets you free, you will be free indeed"...

18

If this happened, then isn't the truth of the statements above by the one who says, "**I am** the truth", LOST as the people look to the book and other's words and other voices, and those other words and voice's nullify, cancel or make of no effect the one who says:

> "*I am* the Way, **the Truth** and the Life...", and "All who are of the truth listen to **MY voice**." ?

If this is so, then is it not true that those eternally valuable truths...

> **"I am the Way, the Truth and the Life, and no one gets to the Father except through me."**

> **"If you continue in *My word*, then you are truly disciples of Mine; and you will know the truth, and the truth will set you free."**

...have been drowned out ... buried ... LOST.

And so, that which is extremely valuable - and which has been lost - has been revealed. The Creator/Father sent One beloved, error-free Messenger who can bring freedom from your hopelessness, confusion, bondage or pain, but his voice has been drowned out, nullified, hidden, obscured, spoken over, made-of-no-effect, ignored...

Lost.

It is a difficult truth to receive, but in truth, the teachings of the One who calls himself the Light of the world have been covered, buried and for all practical purposes, lost. His Voice has been drowned out by thousands of other voices. In fact, at the most essential level, his Voice has been replaced by a book, 'the Bible', by a clever slight-of-hand which says that *the book* IS (or accurately represents) his voice.

His statement, "**All who are of the truth listen to MY voice**", has been changed (and thus corrupted) to, 'All who are of the truth listen to the bible' with all its millions of words and its many

19

contradictory concepts, accounts and teachings. Perhaps the reader has believed the lie that the bible has no contradictions? Here are just a few of many:

"If I sharpen My flashing sword,
And My hand takes hold on justice,
I will render vengeance on My adversaries,
And I will repay those who hate Me.
'I will make My arrows drunk with blood,
And My sword will devour flesh,
With the blood of the slain and the captives,
From the long-haired leaders of the enemy.'
"Rejoice, O nations, with His people;
For He will avenge the blood of His servants,
And will render vengeance on His adversaries,
And will atone for His land and His people." (Deut. 32:41-43)

"There is none like the God of Jeshurun,
Who rides the heavens to your help,
And through the skies in His majesty.
"The eternal God is a dwelling place,
And underneath are the everlasting arms;
And He drove out the enemy from before you,
And said, 'Destroy!' (Deut. 33:26-27)

"Do I not hate those who hate You, O LORD? And do I not loathe those who rise up against you? I hate them with the utmost hatred; they have become my enemies." (Psalms 139:21-22)

Versus

"You have heard that it was said, 'YOU SHALL LOVE YOUR NEIGHBOR and **hate your enemy**.' "But I say to you, **love your enemies** and pray for those who persecute you, so that you may be sons of your Father who is in heaven; for He causes His sun to rise on the evil and the good, and sends rain on the righteous and the unrighteous. (Matthew 5:43-45)

One can pretend there is no contradiction, but that only proves that one is NOT listening to the one who says, "I am the Truth". Paul's teaching of all scripture being inspired by God has God inspiring Moses to bring violent vengeance on his enemies, and David to express his justified hatred for his enemies. Contrast that to the voice of truth which says, "Love your enemies".

And so, the time for the printing of this book is quite long overdue. It should be curious to the reader that there are no similar books easily available given the thousands of books *about* "christ" and many dozens of bible versions available. Why is it that so very few are concerned about focusing whole-heartedly on Jesus and **his** person and **his** teachings ONLY? Perhaps, just perhaps, these things are true...

> **"This is the judgment, that the Light has come into the world, and men loved the darkness rather than the Light, for their deeds were evil."**

> **"But because I speak the truth, you do not believe me."**

Maybe the truth is that the one Voice that brings freedom, offends the vast majority (especially the religious people who claim him as their 'Lord' and 'God'), and they do not want to let his simple and uncompromised truth shine forth? Perhaps most christians/biblians are especially loath to turn to the Light because they very much like believing they are "saved" and "heaven bound" while they continue to ignore the real Light of the world and instead live the way they want?

...beware of the all too common self-justification and self-deception of, 'oh yes, that is true, but not of ME or MY church'...

This commentator hopes that those who are in the darkness of bible and christian religion will allow the Light of the world to shine on their hearts. Seek to understand this key saying of his...

"He who loves his life loses it, and he who hates his life in this world will keep it to life eternal."

...and then, please, come, follow HIM!

Human Beings Fundamental Problem: A Nature of Self-Pride, Fear and Selfishness

Examples from the physical realm: Asking a physically blind person to look at a sunset and appreciate its beauty is irrational - they don't have the capacity to do that. Asking a crippled person who cannot walk to please walk to the store and get some milk, is irrational - they don't have the capacity to do that.

An example from the metaphysical intellectual realm: To ask a five year old child to read and understand Einstein's advanced works on the theory of relatively, is irrational - they don't have the capacity to do that.

An example from the metaphysical moral realm: Asking a person - who is bound up in bitterness towards another person who they believe has wronged them and is the source of their bitterness – to immediately forgive the offender, is irrational - they don't have the capacity to do that.

An example from the metaphysical spiritual realm: Asking a person to seriously and sincerely listen to Joshua/Jesus of Nazareth when they have not placed their faith in him, is irrational – they don't have the capacity to do that. Oh, they can play a game in the intellectual realm and learn many things about Joshua in their mind, but they will not listen to him, nor believe him nor do what he says because they don't have the capacity - faith. Unlike the physical limitation examples above, in this case, the capacity can be chosen or rejected by our free will…we have a choice.

We, as human beings, have limitations. More importantly, we have aspects to our nature that 'cripple' us or 'blind' us or make us far less than what we were intended to be. The three aspects to our normal human nature that bind us and blind us and seek to control us are **self-pride, fear and selfishness**. I challenge the reader to look at the conflict and human-caused wrongness in the world – including the conflict and wrongness that is occurring in **your** life with those you interact with or have relationships with – and find the

23

root cause of the conflict or wrongness. If you do this well, you will arrive - in the vast majority of the cases - at self-pride, and fear and selfishness as the root causes of the wrongness or conflict or hurt.

If we cannot find a way to overcome those three things, we will be part of humanity's problem rather than part of the solution no matter how much our self-pride will spur us to object to the contrary. Said another way, if we are guided by self-pride or fear or selfishness, we simply are not good people as Joshua defines a good person. Ironically and sadly, self-pride will usually prevent us from admitting this simple truth!

What is self-pride? It is believing at the person level, that I am more valuable, more important, more 'enlightened', more worthy or better than other people. Or, that I am a person who has most important things about life figured out better than most people, which results in an unwillingness to learn or consider new beliefs. Or that I deserve more good things than other people. Or that I am more worthy to get this thing – material thing, power, authority, etc. – than others. Here are some examples of how people - who are making decisions or treating others based upon self-pride - think or express themselves.

- 'I am not going to listen to you because I believe I already have a better understanding of the topics you would like to discuss'.
- 'You can't be part of this team/group because you are not worthy or don't have anything significantly valuable to contribute.'
- 'I am just better than you – a have such and such a degree or I scored this on this test, etc. - and thus you ought to so what I say.'
- 'I've already looked into that and I believe I have the answers or the answers cannot be known so I don't want to waste my time talking about that.' (this could also be fear)
- 'Are you going to tell me you know more than that famous subject matter expert? Who are you?' (this could also be fear)
- 'We are just better than you and thus you ought to submit to us or do what we think is good and right.'

24

- 'You ought to just give us that (land, material things, power over others) because we deserve it for these reasons and you don't, and if you don't we are justified in taking it from you forcefully.
- 'Why am I a leader - manager / executive / minister / senator / bishop / captain, etc.? Because I deserve it and am more worthy than you.'
- 'Why would I want to do that…that is beneath me.'
- 'You want me to consider befriending that person? You must be kidding.'
- 'You believe what about God? I have been through seminary and thus I am better equipped to know what is true…'
- 'The people elected/chose me and thus it proves I am more worthy than you to be a leader.'
- 'I've got a bachelor's degree (or masters or doctorate) in that area so who are you to question my knowledge in that area?'
- 'You didn't even attend college…what makes you think you can make a significant contribution to this discussion or work?'
- 'Oh, I would never do or say that to someone…'
- 'You think you are right about everything.'
- 'I am popular, you are not, thus you don't deserve the things I get due to my popularity'.
- 'Don't you know that people with my skin color are just naturally more beautiful people?'.
- 'You have not been to college? Oh well, I guess you won't do much with your life'.
- 'Our church is the largest, most successful church in the city so we are receiving God's blessings more than others'.
- 'My pastor graduated at the top of his class at Ivory Tower Seminary so you really ought to listen to him about God – I mean who are you to question him?'.
- 'Don't you know that I am from the United States, and we have the best nation on the planet?'
- 'I've had all these experiences so you ought to listen to me.'
- 'Oh, my child(ren) did this or that…they accomplished this or that…they are the president of this or that…they are a doctor or a lawyer…' (women often express this vicarious

self-pride, and the unstated thought is, 'because I am such a wonderful parent' or 'didn't we produce a wonderful child')
- 'Oh, I need to post that I went to the bathroom on Facebook because I am so important and all my 'friends' need to know about all the important things I did today.'
- 'Oh, that poor soul...he has so few material things'.
- 'God has blessed us with all this money, and so we must be doing things right in his sight'.

And perhaps the greatest self-deception and self-pride blindness...

- 'I'm not afraid of anything' or 'fear doesn't affect me'.

Of course, there are clever ways to soften or sugar coat the above utterances, but that cleverness or political correctness does not change the fact, no matter how 'humbly' those things might be stated or thought.

Self-pride is one of the great darknesses the people of the earth are captured in.

What is fear? It is a perception that something I value is at risk of being lost, damaged or destroyed. Here are some examples of how people who are making decisions based upon fear think or express themselves.

- 'I can't leave him – I know he treats me badly, but I am afraid of the unknown...at least I know where I stand here.'
- 'But if I give that away, I might not have enough...'
- 'I can't walk away from that job...I might end up on the street...'
- 'I am not going to make that decision because I am afraid I might lose this or that...'
- 'If I say that true or right thing, then I am afraid people will not like me any more...'
- 'I can't believe that about God because I am afraid I will be rejected from the comfortable social circles I am part of...'
- 'I can't do (or say that, or believe that) because these people whose approval I value will no longer accept me...'

- 'But if I don't treat that person this way, I am afraid I will not get what I want from them...' (also selfishness)
- 'I'm not going to give up control of those people because I am afraid I will be worthless without it...'
- 'If I change in that way, I don't know what my life will be like and I am afraid of change or what it might bring...'
- 'I simply do not want to consider that because I fear what it might mean...'
- 'I'm just not going to go there...'
- 'I am not generous because I must save up for retirement or else I won't have adequate funds for the last years of my life.'
- 'There is no way I am going to believe that, because if I believe that, that means all these people I love or respect are wrong and I can't face that possibility and what that would mean.'
- 'I need the material security that my parent's provide so I can't believe or do that even though it is right because they will punish or reject me...'
- 'Jesus can't mean that...that would mean I need to....'
- 'I am afraid to change because I don't know what that will mean for the way I want to live my life.'
- 'All those people can't be wrong...I am afraid to consider that possibility and its implications.'
- 'I'm afraid if I don't look like that, I will not be attractive to others.'
- 'Jesus can't mean that...that would mean these people I esteem would be wrong and that would mean...'
- 'If I don't please that person, they will reject me and then what?'
- 'If I don't get that job, I'll be out on the street.'
- 'There is just no way I will consider that.'
- 'If I am wrong about that, I might be wrong about some other important things and that will mean...'

Fear is one of the great darknesses the people of the earth are captured by.

What is selfishness? It is believing that my wants are more important than others…or stated another way, I am not going to take actions that cause me to lose something I consider valuable…my decisions are going to be based on what I gain or get out of it. Here are some examples of how people who are making decisions or treating others based upon selfishness think or express themselves.

- 'I know you think that is a good idea, but what do I get out of it?'
- 'If there is nothing in it for me/us, then it just doesn't make sense to pursue it…'
- 'Why should I give that away, are you crazy?'
- 'If I don't take care of myself, who will?'
- 'I need my personal space, for that is only good and right and you ought to respect that…'
- 'I only have one life to live, and I am going to live it to its fullest and that means having fun and spending money on myself…'
- 'Hey, we deserve this…'
- 'That seems like the right thing to do - look at what we lose if we don't do that…'
- 'I have to look after number one…'
- 'I just have to do what it takes in order to get what I want…I cannot be concerned about its impact on others…'
- 'I deserve some personal time…that other person is going to have to take care of themselves…'
- 'I know it seems selfish, but if you really look at it, it is for the greater good…'
- 'I worked hard for that and so I have no obligation to share it with others…'
- 'It's a dog-eat-dog world – you need to take care of yourself…'
- 'Sometimes, we just have to take care of ourselves and trust God to take care of the other person…'
- 'Don't call me selfish – I am just living out survival of the fittest…'
- 'At the end of the day, if I don't take care of myself, no one else will…'

28

- 'It all depends upon your perspective…maybe taking from others is what will be best for them in the end…'
- 'If I do that small task, then the others whose job it is to do it will likely lose their jobs…I create work for people.'

These examples are merely a small sampling of statements and justifications that are **thought and uttered billions – perhaps trillions - of times each day in various forms by the people of the earth**. Perhaps you have made statements like these or have thought them?

Self-pride and fear and selfishness oftentimes work together to keep us blind, in darkness and unable to advance on becoming a better human being. For example, if I am afraid to go on a boat due to my fear of drowning, I might say to the person who is offering to take me on a boat, 'well, I really don't care for that type of boat'. Self-pride prevents me from admitting my fear, and causes me to provide an excuse rather than admit the simple truth that I am afraid of drowning. The person might have a good reason to take me on the boat – perhaps to transfer me to an island where I could help people – but my fear causes my pride to provide an excuse for my selfishness!

Self-pride and fear and selfishness are 'enemies' of two very important aspects to human life – love and reason. All three work against our ability to love other people. And all three work against reason to determine what is true and right. And without practicing love and reason and it's fruit, acting rightly, we are truly falling short of being what we were intended to be as human beings…we are failing at life itself!

The simple truth is that people who live according to their natural nature of self-pride or fear or selfishness are the reason and cause for most of the suffering, coldness, injustice, pain, neglect, discord, conflict, abuse and violence – in short, loveless-ness - that occurs in the world each day. I challenge the reader to think this through and consider the possibility that **you are part of the problem rather than part of the solution**…and then ask, 'how can I overcome and be free of my nature of self-pride and fear and selfishness and the hurt that causes other people?'

Can you really experience this world and watch the news and say, "Oh, people are doing well"? Is your standard so low (or in reality you have no standard to judge such things), or are you in such a self-made bubble of self-pride and/or fear and/or selfishness that you refuse to see things how they really are? Perhaps your standard to judge how YOUR life is going is, "If I am comfortable, well fed and entertained, all is well in the world". That kind of thinking is the epitome of a selfish life…a life with no consideration for others…a life lived in the darkness of self-pride and fear and selfishness…a life without any or very little true love…a 'life' that will lead to self-condemnation and destruction…a 'life' that forfeits Life everlasting.

Is that the kind of life you want to live? Do you really want to miss the most important aspect to human life? Are you really sure there is no one who will hold us accountable for how we live the life we are given? Are you certain that by ignoring and denying the Standard we were given you will be excused from being accountable? Do you really want to reject reason and thus deny the simple truths in this section? I urge you not to do that and instead have a truly open mind, meaning you are not afraid to consider new things…meaning that you are not afraid to look at the Light…

Principles of Understanding what Jesus/Joshua Says:

1. **Give Joshua an open, honest, innocent read.**

If we approach Joshua and his teaching as a child that really wants to hear what he has to say, then we will hear what he has to say. Try not to listen primarily with your intellect, but rather with your heart. Young children don't question a mature adult's teachings. If you are truly open-minded, then you will give Joshua the best part of that open-mindedness. This is the most important principle for hearing and understanding Joshua and his teachings.

See supporting principle in Matt. 11:25.

2. **Only Joshua knows for certain the reasons or answers to the 'why' questions of what he said and did, therefore listen to him only to understand him.**

Nobody knows Joshua better than Joshua, so listen to HIS words and teachings only. Only he knows for certain the "why" behind what he said, taught or did. The book author's – like Matthew, Mark, Luke & John – recorded what Joshua said and did, but they had their own religious beliefs through which they viewed Joshua. There are many examples of the book author's not having a proper understanding of what Joshua was trying to convey due to their bringing what THEY wanted to hear versus letting HIM shape their beliefs. For example, see Luke 9:54. Avoid the second greatest error of listening to others tell you what THEY think Joshua means, instead of listening to Joshua in context to understand Joshua.

See supporting principle in Matt. 11:27 & 17:5.

3. **Read things in context.**

Without context, things are easily distorted. For example, Joshua says, "I came that they may have life, and have it abundantly." This saying is very often used by those who love money and material things to justify a selfish, materialistic life. They twist that saying to mean God wants people to be materially wealthy. That saying was taken from John 10, and in context, that saying has absolutely nothing to do with having material wealth. Rather it is clearly a contrast between one who seeks to bring death and the only Good Shepherd/Pastor who brings life – the Life he speaks of elsewhere in John 4:14.

4. **Try and adjust your understandings to Joshua's view of the important things of life instead of trying to force Joshua to fit your understandings of the important things of life.**

You can 'approach' Joshua in two basic ways. You can bring your religious and/or spiritual and/or life and/or moral beliefs to him and try and use his teachings to sort through your beliefs. Or, you can try and start with a clean slate and allow him to give you your beliefs about God and mankind (or at least sincerely consider his teaching without undo bias). The latter method is the one that will allow you to hear what he says. The former method will, at a minimum, hide things he wants to convey, and at worst, prevent you from understanding perhaps the most important things he has to say.

See supporting principles in John 14:6 & Matt. 24:35

5. **Just because Joshua went to the Jewish people does not mean he endorses all their religious beliefs and practices.**

Joshua came to a religious people, the Jews. They had many religious beliefs and practices that were interwoven into their culture. Joshua taught the people the eternal truths and principles he wanted and without unnecessarily offending their religious beliefs. Therefore, he did not address those things which he viewed as not interfering with his primary teachings. He certainly did, however, address those religious beliefs and practices which interfered with his primary teachings, and this is what angered the religious leaders so much. Joshua was killed because he contradicted the religious leader's beliefs about who God is, what He is like, and what He wants. For example, God does not care about keeping a day (the revered sabbath) but He is very concerned about people loving one another.

See supporting principle in Mark 7: 1-13; John 8:31-32.

6. **Just because Joshua visited a certain place or was present at a particular event does not mean he endorses the traditions of that place or the religious beliefs or practices associated with that place or event.**

Because Joshua went to that area of the earth – what people currently call 'the middle east' - does not mean he does not care about the other people of the earth. Because Joshua visited the places people used to 'worship' or engage in their religion - like the Jewish synagogue or temple - does not mean he wants people to congregate in synagogues or temples. Because Joshua was present during certain religious feast days of the Jews does not me he advocates, approves or teaches they ought to be observed. **All it means is that he went where people were congregating to try and reach them with his message**...Joshua was regularly thrown out of, or forced to leave, the places of religious practices. God is not constrained to a particular people group, but rather "loves the people of the earth" (John 3:16). This author's opinion is that God sent his messenger to Israel because He knew His Son's life and teachings would be accurately recorded, preserved and propagated that way.

See supporting principles in Luke 4:28-30; 20:9-16.

7. **Just because Joshua mentioned in his teachings certain famous or revered people of the Jew's history or recorded in their scripture does not mean he says to look to those people to understand his Father.**

For example, Joshua did speak about Moses, but he certainly does not point to Moses as someone to look to in order to know God or what God wants. See Matt. 5 to make this abundantly clear as he corrects Moses' unfulfilled, incomplete and imperfect view of what God wants of people.

See supporting principle in Matt. 5:21-44; 12:38-42 .

8. **Joshua's commands, directives and instructions are plainly given. A command, directive or instruction is a simple saying of the nature, "You ought to do this" or "Don't do that". A very important directive or instruction that he is especially concerned about is preceded by something like, "This command I give you...".**

A primary error people make is to turn something that is not a command or directive, into a command or directive. For example, Joshua says in regard to the sabbath, "The sabbath was made for man, and not man for the sabbath. So the Son of Man is Lord even of the sabbath." This is clearly not an instruction or directive, let alone a command. His point in context is clear. Moses gave the sabbath for people to rest, not for men to be ruled by a day. And Joshua is over – not ruled by - even their beloved day/sabbath. Yet those who seek to have Joshua affirm their religious day, will say this saying is a "command" of his to observe the sabbath. Clearly it is not. Rather, it is a teaching of his regarding his position to something, in this case a revered religious day, the sabbath- and he is a ruler over this thing not given by God, but rather by Moses.

34

The Re-Ordering of the Traditional Sequence of the Four Books:

Most bibles order the four gospel books at the beginning of the New Testament as follows – Matthew, Mark, Luke & John. As a disciple of Joshua, I believe that ordering is sub-optimal for the following reasons.

The gospel of John has the richest content in terms of Joshua speaking to his disciples and his direct explanations about his teachings to them. The other books have more of Joshua speaking to the people in general. John also provides a larger context to the readers than the other four books. In other words, John recorded more of Joshua's sayings which transcended the Jewish culture or that region of the world. In John, Joshua speaks more about human beings in general and our place in this world than the other authors provide.

I place the gospel of Luke next due to his not being Jewish and thus not having to overcome Jewish religious belief baggage biasing his thoughts.

I place the gospel of Mark next due to the simplicity of his account.

I list Matthew last due to what I believe was his Jewish religious belief bias. It seems to me that Matthew had the most difficultly understanding Joshua's teachings due to his upbringing and training in the Jewish religion of the day.

The Life and Words of Joshua* of Nazareth According to John:

* Joshua is a more accurate translation of what has been traditionally translated "Jesus"

Basic Book Introduction:
Distinguish between the Author and his Subject

The author is believed to be Joshua's disciple John, who lived and traveled with Joshua for over three years as Joshua brought his message to the world, starting with the people of Israel.

John, the assumed author of this book, no doubt had most things correct about Joshua since he was with him and taught by him for over three years. This author believes that he accurately remembered and wrote down what Joshua said and did (John 14:26). However, the reader must understand the distinction between his accurately recording what Joshua said and did versus his having a *perfect understanding* of what Joshua said and did. For example, a person can see a man running down a street in an urgent fashion yelling 'fire'. The person witnessing the man running can accurately identify the time and place and other facts associated with the event, but the witness cannot know for sure **why** the man is running and yelling 'fire'.

In like manner, let the reader understand, all men, including the men who were with Joshua (and including this commentator) - had beliefs, religious baggage so to speak – that hindered them from having a perfect understanding of Joshua and his purpose. They, like us, had minds containing things (particularly religious things) which are not from Joshua, which things they could not reconcile with some of the things Joshua said (one example is Acts 1:6), **even while they accurately recorded what he said and did. Therefore, the reader should place full confidence in Joshua and his Words only, in terms of having as close to a perfect understanding of Joshua as is possible**. This is only reasonable as no one but Joshua could have a perfect understanding of Joshua. While John's narrative and commentary (in contrast to Joshua's own words and teachings) is almost certainly accurate in regard to historical details of the circumstances of Joshua's Life, only the Words of Joshua alone should have the reader's full trust in regard to **understanding Joshua and his purposes...revealing the 'why's' regarding Joshua's words and actions**. To assist the reader in this endeavor, Joshua's words are **in bold** in this publishing of John's book.

This commentator's comments are *italicized* and either contained in parenthesis or preceded by a superscripted number. Sections of text that are in title case (where the first letter of each word in a phrase or sentence is capitalized e.g. Thus Said the Lord), are quotes of the old testament scripture.

The purpose of this commentator's comments is threefold. First, is to try and define terms according to Joshua's own usage in the four gospels and to do so using simpler or clarified terms or phrases that avoid religious vocabulary. This is necessary for readers with little or no exposure to concepts they have not encountered before or terms or concepts that have been given an incorrect meaning through current religious culture. For example, an important concept – "religious leaders" - has been hidden by using the name of a specific religious sect's leadership, the "Pharisees". The modern reader will have little idea what "Pharisees" were, but they can certainly grasp the concept, "religious leaders", which is exactly what the Pharisees were.

An example of a term that has been modified by current religious culture would be "prophet". This term has come to mean in the current religious culture, a person who foretells future events. The term as Joshua uses it, simply means someone who speaks God's truths.

Second, is to bring to the reader's attention the important teachings of Joshua which are nullified (cancelled out, or made of no effect)

37

by contradictions with other passages in the bible or by contemporary religious teaching. This is not exhaustive, but rather brings to light the contradictions which, in this commentator's opinion, nullify some of the more important teachings of Joshua.

Third, is to 'clear the dirt off his person and sayings', so to speak, for those who want to hear but have been confused or deceived by the myriad of other voices that claim they understand Joshua better than Joshua understands Joshua. For those people who participate in the religious system, perhaps the most commonly used mantra of the bible based religious system's leadership is, "Jesus doesn't mean that...you need us, your educated clergy, to understand what Jesus really meant". This commentator has news for you – Jesus does mean that! No, I don't mean that you turn figurative language into literal language, like when he says, "if your right eye causes you to sin, rip it from your head". Rather, I am referring to his teachings that go against human kind's normal inclination or that challenge some aspect of the way I am living. For example, the simple teaching, "love your enemies". Yes, it does mean that...no, joining a military and killing the 'enemy' cannot be reconciled with "love your enemies". You may not like what Joshua has to say, but let him say it and don't twist his words. After all, if Joshua is who he says he is, we would do well to listen.

This book opens with John writing about who he believes Joshua is, as well as what he understood Joshua did prior to, and in coming to, the earth. We pick right up at the beginning of the book.

Beginning of the Book:

(1:1) In the beginning was the Word, and the Word was with God, and the Word was God ('s Son).[*1][*2] (2) He was in the beginning with God. (3) All things came into being through him, and apart from him nothing came into being that has come into being. (4) In him was life, and the life was the Light of men. (5) The Light shines in the darkness, and the darkness did not comprehend it.

(6) There came a man sent from God, whose name was John (the baptist). (7) He came as a witness, to testify about the Light, so that all might believe through him. (8) He was not the Light, but he came to testify about the Light.

[*1] *Please note the most important thing about this passage is that it is not Joshua's words. Most translations end the first verse with a contradiction e.g. "the Word was with God...and the Word was God". Using Joshua's own teachings and sayings, he himself did not teach that he and his Father were the same person/being, therefore it appears either John came to believe this after Joshua left or the verse was altered at some point due to a trinitarian bias. The trinity doctrine serves to keep the 'lay people' dependent upon the religious leaders to understand the kingdom of God since the doctrine teaches that three equals one, a contradiction which no one can understand since it breaks a basic rule of logic. If 3 = 1 in God's kingdom, then we need people who say they understand that type of 'truth' to explain God's kingdom to us - and the religious leaders are only too quick to fill that role and thus usurp Joshua as our Teacher and Leader. For a full explanation of why the trinity doctrine is false, see http://www.thepeacefulrevolution.info/trinity.html*

[*2] *What is crystal clear from this passage is that "the Word" is Joshua of Nazareth, NOT the bible! See also verse 14 below and Luke 1:1.*

(9) There was the true Light which, coming into the world (*context clarifies definition: world in this sense would mean "earth"*), enlightens every man. (10) He was in the world, and the world was made through him, and the world (*the people of the earth*) did not know him. (11) He came to his own (*the descendants of Jacob or*

Israel, known as the Jews), and those who were his own did not receive him. (12) But as many as received him, to them he gave the right to become children of God, even to those who believe in his name, (13) who were born, not of blood nor of the will of the flesh nor of the will of man, but of God.*3

*3 *See John chapter three for "born of God".*

(14) And the Word (*of God, Joshua*) became flesh (*a human being*), and dwelt among us, and we saw his glory, glory as of the only spiritually birthed directly from the Father, full of favor towards others and truth. (15) John (*the baptist*) testified about him and cried out, saying, "This was he of whom I said, 'He who comes after me has a higher rank than I, for he existed before me.'" (16) For of his fullness we have all received, and favor after favor. (17) For the law was given through Moses; favor and truth were realized through Messiah (*"Messiah" means the anointed One who delivers people out of something bad*) Joshua.

(18) No one has seen God at any time*4 ; the only begotten Son who is in the bosom of the Father, he has revealed the Father. (19) This is the testimony of John (*the baptist*), when the Jews sent to John religious men from Jerusalem to ask him, "Who are you?" (20) And he confessed and did not deny, but confessed, "I am not the Messiah." (21) They asked him, "What then? Are you Elijah?" And he said, "I am not." "Are you the Prophet?" And he answered, "No." (22) Then they said to him, "Who are you, so that we may give an answer to those who sent us? What do you say about yourself?" (23) He said, "I am A VOICE OF ONE CRYING IN THE WILDERNESS, 'MAKE STRAIGHT THE WAY OF THE LORD,' as Isaiah the prophet (*a prophet is a person who spoke God's truths, especially of future events*) said."

*4 *This teaching would contradict the trinitarian doctrine as Joshua was seen and thus was not God (see also John 4:24, "God is spirit").*

(24) Now they who had been sent from the religious leaders (25) asked him, and said to him, "Why then are you baptizing, if you are not the Messiah, nor Elijah, nor the Prophet?" (26) John answered them saying, "I baptize in water, but among you stands One (*Joshua*) whom you do not know. (27) "It is he who comes after me, the laces of whose sandal I am not worthy to untie." (28) These things took place in Bethany beyond the Jordan, where John was baptizing.

(29) The next day John saw Joshua coming to him and said, "Behold, the Lamb of God (*a phrase/description reflecting a deeply held Jewish religious belief regarding sacrifice*) who takes away the sin of the world! (30) "This is he on behalf of whom I said, 'After me comes a Man who has a higher rank than I, for he existed before me.' [*5] (31) "I did not recognize him, but so that he might be manifested (*revealed*) to Israel, I came baptizing in water." (32) John testified saying, "I have seen the Spirit descending as a dove out of heaven, and He remained upon him. (33) "I did not recognize him, but He who sent me to baptize in water said to me, 'He upon whom you see the Spirit descending and remaining upon him, this is the One who baptizes in the Holy Spirit.' (34) "I myself have seen, and have testified that this is the Son of God.[*6]

[*5] *See John 8:58 regarding "existed before me".*
[*6] *Another confession that contradicts the trinity doctrine, for John did not say, "...this is God" but rather, "this is the Son of God".*

(35) Again the next day John was standing with two of his disciples, (36) and he looked at Joshua as he walked, and said, "Behold, the Lamb of God!" (37) The two disciples heard him speak, and they followed Joshua. (38) And Joshua turned and saw them following, and said to them, "**What do you seek?**" They said to him, "Rabbi (which translated means Teacher), where are you staying?" (39) He said to them, "**Come, and you will see.**" So they came and saw where he was staying; and they stayed with him that day, for it was about the tenth hour. (40) One of the two who heard John speak and followed him, was Andrew, Simon Peter's brother. (41)

He found first his own brother Simon and said to him, "We have found the Messiah". (42) He brought him to Joshua. Joshua looked at him and said, "**You are Simon the son of John; you shall be called Cephas**" (*which is translated Peter*).

(43) The next day Joshua purposed to go into Galilee, and he found Philip. And Joshua said to him, "**Follow me.**" (44) Now Philip was from Bethsaida, of the city of Andrew and Peter. (45) Philip found Nathanael and said to him, "We have found him of whom Moses in the Law and also the Prophets (*people who spoke God's truths*) wrote--Joshua of Nazareth, the son of Joseph." (46) Nathanael said to him, "Can any good thing come out of Nazareth?" Philip said to him, "Come and see." (47) Joshua saw Nathanael coming to him, and said of him, "**Behold, an Israelite indeed, in whom there is no deceit!**" (48) Nathanael said to him, "How do you know me?" Joshua answered and said to him, "**Before Philip called you, when you were under the fig tree, I saw you.**" (49) Nathanael was astonished and said, "Teacher, you are the Son of God; you are the King of Israel." [*7] (50) Joshua answered and said to him, "**Because I said to you that I saw you under the fig tree, do you believe? You will see greater things than these.**" (51) And he said to him, "**Truly, truly, I say to you, you will see the heavens opened and the angels of God ascending and descending on the Son of Man** (*Joshua's favorite title for himself*)."

[*7] *Another witness that contradicts the trinity doctrine – "Son of God" not "God".*

(2:1) On the third day there was a wedding in Cana of Galilee, and the mother of Joshua was there; (2) and both Joshua and his disciples were invited to the wedding. (3) When the wine ran out, the mother of Joshua said to him, "They have no wine." (4) And Joshua said to her, "**Woman, what does that have to do with me? My hour has not yet come**." (5) His mother said to the servants, "Whatever he says to you, do it." (6) Now there were six stone water pots set there for the Jewish custom of purification, containing twenty or thirty gallons each. (7) Joshua said to them, "**Fill the water pots with water**." So they filled them up to the brim. (8) And he said to them, "**Draw some out now and take it to the headwaiter**." So they took it to him. (9) When the headwaiter tasted the water which had become wine, and did not know where it came from (but the servants who had drawn the water knew), the headwaiter called the bridegroom, (10) and said to him, "Every man serves the good wine first, and when the people have drunk freely, then he serves the poorer wine; but you have kept the good wine until now." (11) This beginning of his signs Joshua did in Cana of Galilee, and manifested his glory, and his disciples believed in him.

(12) After this he went down to Capernaum, he and his mother and his brothers and his disciples[*8]; and they stayed there a few days. (13) The Passover (*religious holiday*) of the Jews was near, and Joshua went up to Jerusalem. (14) And he found in the temple those who were selling oxen and sheep and doves, and the money changers seated at their tables. (15) And he made a whip of cords, and drove them all out of the temple, with the sheep and the oxen; and he poured out the coins of the money changers and overturned their tables; (16) and to those who were selling the doves he said, "**Take these things away; stop making my Father's house a place of business**." (17) His disciples remembered that it was written, "ZEAL FOR YOUR HOUSE WILL CONSUME ME." (18) The Jews then said to him, "What sign do you show us as your authority for doing these things?" (19) Joshua answered them, "**Destroy this temple, and in three days I will raise it up**." (20) The Jews then said, "It took forty-six years to build this

temple, and will you raise it up in three days?" (21) But he was speaking of the temple of his body. (22) So when he was raised from the dead, his disciples remembered that he said this; and they believed the scripture and the word which Joshua had spoken.

*8 *Note the text says "his mother and brothers and disciples", thus proving that Joshua had siblings and thus Mary had other children in addition to Joshua.*

(23) Now when he was in Jerusalem at the Passover, during the feast, many believed in his name, observing his signs which he was doing. (24) But Joshua, on his part, was not entrusting himself to them, for he knew all men, (25) and because he did not need anyone to testify concerning man, for he himself knew what was in man.

(3:1) Now there was a man of the religious leaders, named Nicodemus, a ruler of the Jews; (2) this man came to Joshua by night and said to him, "Rabbi, we know that you have come from God as a teacher; for no one can do these signs that you do unless God is with him." (3) Joshua answered and said to him, "**Truly, truly, I say to you, unless one is born from above he cannot see the kingdom of God.**" *9 (4) Nicodemus said to him, "How can a man be born when he is old? He cannot enter a second time into his mother's womb and be born, can he?" (5) Joshua answered, "**Truly, truly, I say to you, unless one is born of water and the Spirit he cannot enter into the kingdom of God. (6) "That which is born of the flesh is flesh, and that which is born of the Spirit is spirit.**"*10 (7) "**Do not be amazed that I said to you, 'You must be born from above.' (8) "The wind blows where it wishes and you hear the sound of it, but do not know where it comes from and where it is going; so is everyone who is born of the Spirit.**" (9) Nicodemus said to him, "How can these things be?" (10) Joshua answered and said to him, "Are you the teacher of Israel and do not understand these things? (11) "**Truly, truly, I say to you, we speak of what we know and testify of what we have seen, and you do not accept our testimony. (12) "If I told you earthly things and you do not believe, how will you believe if I tell you heavenly things?**

*9 *If we have not had a re-birth experience as an adult, where we had a significant change in how we view the existence or reality of God and the purpose of our life, then we have not been born from above. This birth is triggered by our seeing our need and the beginning of faith.*

*10 *Verses 5 and 6 present a simple contrast of natural birth versus spiritual birth. The natural birth being marked by the woman's water breaking ("born of water" & "born of the flesh is flesh") in contrast to the spiritual birth ("born of the Spirit").*

(13) "**No one has ascended into heaven, but he who descended from heaven: the Son of Man** (*Joshua's favorite*

title for himself). (14) **"As Moses lifted up the serpent in the wilderness, even so must the Son of Man be lifted up; (15) so that whoever believes will in him have eternal life. (16) "For God so loved the people of the earth, that He gave his only spiritually birthed Son, that whoever trusts in him shall not perish, but have eternal life. (17) "For God did not send the Son into the world to judge the world, but that the world might be saved through him. (18) "He who believes in him is not condemned; he who does not believe has been condemned already, because he has not believed in the name of the only spiritually birthed Son of God.**[*11] (19) **"This is the judgment, that the Light has come into the world, and men loved the darkness rather than the Light, for their deeds were evil. (20) "For everyone who does evil hates the Light, and <u>does not come to the Light</u> for fear that his deeds will be exposed. (21) "But he who practices the truth comes to the Light, so that his deeds may be shown as having been formed in God."**

[*11] *You must ask yourself, why don't you believe what he says? What does he say that is wrong, unreasonable, bad or false?*

(22) After these things Joshua and his disciples came into the land of Judea, and there he was spending time with them and baptizing. (23) John also was baptizing in Aenon near Salim, because there was much water there; and people were coming and were being baptized-- (24) for John had not yet been thrown into prison. (25) Therefore there arose a discussion on the part of John's disciples with a Jew about purification. (26) And they came to John and said to him, "Rabbi, he who was with you beyond the Jordan, to whom you have testified, behold, he is baptizing and all are coming to him." (27) John answered and said, "A man can receive nothing unless it has been given him from heaven. (28) "You yourselves are my witnesses that I said, 'I am not the Messiah,' but, 'I have been sent ahead of him.' (29) "He who has the bride is the bridegroom; but the friend of the bridegroom, who stands and hears him, rejoices greatly because of the bridegroom's voice. So this joy of

mine has been made full. (30) "He must increase, but I must decrease. (31) "He who comes from above is above all, he who is of the earth is from the earth and speaks of the earth. He who comes from heaven is above all. (32) "What he has seen and heard, of that he testifies; and (*virtually*) no one receives his testimony. (33) "He who has received his testimony has set his seal to this, that God is true. (34) "For he whom God has sent speaks the words of God; for He gives the Spirit without measure. (35) "The Father loves the Son and has given all things into his hand. (36) "He who believes in the Son has eternal life; but he who does not obey the Son will not see life, but the wrath of God abides on him." [12]

[12] *Here is a good example of the old testament or Hebrew scripture view of God being held and repeated in the 'new testament' by John the baptist. For this reason, Joshua said that even the least of those who have come into and understand the Kingdom of God as given and demonstrated by Joshua, are greater than even John, the greatest of the Hebrew prophets. God is not angry or wrathful, and it is we who send ourselves to our destiny, not God.*

(4:1) Therefore when the Lord knew that the religious leaders had heard that Joshua was making and baptizing more disciples than John (2) (although Joshua himself was not baptizing, but his disciples were)*13 , (3) he left Judea and went away again into Galilee. (4) And he had to pass through Samaria. (5) So he came to a city of Samaria called Sychar, near the parcel of ground that Jacob gave to his son Joseph; (6) and Jacob's well was there. So Joshua, being wearied from his journey, was sitting thus by the well. It was about six o'clock in the morning. (7) There came a woman of Samaria to draw water. Joshua said to her, "**Please give me a drink.**" (8) For his disciples had gone away into the city to buy food. (9) Therefore the Samaritan woman said to him, "How is it that you, being a Jew, ask me for a drink since I am a Samaritan woman?" (*For Jews hated and thus have no dealings with Samaritans.*) (10) Joshua answered and said to her, "**If you knew the gift of God, and who it is who says to you, 'Give me a drink,' you would have asked him, and he would have given you living water.**" (11) She said to him, "Sir, you have nothing to draw with and the well is deep; where then do you get that living water? (12) "You are not greater than our father Jacob, are you, who gave us the well, and drank of it himself and his sons and his cattle?" (13) Joshua answered and said to her, "**Everyone who drinks of this water will thirst again; (14) but whoever drinks of the water that I will give him shall never thirst; but the water that I will give him will become in him a well of water springing up to eternal life.**" (15) The woman said to him, "Sir, give me this water, so I will not be thirsty nor come all the way here to draw." (16) He said to her, "**Go, call your husband and come here.**" (17) The woman answered and said, "I have no husband." Joshua said to her, "**You have correctly said, 'I have no husband'; (18) for you have had five husbands, and the one whom you now have is not your husband; this you have said truly.**" (19) The woman said to him, "Sir, I perceive that you are a prophet (*a person who speaks God's truths*).

*13 *This statement plainly says that Joshua did not water baptize his disciples. This author's opinion is that he did not do that so that people would not think it had anything to do with entering into eternal life – that the physical act does not enter a person into spiritual life, but is merely symbolic. Many religious sects have traditionally held sway over the people saying that water baptism' is "necessary for salvation" and that only their 'ordained' people can perform it. Joshua teaches no such thing and in fact refuses to baptize people, indicating it mean's nothing in regard to eternal life.*

(20) "Our fathers worshiped in this mountain, and you people say that in Jerusalem is the place where men ought to worship." (21) Joshua said to her, "**Woman, believe me, an hour is coming when neither in this mountain nor in Jerusalem will you worship the Father. (22) "You worship what you do not know; we worship what we know, for salvation came through the Jews. (23) "But an hour is coming, and now is, when the true worshipers will worship the Father in spirit and truth; for such people the Father seeks to be His worshipers. (24) "God is spirit, and those who worship Him must worship in spirit and truth."** *14 (25) The woman said to him, "I know that Messiah is coming; when that One comes, he will declare all things to us." (26) Joshua said to her, "**I who speak to you am he.**"

*14 *God wants people to worship him with their real, inner self (spirit) and in truth, not with old, repetitive, non-meaningful or impersonal songs or by saying or singing false things about him which is the norm with many christian lyrics. Please note he does not say 'worship him with singing and favorite doctrines'. It is good to worship God with song, but this is unlikely to happen at a meeting when the leader tells everyone, 'OK, time to worship'.*

(27) At this point his disciples came, and they were amazed that he had been speaking with a woman (*for Joshua was showing that his Father loved Samaritans and women just like he loved male Jews*), yet no one said, "What do you seek?" or, "Why do you speak with her?" (28) So the woman left her waterpot, and went into the city and said to the men, (29) "Come, see a man who told me the things

that I have done; this is not the Messiah, is it?" (30) They went out of the city, and were coming to him.

(31) Meanwhile the disciples were urging him, saying, "Rabbi, eat." (32) But he said to them, "**I have food to eat that you do not know about**." (33) So the disciples were saying to one another, "No one brought him anything to eat, did he?" (34) Joshua said to them, "**My food is to do the will of Him who sent me and to accomplish His work. (35) "Do you not say, 'There are yet four months, and then comes the harvest'? Behold, I say to you, lift up your eyes and look on the fields, that they are white for harvest. (36) "Already he who reaps is receiving wages and is gathering fruit for life eternal; so that he who sows and he who reaps may rejoice together. (37) "For in this case the saying is true, 'One sows and another reaps.' (38) "I sent you to reap that for which you have not worked; others have worked and you have entered into their work**." (39) From that city many of the Samaritans believed in him because of the word of the woman who testified, "He told me the things that I have done." (40) So when the Samaritans came to Joshua, they were asking him to stay with them; and he stayed there two days. (41) Many more believed because of his word; (42) and they were saying to the woman, "It is no longer because of what you said that we believe, for we have heard for ourselves and know that this One is indeed the Savior of the world."

(43) After the two days he went forth from there into Galilee. (44) For Joshua himself testified that a prophet (*a person who speaks God's truths*) has no honor in his own country. (45) So when he came to Galilee, the Galileans received him, having seen all the things that he did in Jerusalem at the feast; for they themselves also went to the feast. (46) Therefore he came again to Cana of Galilee where he had made the water wine. And there was a royal official whose son was sick at Capernaum. (47) When he heard that Joshua had come out of Judea into Galilee, he went to him and was imploring him to come down and heal his son; for he was at the point of death. (48) So Joshua said to him, "**Unless you people**

see signs and wonders, you simply will not believe." (49)
The royal official said to him, "Sir, come down before my child
dies." (50) Joshua said to him, "**Go; your son lives**." The man
believed the word that Joshua spoke to him and started off. (51) As
he was now going down, his servants met him, saying that his son
was living. (52) So he inquired of them the hour when he began to
get better. Then they said to him, "Yesterday at the seventh hour the
fever left him." (53) So the father knew that it was at that hour in
which Joshua said to him, "Your son lives"; and he himself believed
and his whole household. (54) This is again a second sign that
Joshua performed when he had come out of Judea into Galilee.

(5:1) After these things there was a feast of the Jews, and Joshua went up to Jerusalem. (2) Now there is in Jerusalem by the sheep gate a pool, which is called in Hebrew Bethesda, having five patios. (3) In these lay many people who were sick, blind, lame, and withered, [waiting for the moving of the waters; (4) for the people believed an angel of the Lord went down at certain seasons into the pool and stirred up the water; whoever then first, after the stirring up of the water, stepped in was made well from whatever disease with which he was afflicted.] (5) A man was there who had been ill for thirty-eight years. (6) When Joshua saw him lying there, and knew that he had already been a long time in that condition, he said to him, **"Do you wish to get well?"** (7) The sick man answered him, "Sir, I have no man to put me into the pool when the water is stirred up, but while I am coming, another steps down before me." (8) Joshua said to him, **"Get up, pick up your mattress and walk."** (9) Immediately the man became well, and picked up his mattress and began to walk. Now it was the Sabbath on that day. (10) So the Jews were saying to the man who was cured, "It is the Sabbath, and it is not allowed for you to carry your mattress." (11) But he answered them, "He who made me well was the one who said to me, 'Pick up your mattress and walk.'" (12) They asked him, "Who is the man who said to you, 'Pick up your mattress and walk'?" (13) But the man who was healed did not know who it was, for Joshua had slipped away while there was a crowd in that place.

(14) Afterward Joshua found him in the temple and said to him, **"Behold, you have become well; do not sin anymore, so that nothing worse happens to you."** *15 (15) The man went away, and told the Jews that it was Joshua who had made him well.

*15 *Some sins or wrong behavior cause harm to our bodies. For example, sexually transmitted diseases spread between unmarried people or unfaithful spouses.*

(16) For this reason the Jews were persecuting (*seeking to harm*) Joshua, because he was doing these things on the Sabbath. (17) But he answered them, **"My Father is working until now, and I**

myself am working." *16 (18) For this reason therefore the Jews were seeking all the more to kill him, because he not only was breaking the Sabbath, but also was calling God his own Father, making himself God's unique Son. (19) Therefore Joshua answered and was saying to them, "**Truly, truly, I say to you, the Son can do nothing of himself, unless it is something he sees the Father doing; for whatever the Father does, these things the Son also does in like manner.** (20) "**For the Father loves the Son, and shows him all things that He Himself is doing; and the Father will show him greater works than these, so that you will marvel.** (21) "**For just as the Father raises the dead and gives them life, even so the Son also gives life to whom he wishes.** (22) "**For not even the Father judges anyone, but He has given all judgment to the Son,** (23) **so that all will honor the Son even as they honor the Father. He who does not honor the Son does not honor the Father who sent him.**

*16 *This saying of Joshua rebukes any bible-based "do not work on the Sabbath" teaching IF Joshua is your Master. The context is clear. They were accusing Joshua of working on their Sabbath with his healing works. Joshua's response was that both he and his Father work on your Sabbath, thus proving it is perfectly fine to work on their Sabbath.*

(24) "**Truly, truly, I say to you, he who hears my word, and believes Him who sent me, has eternal life, and does not come into judgment, but has passed out of death into life.** (25) "**Truly, truly, I say to you, an hour is coming and now is, when the** (*spiritually*) **dead will hear the voice of the Son of God, and those who hear will live.** (26) "**For just as the Father has life in Himself, even so He gave to the Son also to have life in himself;** (27) **and He gave him authority to execute judgment, because he is the Son of Man** (*Joshua's favorite title for himself*). (28) "**Do not marvel at this; for an hour is coming, in which all who are in the tombs** (*both physically and spiritually dead*) **will hear his voice,** (29) **and will come forth; those who did the good deeds to a**

resurrection of life, those who committed the evil deeds to a resurrection of condemnation.[*17]

[*17] *This saying of Joshua directly contradicts Paul's "saved by grace" teaching. Joshua plainly says that those who partake in the resurrection of life are those who "did the good deeds" not those 'saved by grace'. Nowhere in all four gospels does Joshua mention the concept of salvation by grace – and yet he does speak frequently on what a person must do to inherit eternal life as he does here. Who knows better, Paul or Joshua? Why would the key to protestant bible religion's salvation – a salvation concept called "grace" - be utterly absent from Joshua's teachings? Paul's 'grace' teaching certainly does make an easy way to heaven which of course would be very popular with people. In contrast Joshua speaks of the difficult way of losing our life in this world in order to gain eternal Life. See Matt. 7:13 & 10:39.*

(30) **"I can do nothing on my own initiative. As I hear, I judge; and my judgment is just, because I do not seek my own will, but the will of Him who sent me. (31) "If I alone testify about myself, my testimony is not true. (32) "There is another who testifies of me, and I know that the testimony which He gives about me is true. (33) "You have sent to John, and he has testified to the truth. (34) "But the testimony which I receive is not from man, but I say these things so that you may be saved. (35) "He was the lamp that was burning and was shining and you were willing to rejoice for a while in his light. (36) "But the testimony which I have is greater than the testimony of John; for the works which the Father has given me to accomplish--the very works that I do--testify about me, that the Father has sent me. (37)** [*18]

[*18] *A clear statement and validation of Joshua as the Designer's Messenger.*

"And the Father who sent me, He has testified of me. You have neither heard His voice at any time nor seen His form. (38) "You do not have His word abiding in you, for you do not believe him whom He sent. (39) "You search

(or study) **the scriptures** (*the bible*) **because you think that in them** (*the scripture or the bible*) **you have eternal life; yet it is these** (*the scripture referring to Messiah*) **that testify about me;** (40) **and you are unwilling to come to me so that you may have life.**[19] (41) **"I do not receive glory from men;** (42) **but I know you, that you do not have the love of God in yourselves.** (43) **"I have come in my Father's name, and you do not receive me; if another comes in his own name, you will receive him.** (44) **"How can you believe, when you receive glory from one another and you do not seek the glory that is from the one and only God?** (45) **"Do not think that I will accuse you before the Father; the one who accuses you is Moses, in whom you have set your hope.**[20] (46) **"For if you believed Moses, you would believe me, for he wrote about me.** (47) **"But if you do not believe his writings, how will you believe my words?"**

[19] *They possessed and studied and knew the scripture (or the bible) and yet they were without "life" since they did not go to Joshua as their Master and source of truth – instead they clung to the scripture, the very same mistake committed today by the biblians and Christians who look to 'God's Word' (the bible) even while they ignore the true Word of God, Joshua of Nazareth. See John 1:1-3.*

[20] *Here Messiah says that it is a grave error for a person to set one's hope in Moses, for to do so means he can only serve as that person's accuser since Moses taught to place one's hope in God and His Messiah, and Joshua is the Father's Messiah. What does it mean to place one's hope in Moses? It would include looking to Moses' teachings to understand God. Messiah came and showed the imperfection and inadequacy of Moses' teachings – see Joshua's teachings in Matt. 5 contrasting Moses' imperfect teachings with his own perfect teachings. Therefore, it would be foolish to continue to look to Moses to understand the Creator.*

(6:1) After these things Joshua went away to the other side of the Sea of Galilee (or Tiberias). (2) A large crowd followed him, because they saw the miracles which he was performing on those who were sick. (3) Then Joshua went up on the mountain, and there he sat down with his disciples. (4) Now the Passover, the feast of the Jews, was near. (5) Therefore Joshua, lifting up his eyes and seeing that a large crowd was coming to him, said to Philip, **"Where are we to buy bread, so that these may eat?"** (6) This he was saying to test him, for he himself knew what he was intending to do. (7) Philip answered him, "Fifteen hundred dollars' worth of bread is not sufficient for them, for everyone to receive a little." (8) One of his disciples, Andrew, Simon Peter's brother, said to him, (9) "There is a lad here who has five barley loaves and two fish, but what are these for so many people?" (10) Joshua said, **"Have the people sit down."** Now there was much grass in the place. So the men sat down, in number about five thousand. (11) Joshua then took the loaves, and having given thanks, he distributed to those who were seated; likewise also of the fish as much as they wanted. (12) When they were filled, he said to his disciples, **"Gather up the leftover fragments so that nothing will be wasted."** *21 (13) So they gathered them up, and filled twelve baskets with fragments from the five barley loaves which were left over by those who had eaten.

*21 *This is a much forgotten or ignored teaching by people in the wealthy nations of the world, where throwing away food is common practice. It is a sin to waste food as the Light here points out, but is particularly bad when there are so many children and adults starving and malnourished across the planet. With global media, we cannot claim ignorance, only hardness of heart or selfish apathy.*

(14) Therefore when the people saw the sign which he had performed, they said, "This is truly the Prophet who is to come into the world." (15) So Joshua, perceiving that they were intending to come and take him by force to make him king, withdrew again to the mountain by himself alone. (16) Now when evening came, his disciples went down to the sea, (17) and after getting into a boat, they started to cross the sea to Capernaum. It had already become

dark, and Joshua had not yet come to them. (18) The sea began to get rough because a strong wind was blowing. (19) Then, when they had rowed about three or four miles, they saw Joshua walking on the sea and drawing near to the boat; and they were frightened. (20) But he said to them, "**It is I; do not be afraid**." (21) So they were willing to receive him into the boat, and immediately the boat was at the land to which they were going.

(22) The next day the crowd that stood on the other side of the sea saw that there was no other small boat there, except one, and that Joshua had not entered with his disciples into the boat, but that his disciples had gone away alone. (23) There came other small boats from Tiberias near to the place where they ate the bread after the Lord had given thanks. (24) So when the crowd saw that Joshua was not there, nor his disciples, they themselves got into the small boats, and came to Capernaum seeking Joshua. (25) When they found him on the other side of the sea, they said to him, "Rabbi, when did you get here?" (26) Joshua answered them and said, "**Truly, truly, I say to you, you seek me, not because you saw signs, but because you ate of the loaves and were filled. (27) "Do not work for the food which perishes, but for the food which endures to eternal life, which the Son of Man will give to you, for on him the Father, God, has set His seal**." (28) Therefore they said to him, "What shall we do, so that we may work the works of God?" (29) Joshua answered and said to them, "**This is the work of God, that you trust in him whom He has sent**." [22]

[22] *The primary work of God is not 'christian ministry' or believing the christian gospel or going to church, but rather trusting in, and then listening to Joshua – if we do this, then we will do what is right and love!*

(30) So they said to him, "What then do you do for a sign, so that we may see, and believe you? What work do you perform? (31) "Our fathers ate the manna in the wilderness; as it is written, 'HE GAVE THEM BREAD OUT OF HEAVEN TO EAT.'" (32) Joshua then said to them, "**Truly, truly, I say to you, it is not Moses**

who has given you the bread out of heaven, but it is my Father who gives you the true bread out of heaven.** (33) **"For the bread of God is that which comes down out of heaven, and gives life to the world."** (34) Then they said to him, "Lord, always give us this bread." (35) Joshua said to them, "**I am the bread of life; he who comes to me will not hunger, and he who believes in me will never thirst.** (36) **"But I said to you that you have seen me, and yet do not believe.** (37) **"All that the Father gives me will come to me, and the one who comes to me I will certainly not cast out.** (38) **"For I have come down from heaven, not to do my own will, but the will of Him who sent me.** (39) **"This is the will of Him who sent me, that of all that He has given me I lose nothing, but raise it up on the last day.** (40) **"For this is the will of my Father, that everyone who beholds the Son and trusts in him will have eternal life, and I myself will raise him up on the last day."** [*23]

[*23] *What a beautiful truth for those with faith that provides true Hope :)*

(41) Therefore those who would not trust in him were grumbling about him, because he said, "**I am the bread that came down out of heaven**." (42) They were saying, "Is not this Joshua, the son of Joseph, whose father and mother we know? How does he now say, 'I have come down out of heaven'?" (43) Joshua answered and said to them, "**Do not grumble among yourselves.** (44) **"No one can come to me unless the Father who sent me draws him; and I will raise him up on the last day.** (45) **"It is written in the prophets** (*books of the old testament written by people who spoke God's truths*), **'AND THEY SHALL ALL BE TAUGHT OF GOD.' Everyone who has heard and learned from the Father, comes to me.** (46) **"Not that anyone has seen the Father, except the One who is from God; he has seen the Father.** (47) **"Truly, truly, I say to you, he who believes what I say has eternal life.**[*24]

*24 "...what I say...", not, 'what the bible or scriptures say' or 'what christian
leader says'. Disciples trust in a person and his words, not a book and its
scripture or those who say they represent the Light. Yes, his words were placed in
a book and are called scripture, but only Joshua's words will "never pass away".
Disciples trust in a person and his words, Joshua of Nazareth.

(48) **"I am the bread of life.** (49) **"Your fathers ate the
manna in the wilderness, and they died.** (50) **"This is the
bread which comes down out of heaven, so that one may
eat of it and not die.** (51) **"I am the living bread that came
down out of heaven; if anyone eats of this bread, he will
live forever; and the bread also which I will give for the life
of the world is my flesh** (*speaking of his physical death and
spiritual ransom – see Matt. 20:28*)**."** (52) Then those who would
not trust him could not understand what he was saying and thus
began to argue with one another, saying, "How can this man give us
his flesh to eat?" (53) So Joshua, continuing with his manna-food
metaphor, said to them, **"Truly, truly, I say to you, unless you
eat the flesh of the Son of Man and drink his blood, you
have no life in yourselves.** (54) **"He who eats my flesh and
drinks my blood has eternal life, and I will raise him up on
the last day.** (55) **"For my flesh is true food, and my blood
is true drink.** (56) **"He who eats my flesh and drinks my
blood abides in me, and I in him.** (57) **"As the living
Father sent me, and I live because of the Father, so he who
eats me, he also will live because of me.** (58) **"This is the
bread which came down out of heaven; not as the fathers
ate and died; he who eats this bread will live forever."** (*See
verse 63 below regarding the metaphorical language used in this
passage.*)

(59) These things he said in the synagogue as he taught in
Capernaum. (60) Therefore many of his disciples, when they heard
this said, "This is a difficult statement; who can listen to it?" (61)
But Joshua, conscious that his disciples grumbled at this, said to
them, **"Does this cause you to stumble?** (62) **"What then if
you see the Son of Man ascending to where he was before?**

(63) **"It is the Spirit who gives life; the flesh profits nothing; the words that I have spoken to you <u>are spirit</u> and are life. (64) "But there are some of you who do not believe."** For Joshua knew from the beginning who they were who did not believe, and who it was that would betray him. (65) And he was saying, **"For this reason I have said to you, that no one can come to me unless it has been granted him from the Father."** (66) As a result of this many of his disciples withdrew and were not walking with him anymore. (67) So Joshua said to the twelve, **"You do not want to go away also, do you?"** (68) Simon Peter answered him, "Lord, to whom shall we go? You have words of eternal life. (69) "We have believed and have come to know that you are the Holy One of God." (70) Joshua answered them, **"Did I myself not choose you, the twelve, and yet one of you is a devil?"** (71) Now he meant Judas the son of Simon Iscariot, for he, one of the twelve, was going to betray him.

(7:1) After these things Joshua was walking in Galilee, for he was unwilling at that time to walk in Judea because the religious leaders were aggressively seeking to kill him. (2) Now a feast of the Jews, the Feast of Booths, was near. (3) Therefore his brothers said to him, "Leave here and go into Judea, so that your disciples also may see your works which you are doing. (4) "For no one does anything in secret when he himself seeks to be known publicly. If you do these things, show yourself to the world." (5) For not even his brothers were believing in him. (6) So Joshua said to them, "**My time is not yet here, but your time is always opportune. (7) "The world cannot hate you, but it hates me because I testify of it, that its deeds are evil.**"[*25] **(8) "Go up to the feast yourselves; I do not go up to this feast because my time has not yet fully come.**" (9) Having said these things to them, he stayed in Galilee. (10) But when his brothers had gone up to the feast, then he himself also went up, not publicly, but as if, in secret.

[*25] *See John 3:19-21.*

(11) So the Jews were seeking him at the feast and were saying, "Where is he?" (12) There was much grumbling among the crowds concerning him; some were saying, "He is a good man"; others were saying, "No, on the contrary, he leads the people astray." (13) Yet no one was speaking openly of him for fear of the Jewish leadership. (14) But when it was the middle of the feast Joshua went up into the temple, and began to teach. (15) The Jews then were astonished, saying, "How has this man become learned, having never been educated?" (16) So Joshua answered them and said, "**My teaching is not Mine, but His who sent me. (17) "If anyone is willing to do His will, he will know of the teaching, whether it is of God or whether I speak from myself. (18) "He who speaks from himself seeks his own glory; but he who is seeking the glory of the One who sent him, he is true, and there is no unrighteousness in Him. (19) "Did not Moses give you the Law, and yet none of you carries out the Law? Why do you seek to kill me?**" (20) The crowd answered, "You have a demon (*bad angel*)! Who seeks to kill

you?" (21) Joshua answered them, "**I did one deed, and you all marvel. (22) "For this reason Moses has given you circumcision (not because it is from Moses, but from the fathers), and on the Sabbath you circumcise a man. (23) "If a man receives circumcision on the Sabbath so that the Law of Moses will not be broken, are you angry with me because I made an entire man well on the Sabbath? (24) "Do not judge according to appearance, but judge with righteous judgment.**" *26

*26 *This statement clarifies Joshua's "do not judge" statements in Matt. 7:1-3. Here he is exhorting his listeners to make a right judgment about what is true or false, right or wrong. So we are to be very careful about judging faults or perceived weaknesses in people but we are to be diligent in making judgments about what is true and false (beliefs), right or wrong (behavior) using Joshua's teachings as our standard to do so.*

(25) So some of the people of Jerusalem were saying, "Is this not the man whom they are seeking to kill? (26) "Look, he is speaking publicly, and they are saying nothing to him. The rulers do not really know that this is the Messiah, do they? (27) "However, we know where this man is from; but whenever the Messiah may come, no one knows where he is from." (28) Then Joshua cried out in the temple, teaching and saying, "**You both know me and know where I am from; and I have not come of myself, but He who sent me is true, whom you do not know. (29) "I know Him, because I am from Him, and He sent me.**" (30) So they were seeking to seize him; and no man laid his hand on him, because his hour had not yet come. (31) But many of the crowd believed in him; and they were saying, "When the Messiah comes, he will not perform more signs than those which this man has, will he?" (32) The religious leaders heard the crowd muttering these things about him, and the religious leaders sent officers to seize him. (33) Therefore Joshua said, "**For a little while longer I am with you, then I go to him who sent me. (34) "You will seek me, and will not find me; and where I am, you cannot come.**" (35) Those who did not understand Joshua said to one

another, "Where does this man intend to go that we will not find him? He is not intending to go to the Dispersion among the Greeks, and teach the Greeks, is he? (36) "What is this statement that he said, 'You will seek me, and will not find me; and where I am, you cannot come'?"

(37) Now on the last day, the great day of the feast, Joshua stood and cried out, saying, "**If anyone is thirsty, let him come to me and drink. (38) "He who believes in me, as the scripture said, 'From his innermost being will flow rivers of living water.**'" (39) But this he spoke of the Spirit, whom those who believed in him were to receive; for the Spirit was not yet given, because Joshua was not yet glorified. (40) Some of the people therefore, when they heard these words, were saying, "This certainly is the Prophet." (41) Others were saying, "This is the Messiah." Still others were saying, "Surely the Messiah is not going to come from Galilee, is he? (42) "Has not the scripture said that the Messiah comes from the descendants of David, and from Bethlehem, the village where David was?" (43) So a division occurred in the crowd because of him. (44) Some of them wanted to seize him, but no one laid hands on him. (45) The officers then came to the religious leaders, and they said to them, "Why did you not bring him?" (46) The officers answered, "Never has a man spoken the way this man speaks." (47) The religious leaders then answered them, "You have not also been led astray, have you? (48) "No one of the political or religious leaders has believed in him, has he? (49) "But this crowd which does not know the Law is accursed." (50) Nicodemus (*he who came to Joshua before, being one of them*) said to them, (51) "Our Law does not judge a man unless it first hears from him and knows what he is doing, does it?" (52) They answered him, "You are not also from Galilee, are you? Search, and see that no prophet (*a person who speaks God's truths*) arises out of Galilee." (53) Then everyone went to his home.

(8:1) But Joshua went to the Mount of Olives. (2) Early in the morning he came again into the temple, and all the people were coming to him; and he sat down and began to teach them. (3) The bible experts and the religious leaders brought a woman caught in adultery (*"adultery" is a married person having sex with someone other than their spouse*), and having set her in the center of the court, (4) they said to him, "Teacher, this woman has been caught in adultery, in the very act. (5) "Now in the Law Moses commanded us to stone such women; what then do you say?" (6) They were saying this, testing him, so that they might have grounds for arresting him. But Joshua stooped down and with his finger wrote on the ground. (7) But when they persisted in asking him, he straightened up, and said to them, "**He who is without sin among you, let him be the first to throw a stone at her.**" (8) Again he stooped down and wrote on the ground. (9) When they heard it, they began to go out one by one, beginning with the older ones, and he was left alone, and the woman, where she was, in the center of the court. (10) Straightening up, Joshua said to her, "**Woman, where are they? Did no one condemn you?**" (11) She said, "No one, Lord." And Joshua said, "**Neither do I condemn you. Go. From now on sin no more.**"

(12) Then Joshua again spoke to them, saying, "**I am the Light of the world; he who follows me will not walk in the darkness, but will have the Light of life.**" [*27] (13) So the religious leaders said to him, "You are testifying about yourself; your testimony is not true." (14) Joshua answered and said to them, "**Even if I testify about myself, my testimony is true, for I know where I came from and where I am going; but you do not know where I come from or where I am going. (15) "You judge according to the flesh; I am not judging anyone. (16) "But even if I do judge, my judgment is true; for I am not alone in it, but I and the Father who sent me. (17) "Even in your law**[*28] **it has been written that the testimony of two men is true. (18) "I am he who testifies about myself, and the Father who sent me testifies about me.**" (19) So they were saying to him, "Where is your Father?"

Joshua answered, "**You know neither me nor my Father; if you knew me, you would know my Father also.**" (20) These words he spoke in the treasury, as he taught in the temple; and no one seized him, because his hour had not yet come.

*27 *The Creator sent a Light into the world – the model for mankind – and those who know of him and yet don't follow him (who do not do what he says), walk in darkness and do not have the Light of Life.*

*28 *Joshua is referring to Moses' words in Deuteronomy. If 'the bible' or 'the scripture' were his Father's words/thoughts, would Joshua refer to it as "your law" instead of "my Father's words"?*

(21) Then he said again to them, "**I go away, and you will seek me, and will die in your sin; where I am going, you cannot come.**" (22) So those who did not believe him were saying, "Surely he will not kill himself, will he, since he says, 'Where I am going, you cannot come'?" (23) And he was saying to them, "**You are from below, I am from above; you are of this world, I am not of this world.**"*29 (24) "**Therefore I said to you that you will die in your sins; for unless you believe that I am he, you will die in your sins.**" (25) So they were saying to him, "Who are you?" Joshua said to them, "**What have I been saying to you from the beginning? (26) "I have many things to speak and to judge concerning you, but He who sent me is true; and the things which I heard from Him, these I speak to the world.**" (27) They did not realize that he had been speaking to them about the Father. (28) So Joshua said, "**When you lift up the Son of Man, then you will know that I am he,**"*30 **and I do nothing on my own initiative, but I speak these things as the Father taught me. (29) "And He who sent me is with me; He has not left me alone, for I always do the things that are pleasing to Him.**" (30) As he spoke these things, many came to believe in him.

*29 *See John 3:19, 7:7, 8:23, 15:18-19, 17:6, 14-16 regarding the world - those who*
do not take Joshua as their leader - and those who follow the Light and our
relationship to the world.

*30 *In the saying, "lift up the Son of Man" he was referring to his crucifixion and*
the signs accompanying it (see Matt. 27:51-54), possibly including the
resurrection.

(31) So Joshua was saying to those who had believed him, **"If you continue in <u>my Word</u>** (*Joshua's words/teachings and no one else's!*)**, then you are truly disciples of mine; (32) and you will know the truth, and the truth will make you free."**

(33) Those whose pride was great answered him, "We are Abraham's descendants and have never yet been enslaved to anyone; how is it that you say, 'You will become free'?" (34) Joshua answered them, **"Truly, truly, I say to you, everyone who commits sin is the servant of sin. (35) "The servant does not remain in the house forever; the son does remain forever. (36) "So if the Son makes you free, you will be free indeed. (37) "I know that you are Abraham's descendants; yet you seek to kill me, because my Word has no place in you. (38) "I speak the things which I have seen with my Father; therefore you also do the things which you heard from your father."** (39) They answered and said to him, "Abraham is our father." Joshua said to them, **"If you are Abraham's children, do the deeds of Abraham. (40) "But as it is, you are seeking to kill me, a man who has told you the truth, which I heard from God; this Abraham did not do. (41) "You are doing the deeds of your father."** They said to him, "We were not born of fornication (*non-married people having sex*); we have one Father: God." (42) Joshua said to them, **"If God were your Father, you would love me, for I proceeded forth and have come from God, for I have not even come on my own initiative, but He sent me. (43) "Why do you not understand what I am saying? It is because you cannot hear my word. (44) "You are of your**

father the devil, and you want to do the desires of your father. He was a murderer from the beginning, and does not stand in the truth because there is no truth in him. Whenever he speaks a lie, he speaks from his own nature, for he is a liar and the father of lies. (45) "But because I speak the truth, you do not believe me. (46) "Which one of you convicts me of sin? If I speak truth, why do you not believe me? (47) "He who is of God hears the words of God; for this reason you do not hear them, because you are not of God."

(48) Those who refused to listen to Joshua said to him, "Do we not say rightly that you are a Samaritan and have a demon?" (49) Joshua answered, "**I do not have a demon** (*bad angel*); **but I honor my Father, and you dishonor me. (50) "But I do not seek my glory; there is One who seeks and judges. (51) "Truly, truly, I say to you, if anyone keeps my word he will never see death**." *31 (52) Those proud of heart said to him, "Now we know that you have a demon (*bad angel*). Abraham died, and the prophets also; and you say, 'If anyone keeps my word, he will never taste of death.' (53) "Surely you are not greater than our father Abraham, who died? The prophets died too; whom do you make yourself out to be?" (54) Joshua answered, "**If I glorify myself, my glory is nothing; it is my Father who glorifies me, of whom you say, 'He is our God'; (55) and you have not come to know Him, but I know Him; and if I say that I do not know Him, I will be a liar like you, but I do know Him and keep His word. (56) "Your father Abraham rejoiced to see my day, and he saw it and was glad**." (57) So the unbelieving said to him, "You are not yet fifty years old, and have you seen Abraham?" (58) Joshua said to them, "**Truly, truly, I say to you, before Abraham was born, I existed**." *32 (59) Therefore they picked up stones to throw at him, but Joshua hid himself and went out of the temple.

*31 "...*keeps* **my word** (*NOT 'the bible'*) *he will never see death" is far different from 'who accepts God's grace will go to heaven'. The first ("who keeps my* word") is from the one who claims to know the Father better than any person, being the Father's unique and only Son – and who defeated death to prove that what he said was true. The latter ('who believes this doctrine of grace') is from Paul of Tarsus. Who are you going to believe and why?

*32 This is one of the few verses that those who believe the trinity doctrine use to justify their doctrine. Does Joshua say, "I am God" here? No, he does not. What about the **hundreds of times** Joshua refers to, speaks to, and talks about his "Father"? See John 7:28-29 and 8:54-55 as two examples of the hundreds of such references Joshua makes to his "Father". The most the saying can be said to prove is that Joshua existed before Abraham – consistent with John 1:1-3, 10, 14. To turn it into something more requires religious imagination and original language sleight-of-hand that the religious leaders will be only too quick to provide.

(9:1) As Joshua passed by, he saw a man blind from birth. (2) And his disciples asked him, "Teacher, who sinned, this man or his parents, that he would be born blind?" (3) Joshua answered, "**It was neither that this man sinned, nor his parents; but it was so that the works of God might be displayed in him. (4) "We must work the works of Him who sent me as long as it is day; night is coming when no one can work. (5) "While I am in the world, I am the Light of the world**." *33 (6) When he had said this, he spat on the ground, and made clay of the spittle, and applied the clay to his eyes, (7) and said to him, "**Go, wash in the pool of Siloam**" (which is translated, Sent). So he went away and washed, and came back seeing! (8) Therefore the neighbors, and those who previously saw him as a beggar, were saying, "Is not this the blind one who used to sit and beg?" (9) Others were saying, "This is he," still others were saying, "No, but he is like him." He kept saying, "I am the one." (10) So they were saying to him, "How then were your eyes opened?" (11) He answered, "The man who is called Joshua made clay, and anointed my eyes, and said to me, 'Go to Siloam and wash'; so I went away and washed, and I received sight." (12) They said to him, "Where is he?" He said, "I do not know."

*33 *The work Joshua is referring to in these verses is miracles. When the Light left the world it got dark – night came. And when night came, no one could/can do the works of the Light, miracles. The work of miracles that Joshua did was to validate who Joshua was – that was their primary purpose. And with that purpose fulfilled, the night came and "no one can work" miracles. There are no miracles after Joshua went back to be with the Father.*

(13) They brought to the religious leaders the man who was formerly blind. (14) Now it was a Sabbath on the day when Joshua made the clay and opened his eyes. (15) Then the religious leaders also were asking him again how he received his sight. And he said to them, "He applied clay to my eyes, and I washed, and I see." (16) Therefore some of the religious leaders were saying, "This man is not from God, because he does not keep the Sabbath." (*See John 5:17*) But others were saying, "How can a man who is a sinner

perform such signs?" And there was a division among them. (17) So they said to the blind man again, "What do you say about him, since he opened your eyes?" And he said, "He is a prophet." (18) The Jews then did not believe it of him, that he had been blind and had received sight, until they called the parents of the very one who had received his sight, (19) and questioned them, saying, "Is this your son, who you say was born blind? Then how does he now see?" (20) His parents answered them and said, "We know that this is our son, and that he was born blind; (21) but how he now sees, we do not know; or who opened his eyes, we do not know. Ask him; he is of age, he will speak for himself." (22) His parents said this because they were afraid of the religious leaders and their congregants; for they had already agreed that if anyone confessed him to be Messiah; he was to be put out of the local religious organization (or synagogue). (23) For this reason his parents said, "He is of age; ask him."

(24) So a second time they called the man who had been blind, and said to him, "Give glory to God; we know that this man is a sinner." (25) He then answered, "Whether he is a sinner, I do not know; one thing I do know, that though I was blind, now I see." (26) So they said to him, "What did he do to you? How did he open your eyes?" (27) He answered them, "I told you already and you did not listen; why do you want to hear it again? You do not want to become his disciples too, do you?" (28) They got very angry at him and said, "You are his disciple, but we are disciples of Moses. (29) "We know that God has spoken to Moses, but as for this man, we do not know where he is from." (30) The man answered and said to them, "Well, here is an amazing thing that you do not know where he is from, and yet he opened my eyes. (31) "We know that God does not hear sinners; but if anyone is God-fearing and does His will, He hears him. (32) "Since the beginning of time it has never been heard that anyone opened the eyes of a person born blind. (33) "If this man were not from God, he could do nothing." (34) They answered him, "You were born entirely in sins, and are you teaching us?" So they threw him out.

(35) Joshua heard that they had thrown him out of the temple, and finding him, he said, "**Do you believe in the Son of Man?**" (36) He answered, "Who is he, Lord, that I may believe in him?" (37) Joshua said to him, "**You have both seen him, and he is the one who is talking with you.**" (38) And he said, "Lord, I believe." And he bowed before him. (39) And Joshua said, "**For judgment I came into this world, so that those who do not see may see, and that those who see may become blind.**" (40) Those of the religious leaders who were near him heard these things and said to him, "We are not blind too, are we?" (41) Joshua said to them, "**If you were blind, you would have no sin; but since you say, 'We see,' your sin remains.**"[*34]

*34 *"...those who do not see..." – the humble, powerless, ignored, used, meek – may see their Hope and Life. "...those who see..." – those looked to as the brightest of humanity, the intellectual elite, those in power who love their world and who are proud of their positions and their religion and politics and science and technology and laws – "may become blind" to Joshua's Way. Verse 41, "We see" - the proud people who think they know what life is about even while they ignore the Light and instead hold to their religious traditions and doctrine and thus remain guilty and unjustified.*

(10:1) "Truly, truly, I say to you, he who does not enter by the door into the pen of the sheep, but climbs up some other way, he is a thief and a robber. (2) "But he who enters by the door is a shepherd (*"shepherd" is translated from the Greek term "poimen", which is wrongly and interestingly translated elsewhere in the new testament as "pastor" – see Eph. 4:11*) of the sheep. (3) "To him the doorkeeper opens, and the sheep hear his voice, and he calls his own sheep by name and leads them out. (4) "When he lets all his sheep out, he goes ahead of them, and the sheep follow him because they know his voice. (5) "A stranger they simply will not follow, but will flee from him, because they do not know the voice of strangers.** (6) This figure of speech Joshua spoke to them, but they did not understand what those things were which he had been saying to them. (7) So Joshua said to them again, **"Truly, truly, I say to you, I am the door of the sheep. (8) "All who came before me are thieves and robbers, but the sheep did not hear them. (9) "I am the door; if anyone enters through me, he will be saved, and will go in and out and find pasture. (10) "The thief comes only to steal and kill and destroy; I came that they may have life, and have it abundantly."** [*35]

[*35] *Eternal Life IS abundant Life, not the material wealth or the other things of the world or flesh that the religious leaders like to corrupt this saying to mean.*

(11) **"I am the good shepherd-pastor; the good shepherd-pastor lays down his life for the sheep. (12) "He who is a hired hand** (*who insists on being paid money to 'care for the sheep' i.e. religious leaders*)**, and not a shepherd, who is <u>not the owner of the sheep</u>,** [*36] **sees the wolf coming, and leaves the sheep and flees, and the wolf snatches them and scatters them. (13) "He flees because he is a hired hand and is not concerned enough about the sheep. (14) "I am the good shepherd-pastor, and I know my own and my own know me, (15) even as the Father knows me and I know the Father; and I lay down my life for the sheep.**

(16) "I have other sheep (*non-Jews*), which are not of this fold (*the fold of Israel*); I must bring them also, and they will hear my voice; and they will become one flock with one shepherd-pastor."[*37] **(17)** "For this reason the Father loves me, because I lay down my life so that I may take it again. **(18)** "No one has taken it away from me, but I lay it down on my own initiative. I have authority to lay it down, and I have authority to take it up again. This commandment I received from my Father."

[*36] *Only the Son of Man and his Father own the sheep/people, not religious leaders.*

[*37] *Paul's teachings in Ephesians 4:11 is in direct contradiction to this teaching of Joshua and thus seeks to nullify the Good Shepherd's-Pastor's words. Who are YOU going to listen to and follow? Paul says that God has given many shepherds-pastors. Joshua says that only he, and no one else, is the one good Shepherd-Pastor who owns his sheep. Also please note that Joshua's flock is ONE flock, not the thousands of divisions of Christianity; and ONE shepherd/pastor – only ONE, Joshua.*

(19) A division occurred again among the Jews because of these words. (20) Many of them were saying, "He has a demon (*bad angel*) and is insane. Why do you listen to him?" (21) Others were saying, "These are not the sayings of one demon-possessed. A demon (*bad angel*) cannot open the eyes of the blind, can he?" (22) At that time the Feast of the Dedication took place at Jerusalem; (23) it was winter, and Joshua was walking in the temple in the portico of Solomon. (24) The Jews then gathered around him, and were saying to him, "How long will you keep us in suspense? If you are the Messiah, tell us plainly." (25) Joshua answered them, "**I told you, and you do not believe; the works that I do in my Father's name, these testify of me.** (26) "**But you do not believe because you are not of my sheep.** (27) "**My sheep hear my voice, and I know them, and they follow me;**"[*38] (28) **and I give eternal life to them, and they will never perish; and no one will snatch them out of my hand.** (29)

"My Father, who has given them to me, is greater than all; and no one is able to snatch them out of the Father's hand. (30) "I and the Father are one." *39

*38 *"My sheep hear MY voice (not the voice of religious leaders or bible authors or scholars)...and they follow ME", not anyone else...not pastor wonderful or minister marvelous, etc. ad nausea.*

*39 *This verse is often used to support the trinity doctrine. Given that Joshua makes a clear distinction between himself and his Father – saying "his Father" is greater than all, including himself – just prior to the last statement, it is only reasonable to understand the last statement to be referring to their **unity** in purpose in protecting the sheep. Without a trinity doctrine to bias a reader, in this author's opinion NO ONE would conclude from reading verses 25 – 30 that the last statement means that "my Father" and Joshua are the same person or being.*

(31) The Jews picked up stones again to stone him. (32) Joshua answered them, "**I showed you many good works from the Father; for which of them are you stoning me?**" (33) The Jews answered him, "For a good work we do not stone you, but for blasphemy; and because you, being a man, make yourself out to be God." (34) Joshua answered them, "**Has it not been written in your Law, 'I SAID, YOU ARE GODS'?** (35) "**If he called them gods** (*referring to the judges at Moses time who could cause the death or life of someone they were judging*) **to whom the word of God came (and the scripture cannot be broken), (36) why do you say of him, whom the Father sanctified and sent into the world, 'You are blaspheming,' because I said, 'I am the Son of God'?** *40 (37) "**If I do not do the works of my Father, do not believe me; (38) but if I do them, though you do not believe me, believe the works, so that you may know and understand that the Father is in me, and I in the Father.**" *41 (39) Therefore they were seeking again to seize him, and he eluded their grasp. (40) And he went away again beyond the Jordan to the place where John was first baptizing, and he was staying there. (41) Many came to him and

were saying, "While John performed no sign, yet everything John said about this man was true." (42) Many believed in him there.

*40 *Joshua is rebuking the Jews claim that he "makes himself out to be God" and replies, "I am the Son of God...sent from the Father into the world" (see John 3:16-17). A clearer rebuke of the trinity doctrine is hard to find. Of course referring to "his Father" many dozens of times throughout the gospels is the stronger natural rebuke to a strange doctrine that his Father and he are the same person or same "God". Again, the purpose of the trinity doctrine is to make the 'common' or 'lay' people dependent upon the religious leaders to understand God.*

*41 *Joshua calls people who refuse to believe his words, to believe him based on the validation he provides – the "works" or miracles. Who else in history performed miracles to validate his or her person or message? No one has in a genuine, authentic way, thus Joshua provides proof that he is the Designers/Creators Messenger.*

(11:1) Now a certain man was sick, Lazarus of Bethany, the village of Mary and her sister Martha, both good friends of Joshua. (2) It was the Mary who anointed the Lord with ointment, and wiped his feet with her hair, whose brother Lazarus was sick. (3) So the sisters sent word to him, saying, "Lord, behold, he whom you love is sick." (4) But when Joshua heard this, he said, "**This sickness is not to end in death, but for the glory of God, so that the Son of God may be glorified by it.**" (5) Now Joshua loved Martha and her sister and Lazarus. (6) So when he heard that he was sick, he then stayed two days longer in the place where he was. (7) Then after this he said to the disciples, "**Let us go to Judea again.**" (8) The disciples said to him, "Master, the Jews were just now seeking to stone you, and are you going there again?" (9) Joshua answered, "**Are there not twelve hours in the day? If anyone walks in the day, he does not stumble, because he sees the light of this world. (10) "But if anyone walks in the night, he stumbles, because the light is not in him.**" (11) This he said, and after that he said to them, "**Our friend Lazarus has fallen asleep; but I go, so that I may awaken him out of sleep.**" (12) The disciples then said to him, "Lord, if he has fallen asleep, he will recover." (13) Now Joshua had spoken of his death, but they thought that he was speaking of literal sleep. (14) So Joshua then said to them plainly, "**Lazarus is dead, (15) and I am glad for your sakes that I was not there, so that you may believe; but let us go to him.**" (16) Therefore Thomas, who is called Didymus, said to his fellow disciples, "Let us also go, so that we may die with him."

(17) So when Joshua came, he found that his body had already been in the tomb four days. (18) Now Bethany was near Jerusalem, about two miles off; (19) and many of the Jews had come to Martha and Mary, to console them concerning their brother. (20) Martha therefore, when she heard that Joshua was coming, went to meet him, but Mary stayed at the house. (21) Martha then said to Joshua, "Lord, if you had been here, my brother would not have died. (22) "Even now I know that whatever you ask of God, God will give you." (23) Joshua said to her, "**Your brother will rise**

again." (24) Martha said to him, "I know that he will rise again in the resurrection on the last day."

(25) Joshua said to her, "**I am the resurrection and the life; he who believes in me will live** (*spiritually*) **even if he dies** (*physically*), (26) **and everyone who lives and believes in me will never die** (*spiritually*). **Do you believe this?**"

(27) She said to him, "Yes, Lord; I have believed that you are the Messiah, the Son of God, even he who comes into the world." (28) When she had said this, she went away and called Mary her sister, saying secretly, "The Teacher is here and is calling for you." (29) And when she heard it, she got up quickly and was coming to him. (30) Now Joshua had not yet come into the village, but was still in the place where Martha met him. (31) Then the Jews who were with her in the house, and consoling her, when they saw that Mary got up quickly and went out, they followed her, supposing that she was going to the tomb to weep there. (32) Therefore, when Mary came where Joshua was, she saw him, and fell at his feet, saying to him, "Lord, if you had been here, my brother would not have died." (33) When Joshua therefore saw her weeping, and the Jews who came with her also weeping, he was deeply moved in spirit and was troubled, (34) and said, "**Where have you laid him?**" They said to him, "Lord, come and see." (35) Joshua wept. (36) So the Jews were saying, "See how he loved him!" (37) But some of them said, "Could not this man, who opened the eyes of the blind man, have kept this man also from dying?" (38) So Joshua, again being deeply moved within, came to the tomb. Now it was a cave, and a stone was lying against it. (39) Joshua said, "**Remove the stone.**" Martha, the sister of the deceased, said to him, "Lord, by this time there will be a stench, for he has been dead four days." (40) Joshua said to her, "**Did I not say to you that if you believe, you will see the glory of God?**" (41) So they removed the stone. Then Joshua raised his eyes, and said, "**Father, I thank You that You have heard me. (42) "I knew that You always hear me; but because of the people standing around I said it, so that they may believe that You sent me.**" (43) When he had said

these things, he cried out with a loud voice, "**Lazarus, come forth**." (44) The man who had died came forth, bound hand and foot with wrappings, and his face was wrapped around with a cloth. Joshua said to them, "**Unbind him, and let him go**." (45) Therefore many of the Jews who came to Mary, and saw what he had done, believed in him. (46) But some of them went to the religious leaders and told them the things which Joshua had done.

(47) Therefore the religious leaders convened a council, and were saying, "What are we doing? For this man is performing many signs. (48) "If we let him go on like this, all men will believe in him, and the Romans will come and take away both our place and our nation." (49) But one of them, Caiaphas, who was the president of the religious leaders council that year, said to them, "You know nothing at all, (50) nor do you take into account that it is expedient for you that one man die for the people, and that the whole nation not perish." (51) Now he did not say this on his own initiative, but being president that year, he prophesied that Joshua was going to die for the nation, (52) and not for the nation only, but in order that he might also gather together into one the children of God who are scattered abroad. (53) So from that day on they planned together to kill him. (54) Therefore Joshua no longer continued to walk publicly among the Jews, but went away from there to the country near the wilderness, into a city called Ephraim; and there he stayed with the disciples.

(55) Now the Passover of the Jews was near, and many went up to Jerusalem out of the country before the Passover to purify themselves. (56) So they were seeking for Joshua, and were saying to one another as they stood in the temple, "What do you think; that he will not come to the feast at all?" (57) Now the religious leaders had given orders that if anyone knew where he was, he was to report it, so that they might seize him.

(12:1) Joshua, therefore, six days before the Passover, came to Bethany where Lazarus was, whom Joshua had raised from the dead. (2) So they made him a supper there, and Martha was serving; but Lazarus was one of those reclining at the table with him. (3) Mary then took a pound of very costly perfume of pure nard, and anointed the feet of Joshua and wiped his feet with her hair; and the house was filled with the fragrance of the perfume. (4) But Judas Iscariot, one of his disciples, who was intending to betray him, said, (5) "Why was this perfume not sold for hundreds dollars and given to poor people?" (6) Now he said this, not because he was concerned about the poor, but because he was a thief, and as he had the money box, he used to pilfer what was put into it. (7) Therefore Joshua said, **"Let her alone, so that she may keep it for the day of my burial. (8) "For you always have the poor with you, but you do not always have me."** [*42] (9) The large crowd of the Jews then learned that he was there; and they came, not for Joshua' sake only, but that they might also see Lazarus, whom he raised from the dead. (10) But the religious leaders planned to put Lazarus to death also; (11) because on account of him many of the Jews were going away and were believing in (*another way of saying, placing their faith in*) Joshua.

[*42] *Loving, respecting, listening to, obeying Joshua is more important that caring for the poor, though caring for the poor is good and right according to Joshua (see Luke 13).*

(12) On the next day the large crowd who had come to the feast, when they heard that Joshua was coming to Jerusalem, (13) took the branches of the palm trees and went out to meet him, and began to shout, "Hosanna! BLESSED IS HE WHO COMES IN THE NAME OF THE LORD, even the King of Israel." (14) Joshua, finding a young donkey, sat on it; as it is written, (15) "FEAR NOT, DAUGHTER OF ZION; BEHOLD, YOUR KING IS COMING, SEATED ON A DONKEY'S COLT." (16) These things his disciples did not understand at the first; but when Joshua was glorified (*defeated death by his resurrection*), then they remembered that these things were written of him, and that they had done these

things to him. (17) So the people, who were with him when he called Lazarus out of the tomb and raised him from the dead, continued to testify about him. (18) For this reason also the people went and met him, because they heard that he had performed this sign. (19) So the religious leaders said to one another, "You see that you are not doing any good; look, the world has gone after him."

(20) Now there were some Greeks among those who were going up to worship at the feast; (21) these then came to Philip, who was from Bethsaida of Galilee, and began to ask him, saying, "Sir, we wish to see Joshua." (22) Philip came and told Andrew; Andrew and Philip came and told Joshua. (23) And Joshua answered them, saying, "**The hour has come for the Son of Man to be glorified. (24) "Truly, truly, I say to you, unless a grain of wheat falls into the earth and dies, it remains alone; but if it dies, it bears much fruit.**

(25) **"He who loves his life loses it, and he who hates his life in this world will keep it to life eternal.**"[*43]

(26) **"If anyone serves me, he must follow me; and where I am, there my servant will be also; if anyone <u>serves me</u>, the Father will honor him. (27) "Now my soul has become troubled; and what shall I say, 'Father, save me from this hour'? But for this purpose I came to this hour. (28) "Father, glorify Your name.**" Then a voice came out of heaven: "**I have both glorified it, and will glorify it again.**" (29) So the crowd of people who stood by and heard it were saying that it had thundered; others were saying, "An angel has spoken to him." (30) Joshua answered and said, "**This voice has not come for my sake, but for your sakes. (31) "Now judgment is upon this world; now the ruler of this world** (*Satan*) **will be cast out.**"[*44] **(32) "And I, if I am lifted up from the earth, will draw all men to myself.**" [*45] (33) But he was saying this to indicate the kind of death by which he was to die. (34) The crowd then answered him, "We have heard out of the Law that the Messiah is to remain forever; and how can you say, 'The Son of Man must be

lifted up'? Who is this Son of Man?" (35) So Joshua said to them, **"For a little while longer the Light is among you. Walk while you have the Light, so that darkness will not overtake you; he who walks in the darkness does not know where he goes. (36)** "While you have the Light (*while Joshua is on the earth*)**, trust in the Light** (*given by the Maker, our Father*)**, so that you may become sons of Light**." These things Joshua spoke, and he went away and hid himself from them.

*43 *Verse 25 provides a key teaching of Joshua of what one must do to be his disciple/follower. This key teaching is repeated in all the gospels (Matt. 10:39, 16:25; Mark 8:35; Luke 9:24, 17:33) and yet is virtually unknown to the masses who take some Christian label. Disciples must ask ourselves, 'are we willing to do this'?*

*44 *In this commentator's opinion, this was fulfilled with the ransom paid at the cross (Joshua's death – see Matt. 20:28), and thus Satan lost his strong ruler-ship over mankind – Joshua opened the door to mankind's prison cell by paying the ransom (Matt. 20:28) and ever since, mankind (each person) is free to choose whom or what they will serve – each person must decide if they are going to walk out of the dark prison cell and go to the Light or not – a cell they have grown accustomed to and feel comfortable in.*

*45 *He **was** lifted up from the earth and thus he does draw all men to himself. See Luke 24:51. Everyone who hears of Joshua has been given an invitation to come. All who have had the opportunity to hear his words have no excuse for rejecting him. Substituting bible or christian religion for him is a clever way to reject him.*

(37) But though he had performed so many signs before them, yet they were not believing in him. (38) This was to fulfill the word of Isaiah the prophet which he spoke: "Lord, Who Has Believed Our Report? And To Whom Has The Arm Of The Lord Been Revealed?" (39) For this reason they could not believe, for Isaiah said again, (40) "He Has Blinded Their Eyes And He Hardened Their Heart, So That They Would Not See With Their Eyes And Perceive With Their Heart, And Be Converted And I Heal Them." (41) These things

Isaiah said because he saw his glory, and he spoke of him."[46] (42) Nevertheless many even of the political rulers believed in him, but because of the religious leaders they were not confessing him, for fear that they would be put out of the synagogue; (43) for they loved the approval of men rather than the approval of God.

[46] *This is a good example of a saying in the scripture being wrong. The writer John quotes the Jewish prophet Isaiah who in this case says that God "Has Blinded Their Eyes And He Hardened Their Heart, So That They Would Not See With Their Eyes And Perceive With Their Heart". The heavenly Father does not blind men nor harden their hearts, rather men do that all by themselves. Listen to Joshua, whose words are from the Father's heart - "For I have come not to destroy men's lives, but to save them". See the next paragraph – "I have come to save the people of the earth" and those words are given by "the Father Himself". All Old Testament sayings should be thought of as potentially painting the wrong picture of God unless the saying is validated by Joshua's Way and teachings.*

(44) And Joshua cried out and said, **"He who believes in me, does not believe in me but in Him who sent me. (45) "He who sees me sees the One who sent me. (46) "I have come as Light into the world, so that everyone who trusts in me will not remain in darkness. (47) "If anyone hears my sayings and does not keep them, I do not judge him; for I did not come to judge the world, but to save the people of the earth. (48) "He who rejects me and does not receive my sayings, has one who judges him; the word I spoke is what will judge him at the last day. (49) "For I did not speak on my own initiative, but the Father Himself who sent me has given me a commandment as to what to say and what to speak. (50) "I know that His commandment is eternal life; therefore the things I speak, I speak just as the Father has told me."** [47]

[47] *What more could he say? He is the Creator's Messenger. He is the Light of the world and the Life that everyone needs. There are consequences for rejecting him and his Light. Why would you reject him? What does he say that is wrong? Which of his primary teachings do you disagree with and why?*

(13:1) Now before the Feast of the Passover, Joshua knowing that his hour had come that he would depart out of this world to the Father, having loved his own who were in the world, he loved them to the end. (2) During supper, the devil having already put into the heart of Judas Iscariot, the son of Simon, to betray him, (3) Joshua, knowing that the Father had given all things into his hands, and that he had come forth from God and was going back to God, (4) got up from supper, and laid aside his garments; and taking a towel, he tied the towel around his waist. (5) Then he poured water into the basin, and began to wash the disciples' feet and to wipe them with the towel which was around his waist. (6) So he came to Simon Peter. He said to him, "Lord, do you wash my feet?" (7) Joshua answered and said to him, "**What I do you do not realize now, but you will understand hereafter.**" (8) Peter said to him, "Never shall you wash my feet!" Joshua answered him, "**If I do not wash you, you have no part with me**." (9) Simon Peter said to him, "Lord, then wash not only my feet, but also my hands and my head." (10) Joshua said to him, "**He who has bathed needs only to wash his feet, but is completely clean; and you are clean, but not all of you**." (11) For he knew the one who was betraying him; for this reason he said, "**Not all of you are clean**."

(12) So when he had washed their feet, and taken his garments and reclined at the table again, he said to them, "**Do you know what I have done to you? (13) "You call me Teacher and Lord; and you are right, for so I am. (14) "If I then, the Lord and the Teacher, washed your feet, you also ought to wash one another's feet. (15) "For I gave you an example that you also should do as I did to you. (16) "Truly, truly, I say to you, a servant is not greater than his master, nor is one who is sent greater than the one who sent him. (17) "If you know these things, you are blessed if you do them. (18) "I do not speak of all of you. I know the ones I have chosen; but it is that the scripture may be fulfilled, 'HE WHO EATS MY BREAD HAS LIFTED UP HIS HEEL AGAINST ME.' (19) "From now on I am telling you before it comes to pass, so that when it does occur, you may**

believe that I am he. **(20) "Truly, truly, I say to you, he who receives whomever I send receives me; and he who receives me receives Him who sent me."**

(21) When Joshua had said this, he became troubled in spirit, and testified and said, **"Truly, truly, I say to you, that one of you will betray me."** (22) The disciples began looking at one another, at a loss to know of which one he was speaking. (23) There was lying on Joshua' chest one of his disciples, whom Joshua loved. (24) So Simon Peter gestured to him, and said to him, "Tell us who it is of whom he is speaking." (25) He, leaning back thus on Joshua' chest, said to him, "Lord, who is it?" (26) Joshua then answered, **"That is the one for whom I shall dip the bread and give it to him."** So when he had dipped the bread, he took and gave it to Judas, the son of Simon Iscariot. (27) After the bread, Satan then entered into him. Therefore Joshua said to him, **"What you do, do quickly."** [*48] (28) Now no one of those laying around the table knew for what purpose he had said this to him. (29) For some were supposing, because Judas had the money box, that Joshua was saying to him, "Buy the things we have need of for the feast"; or else, that he should give something to the poor. (30) So after receiving the bread Judas went out immediately; and it was night.

[*48] *Here is a good example of the author John reading something into a situation that Joshua did not clearly address. John says, "Satan then entered into Judas". If you look at only Joshua's words from verse 1 through verse 30, you certainly could not deduce that "Satan then entered into Judas" – that was John's understanding and not necessarily what actually happened.*

(31) Therefore when he had gone out, Joshua said, **"Now is the Son of Man glorified, and God is glorified in him; (32) if God is glorified in him, God will also glorify him in Himself, and will glorify him immediately. (33) "Little children, I am with you a little while longer. You will seek me; and as I said to the Jews,** [*49] **now I also say to you, 'Where I am going, you cannot come.'**

"...to the Jews..." Joshua did not say, 'to my people' or 'to God's people', or anything of that sort...rather he referred to them in an objective way as he would any people group. The Creator is not a respecter of people - He loves and cares about all people.

(34) **"A new commandment I give to you, that you love one another, even as I have loved you, that you also love one another.** (35) **"By this all men will know that you are my disciples, if you have love for one another."** *50

*50 *This is the only command Joshua described as "new", thus setting it apart - and perhaps rising it above - his other commands. If his followers do not live this command out, then there is no 'witness' to the people of the earth of his existence or the Father's love for people. All the preaching and words and efforts will largely fail if this new command is not lived out by his people...it is the essential rubber-meets-the-road requirement and yet, sadly, this most important manifestation of actual love is all but gone, replaced in large measure by, 'they will know you are Christians by your bible knowledge or your 'church' steeples or your Christmas songs.' Christianity/churchianity is a sad, empty and powerless substitute for the Father's and Joshua's love.*

(36) Simon Peter said to him, "Lord, where are you going?" Joshua answered, **"Where I go, you cannot follow me now; but you will follow later."** (37) Peter said to him, "Lord, why can I not follow you right now? I will lay down my life for you." (38) Joshua answered, **"Will you lay down your life for me? Truly, truly, I say to you, a rooster will not crow until you deny me three times.**

(14:1) "Do not let your heart be troubled; trust in God, trust also in me. (2) "In my Father's house are many dwelling places; if it were not so, I would have told you; for I go to prepare a place for you. (3) "If I go and prepare a place for you, I will come again and receive you to myself, that where I am, there you may be also. (4) "And you know the way where I am going." (5) Thomas said to him, "Lord, we do not know where you are going, how do we know the way?" (6) Joshua said to him, "I am the way, and the truth, and the life; no one comes to the Father but through me.[*51] (7) "If you had known me, you would have known my Father also; from now on you know Him, and have seen Him." (8) Philip said to him, "Lord, show us the Father, and it is enough for us." (9) Joshua said to him, "Have I been so long with you, and yet you have not come to know me, Philip? He who has seen me has seen the Father; how can you say, 'Show us the Father'? (10) "Do you not believe that I am in the Father, and the Father is in me? The words that I say to you I do not speak on my own initiative, but the Father abiding in me does His works. (11) "Believe me that I am in the Father and the Father is in me; otherwise believe because of the works themselves. (12) "Truly, truly, I say to you, he who believes in me, the works that I do, he will do also; and greater works than these he will do; because I go to the Father. (13) "Whatever you ask in my name, that will I do, so that the Father may be glorified in the Son. (14) "If you ask me anything in my name, I will do it.[*52]**

[*51] *He does not say, "All people who are not Christians will go to hell" in this saying. Rather, he simply says that all people who die will go before him as their judge for him to judge how they lived their lives and why they did things – see John 5:22. In addition, this claim is comprehensive and sets him apart from any other human being. He says, "I am the way that humans ought to live, I represent all the spiritual truth that matters, and I am eternal life.*

[*52] *In regard to sayings like this – sayings that don't match reality - only a few possibilities exist - he did not say it; it was recorded incorrectly; it only applied*

while he was on the earth the first time; or we need faith to bring it to pass. See note 64 in this gospel.

(15) "If you love me, you will keep my commandments.[*53]

[*53] *The primary fruit or manifestation of a person's love of Joshua is doing what he says. It is NOT primarily an emotion or feeling, but rather obedience to him and his teachings. We can claim we love Joshua, but if we don't read HIS words – thus showing we care about what he says - and then seek to DO what HE says, then we in fact do not love him. See also John 14:21-24; 15:10.*

(16) "I will ask the Father, and He will give you another helper, that he may be with you forever; (17) that is the Spirit of truth,[*54] **whom the world cannot receive, because it does not see him or know him, but you know him because he abides with you and will be in you. (18) "I will not leave you as orphans; I will come to you. (19) "After a little while the world will no longer see me, but you will see me; because I live, you will live also** (*after the resurrection, he will show himself to his followers*). **(20) "In that day you will know that I am in my Father, and you in me, and I in you.**

[*54] *Contrast "Spirit of truth" with all the emotionally based so-called manifestations of the Spirit so prevalent in many Christian and bible sects. Strange or uncontrolled behavior is a poor substitute for truth.*

(21) "He who has my commandments and keeps them is the one who loves me; and he who loves me will be loved by my Father, and I will love him and will disclose myself to him."

(22) Judas (*not Iscariot, the one who betrayed him*) said to him, "Lord, what then has happened that you are going to disclose yourself to us and not to the people?" (23) Joshua answered and said to him, **"If anyone loves me, he will keep my word; and my Father will love him, and we will come to him and**

make our abode with him. (24) "He who does not love me does not keep my words; and the word which you hear is not mine, but the Father's who sent me. (25) "These things I have spoken to you while abiding with you. (26) "But the Helper, the Holy Spirit, whom the Father will send in my name, he will teach you all things, and bring to your remembrance all that I said to you.[*55] (27) "Peace I leave with you; my peace I give to you; not as the world gives do I give to you. Do not let your heart be troubled, nor let it be fearful. (28) "You heard that I said to you, 'I go away, and I will come to you.' If you loved me, you would have rejoiced because I go to the Father, for the Father is greater than I. (29) "Now I have told you before it happens, so that when it happens, you may believe. (30) "I will not speak much more with you, for the ruler of the world is coming, and he has nothing in me; (31) but so that the world may know that I love the Father, I do exactly as the Father commanded me.[*56] Get up, let us go from here.

[*55] *The promise that those eyewitnesses and other contemporaries who would record the events and sayings of Joshua would do so accurately.*

[*56] *The Father asked the Son to please go pay a ransom to free the people of the earth from the "ruler of the world", Satan (see Matt. 20:28). The Son could have defended himself and not given his physical life to pay the ransom, but to show his love for his Father, he laid down his life for all who consider him a friend and thus accept the freedom that he provides.*

(15:1) "I am the true vine, and my Father is the One who cares for the vine. (2) "Every branch in me that does not bear fruit, He takes away; and every branch that bears fruit, He prunes it so that it may bear more fruit. (3) "You are already clean because of the word which I have spoken to you.*57 (4) "Abide*58 in me, and I in you. As the branch cannot bear fruit of itself unless it abides in the vine, so neither can you unless you abide in me. (5) "I am the vine, you are the branches; he who abides in me and I in him, he bears much fruit, for apart from me you can do nothing. (6) "If anyone does not abide in me, he is thrown away as a branch and dries up; and they gather them, and cast them into the fire and they are burned. (7) "If you abide in me, and my words abide in you, ask whatever you wish, and it will be done for you. (8) "My Father is glorified by this, that you bear much fruit, and so prove to be my disciples. (9) "Just as the Father has loved me, I have also loved you; abide in my love.

*57 *There is one sure way to get spiritually clean, and it is not baptism or other ritual or teaching! Rather, it is listening to the Light and receiving his word/teachings.*

*58 *"Abide" means to spiritually dwell, stay or remain in...to be conscious of his presence and his teachings.*

(10) "If you keep my commandments, you will abide in my love; just as I have kept my Father's commandments and abide in His love.

(11) "These things I have spoken to you so that my joy may be in you, and that your joy may be made full. (12) "This is my commandment, that you love one another, just as I have loved you.*59 (13) "Greater love has no one than this, that one lay down his life for his friends. (14) "You are my friends if you do what I command you. (15) "No longer do I call you servants, for the servant does not know what his

master is doing; but I have called you friends, for all things that I have heard from my Father I have made known to you. (16) "You did not choose me but I chose you, and appointed you that you would go and bear fruit, and that your fruit would remain, so that whatever you ask of the Father in my name He may give to you. (17) "This I command you, that you love one another."*60

*59, 60 *The New Command repeated and spoken as if it was his only command to his followers, "This is my commandment". If we are not doing this, we are failing badly. If it is hard to love our enemies, then it should be easy to love our true brothers and sisters, and yet what does the world see when it looks at the thing that calls itself "Jesus' church"? Certainly not love the way Joshua defines it.*

(18) "If the world (*the people of the earth who don't have Joshua as their leader*) hates you, you know that it has hated me before it hated you. (19) "If you were of the world, the world would love its own; but because you are not of the world, but I chose you out of the world,"*61 because of this the world hates you. (20) "Remember the word that I said to you, 'A servant is not greater than his master.' If they persecuted (*sought to harm*) me, they will also persecute you; if they kept my word, they will keep yours also.

*61 *Joshua's disciples are called out of the world. This does not mean we seclude ourselves in a remote monastery or that we run to the desert and hide from people. Rather it means we do not live like those who don't listen to Joshua, and thus we will be separate since we love/care for others who are not our natural or legal relatives, and people will be offended by our words and ways. We are to be a different, noticeable people who are not part of the world's systems, living according to the teachings of the Light and not valuing what the people of the earth value but rather valuing our heavenly Father and His Son's Way of love and right-ness.*

(21) "But all these things they will do to you for my name's sake, because they do not know the One who sent me. (22) "If I had not come and spoken to them, they would not

have sin, but now they have no excuse for their sin.[*61] (23) "He who hates me hates my Father also. (24) "If I had not done among them the works which no one else did, they would not have sin; but now they have both seen and hated me and my Father as well. (25) "But they have done this to fulfill the word that is written in their Law (see John 8:17), 'THEY HATED ME WITHOUT A CAUSE.' (26) "When the Helper comes, whom I will send to you from the Father, that is the Spirit of truth who proceeds from the Father, he will testify about me,[*62] (27) and you will testify also, because you have been with me from the beginning.

[*61] *Knowledge brings accountability. Those who are in the worst position are those who hear and know Joshua's teachings, but do not do them.*

[*62] *This is the Holy Spirit's – the "Spirit of truth" – primary function, to testify or witness that Joshua of Nazareth is the "truth" like he said he was. See also John 16:13-14. And yet there are millions of Christians listening to Paul's teachings on the Spirit which teachings often contradict the teachings of Joshua and which teachings have nothing to do with testifying about Joshua!*

(16:1) "These things I have spoken to you so that you may be kept from stumbling. (2) "They will make you outcasts from the religious organization, but an hour is coming for everyone who kills you to think that he is offering service to God. (3) "These things they will do because they have not known the Father or me. (4) "But these things I have spoken to you, so that when their hour comes, you may remember that I told you of them. These things I did not say to you at the beginning, because I was with you. (5) "But now I am going to Him who sent me; and none of you asks me, 'Where are you going?' (6) "But because I have said these things to you, sorrow has filled your heart.

(7) "But I tell you the truth, it is to your advantage that I go away; for if I do not go away, the Helper will not come to you; but if I go, I will send Him to you. (8) "And the Holy Spirit, when He comes, will convict the world concerning sin and righteousness and judgment; (9) concerning sin, because they do not believe in me; (10) and concerning righteousness, because I go to the Father and you no longer see me; (11) and concerning judgment, because the ruler of this world has been judged.*63 (12) "I have many more things to say to you, but you cannot bear them now. (13) "But when He, the Spirit of truth, comes, He will guide you into all the truth; for He will not speak on His own initiative, but whatever He hears, He will speak; and He will disclose to you what is to come. (14) "He will glorify me, for He will take of mine and will disclose it to you. (15) "All things that the Father has are mine; therefore I said that He takes of mine and will disclose it to you. (16) "A little while, and you will no longer see me; and again a little while, and you will see me."

*63 *Listen to Joshua if you want to know the real purpose of the Holy Spirit instead of Paul's or christian leaders teachings.*

(17) Some of his disciples then said to one another, "What is this thing he is telling us, 'A little while, and you will not see me; and again a little while, and you will see me'; and, 'because I go to the Father'?" (18) So they were saying, "What is this that he says, 'A little while'? We do not know what he is talking about." (19) Joshua knew that they wished to question him, and he said to them, "**Are you discussing together about this, that I said, 'A little while, and you will not see me, and again a little while, and you will see me'?** (20) **"Truly, truly, I say to you, that you will weep and cry out in pain, but the world will rejoice; you will grieve, but your grief will be turned into joy.** (21) **"Whenever a woman is in labor she has pain, because her hour has come; but when she gives birth to the child, she no longer remembers the pain and anguish because of the joy that a child has been born into the world.** (22) **"Therefore you too have grief now; but I will see you again, and your heart will rejoice, and no one will take your joy away from you.**

(23) **"In that day you will not question me about anything. Truly, truly, I say to you, if you ask the Father for anything in my name, He will give it to you.** (24) **"Until now you have asked for nothing in my name; ask and you will receive,**[*64] **so that your joy may be made full.** (25) **"These things I have spoken to you in figurative language; an hour is coming when I will no longer speak to you in figurative language, but will tell you plainly of the Father.** (26) **"In that day you will ask in my name, and I do not say to you that I will request of the Father on your behalf;** (27) **for the Father Himself loves you, because you have loved me and have believed that I came forth from the Father.** (28) **"I came forth from the Father and have come into the world; I am leaving the world again and going to the Father."**

*64 *When words are attributed to Joshua that don't come true – words like, "ask the Father for anything in my name, He will give it to you" - there are several* *possibilities. Either he didn't actually say it – his words were changed. Or the reasons why it originally applied no longer exist.*

(29) His disciples said, "Alright, now you are speaking plainly and are not using a figure of speech. (30) "Now we know that you know all things, and have no need for anyone to question you; by this we believe that you came from God." (31) Joshua answered them, "**Do you now believe? (32) "Behold, an hour is coming, and has already come, for you to be scattered, each to his own home, and to leave me alone; and yet I am not alone, because the Father is with me. (33) "These things I have spoken to you, so that in me you may have peace. In the world you have great trouble, but take courage; I have overcome the world."** *[65]

---

[65] Disciples need to "take courage" for the world is and will always be against us and therefore bring trouble our way when we speak and live out the Lights truths and thus reveal the darkness of the world. Even in the darkest hour when the world seeks to destroy the bringers of the Light, our courage will not be misplaced since the one we follow has already overcome the world.

(17:1) Joshua spoke these things; and lifting up his eyes to heaven, he said, "**Father, the hour has come; glorify your son, that the son may glorify You,** (2) **even as You gave him authority over all flesh, that to all whom You have given him, he may give eternal life.** (3) **"This is eternal life, that they may know You, the only true God, and Messiah Joshua whom You have sent.**"[66]

[66] *Perhaps the clearest definition of eternal life! We would do well to pay attention to this saying...eternal life is found, gained or remained in by knowing the Father and His Son, and an essential part of that is to read, know and understand the Son's words and teachings, NOT the bible or scripture. See John 8:31-32.*

(4) **"I glorified You on the earth, having accomplished the work which You have given me to do.** (5) **"Now, Father, glorify me together with Yourself, with the glory which I had with You before the world was.** (6) **"I have manifested Your name to the men whom You gave me out of the world; they were Yours and You gave them to me, and they have kept Your word.** (7) **"Now they have come to know that everything You have given me is from You;** (8) **for the words which You gave me I have given to them; and they received them and truly understood that I came forth from You, and they believed that You sent me.** (9) **"I ask on their behalf; I do not ask on behalf of the world, but of those whom You have given me; for they are Yours;** (10) **and all things that are Mine are Yours, and Yours are Mine; and I have been glorified in them.**

(11) **"I am no longer in the world; and yet they themselves are in the world, and I come to You. Holy Father, keep them in Your name, the name which You have given me, that they may be one even as we are.** (12) **"While I was with them, I was keeping them in Your name which You have given me; and I guarded them and not one of them perished but Judas Iscariot, the son of destruction, so that**

the scripture would be fulfilled. (13) "But now I come to You; and these things I speak in the world so that they may have my joy made full in themselves. (14) "I have given them Your word; and the world has hated them, because they are not of the world, even as I am not of the world (*see John 15:18*). (15) "I do not ask You to take them out of the world, but to keep them from the evil one. (16) "They are not of the world, even as I am not of the world. (17) "Sanctify (*set them apart*) them in the truth; Your word is truth. (18) "As You sent me into the world, I also have sent them into the world. [67]

[67] *Disciples have a purpose or work while in the world since we are "sent" into the world to bring people to the Father. There are no "ministries" as the religious sects define that – all disciples have the same mission, to bring people to our Father and spread Joshua's teachings, and we all are to be active in that work since it reflects the passion of our heart. It all starts - and our work is only credible - by keeping the new command. See John 13:34-35.*

(19) "For their sakes I separate myself, that they themselves also may be separated in truth.[68] (20) "I do not ask on behalf of these alone, but for those also who believe in me through their word; (21) that they may all be one; even as You, Father, are in me and I in You, that they also may be in Us, so that the world may believe that You sent me. (22) "The glory which You have given me I have given to them, that they may be one, just as We are one; (23) I in them and You in me, that they may be perfected in unity,[69] so that the world may know that You sent me, and loved them, even as You have loved me. (24) "Father, I desire that they also, whom You have given me, be with me where I am, so that they may see my glory which You have given me, for You loved me before the foundation of the world. (25) "O righteous Father, although the world has not known You, yet I have known You; and these have known that You sent me; (26) and I have made Your name

known to them, and will make it known, so that the love with which You loved me may be in them, and I in them."

*68   *See verses 14, 16, 17, 19 – all speak of the disciples separation from the world – the people of the earth who will not have Joshua as their leader. We will be a separate, distinguishable people, not living according to the world's ways nor chasing what the world considers valuable.*

*69   *The people of the earth who don't believe Joshua will only know that God sent His most beloved Son to save us IF we are in unity. How do the tens of thousands of divided bible/Christian sects represent Joshua's stated desire here? All attempts to explain how the tens of thousands of divisions of people all saying they are somehow part of a unified 'church of christ', are nothing more than empty words of grievous hypocrisy. The little flocks and Families of the good shepherd are the actual representation of the unity brought about by the love spoken of here by Joshua.*

(18:1) When Joshua had spoken these words, he went forth with his disciples over the ravine of the Kidron, where there was a garden, in which he entered with his disciples. (2) Now Judas also, who was betraying him, knew the place, for Joshua had often met there with his disciples. (3) Judas then, having received the Roman representatives and officers from the religious leaders, came there with lanterns and torches and weapons. (4) So Joshua, knowing all the things that were coming upon him, went forth and said to them, **"Whom do you seek?"** (5) They answered him, "Joshua the Nazarene." He said to them, **"I am he."** And Judas also, who was betraying him, was standing with them. (6) So when he said to them, **"I am he,"** they drew back and fell to the ground. (7) Therefore he again asked them, **"Whom do you seek?"** And they said, "Joshua the Nazarene." (8) Joshua answered, **"I told you that I am he; so if you seek me, let these go their way,"** (9) to fulfill the word which he spoke, **"Of those whom You have given me I lost not one."** (10) Simon Peter then, having a sword, drew it and struck the chief religious leader's servant, and cut off his right ear; and the servant's name was Malchus. (11) So Joshua said to Peter, **"Put the sword into the sheath; the cup** (*or work*) **which the Father has given me, shall I not drink it?"** (12) So the Roman representatives and the commander and the officers of the religious and political leaders, arrested Joshua and bound him, (13) and led him to Annas first; for he was father-in-law of Caiaphas, who was chief religious leader that year. (14) Now Caiaphas was the one who had advised the people that it was best for one man to die on behalf of the people.

(15) Simon Peter was following Joshua, and so was another disciple. Now that disciple was known to the chief religious leader, and entered with Joshua into the court of the chief religious leader, (16) but Peter was standing at the door outside. So the other disciple, who was known to the chief religious leader, went out and spoke to the doorkeeper, and brought Peter in. (17) Then the servant-girl who kept the door said to Peter, "You are not also one of this man's disciples, are you?" He said, "I am not." (18) Now the servants and the officers were standing there, having made a

charcoal fire, for it was cold and they were warming themselves; and Peter was also with them, standing and warming himself. (19) The chief religious leader then questioned Joshua about his disciples, and about his teaching. (20) Joshua answered him, "**I have spoken openly to the world; I always taught in the religious buildings and in the temple, where all the people come together; and I spoke nothing in secret. (21) "Why do you question me? Question those who have heard what I spoke to them; they know what I said.**" (22) When he had said this, one of the officers standing nearby struck Joshua, saying, "Is that the way you answer the high priest?" (23) Joshua answered him, "**If I have spoken wrongly, testify of the wrong; but if rightly, why do you strike me?**" (24) So Annas sent him bound to Caiaphas the chief religious leader. (25) Now Simon Peter was standing and warming himself. So they said to him, "You are not also one of his disciples, are you?" He denied it, and said, "I am not." (26) One of the servants of the chief religious leader, being a relative of the one whose ear Peter cut off, said, "Did I not see you in the garden with him?" (27) Peter then denied it again, and immediately a rooster crowed.

(28) Then they led Joshua from Caiaphas into the Praetorium (*the place of Roman judgment*), and it was early; and they themselves (*the Jewish religious, judicial and political leaders*) did not enter into the Praetorium so that they would not be defiled (*be made unclean in their eyes*), but might eat the Passover. (29) Therefore Pilate (*the Roman governor*) went out to them and said, "What accusation do you bring against this Man?" (30) They answered and said to him, "If this Man were not an evildoer, we would not have delivered him to you." (31) So Pilate said to them, "Take him yourselves, and judge him according to your law." The Jews said to him, "We are not permitted to put anyone to death," (32) to fulfill the word of Joshua which he spoke, signifying by what kind of death he was about to die. (33) Therefore Pilate entered again into the Praetorium, and summoned Joshua and said to him, "Are you the King of the Jews?" (34) Joshua answered, "**Are you saying this on your own initiative, or did others tell you about me?**"

(35) Pilate answered, "I am not a Jew, am I? Your own nation and the chief religious leaders delivered you to me; what have you done?" (36) Joshua answered, **"My kingdom is not of this world. If my kingdom were of this world, then my servants would be fighting so that I would not be handed over to those who hate me; but as it is, my kingdom is not of this world."** [*70] (37) Therefore Pilate said to him, "So you are a king?" Joshua answered, **"You say correctly that I am a king. For this I have been born, and for this I have come into the world, to testify to the truth. Everyone who is of the truth hears my voice."** [*71] (38) Pilate said to him, "What is truth?" And when he had said this, he went out again to the Jews and said to them, "I find no guilt in him. (39) "But you have a custom that I release someone for you at the Passover; do you wish then that I release for you the King of the Jews?" (40) So they cried out again, saying, "Not this Man, but Barabbas." Now Barabbas was a robber and accused murderer.

[*70] *Are not the religious system's (Roman Catholic, Anglican, Orthodox, Baptist, Methodist, Lutheran, Non-Denominational, etc.) kingdoms in this world, with their leaders/kings and properties and buildings and programs and money that make up those systems? Do not those religious kingdoms operate by the world's rules? Are they not accepted by the world as good religious institutions? In contrast, Joshua's kingdom is not of this world and is not represented by the world's bible or Christian religious sects.*

[*71] *If you are of the truth – if you care about that which is true and hate that which is false – you will hear Joshua's voice through his teachings and you will react appropriately, which is to agree with and do what Joshua says.*

(19:1) Pilate then took Joshua and had him whipped. (2) And the soldiers twisted together a crown of thorns and put it on his head, and put a purple robe on him; (3) and they began to come up to him and say, "Hail, King of the Jews!" and to give him hard slaps in the face. (4) Pilate came out again and said to them, "Behold, I am bringing him out to you so that you may know that I find no guilt in him." (5) Joshua then came out, wearing the crown of thorns and the purple robe. Pilate said to them, "Behold, the Man!" (6) So when the chief religious leaders and politicians saw him, they cried out saying, "Crucify, crucify!" Pilate said to them, "Take him yourselves and crucify him, for I find no guilt in him." (7) The religious leaders answered him, "We have a law, and by that law he ought to die because he made himself out to be the Son of God." *72

*72 *Even the religious leaders – after hearing all the claims of the people over many months – did not accuse him of blasphemy saying he claimed to be "God". A plain confession/accusation of his enemies in a legal setting having carefully calculated their words saying he claimed he was "the Son of God", is a very strong confirmation that Joshua did NOT claim to be "God", yet another refutation of the trinity doctrine.*

(8) Therefore when Pilate heard this statement, he was even more afraid; (9) and he entered into the Praetorium again and said to Joshua, "Where are you from?" But Joshua gave him no answer. (10) So Pilate said to him, "You do not speak to me? Do you not know that I have authority to release you, and I have authority to crucify you?" (11) Joshua answered, "**You would have no authority over me, unless it had been given you from above; for this reason he who delivered me to you** (*Judas Iscariot*) **has the greater sin.**" (12) As a result of this Pilate made efforts to release him, but the Jews cried out saying, "If you release this Man, you are no friend of Caesar; everyone who makes himself out to be a king opposes Caesar."

(13) Therefore when Pilate heard these words, he brought Joshua out, and sat down on the judgment seat at a place called The Pavement, but in Hebrew, Gabbatha. (14) Now it was the day of

preparation for the Passover; it was about six o'clock in the morning. And he said to the Jews, "Behold, your King!" (15) So they cried out, "Away with him, away with him, crucify him!" Pilate said to them, "Shall I crucify your King?" The chief religious leaders answered, "We have no king but Caesar." (16) So he then handed him over to them to be crucified.

(17) They took Joshua, therefore, and he went out, bearing his own cross, to the place called the Place of a Skull, which is called in Hebrew, Golgotha. (18) There they crucified him, and with him two other men, one on either side, and Joshua in between. (19) Pilate also wrote an inscription and put it on the cross. It was written, "JOSHUA THE NAZARENE, THE KING OF THE JEWS." (20) Therefore many of the Jews read this inscription, for the place where Joshua was crucified was near the city; and it was written in Hebrew, Latin and in Greek. (21) So the religious leaders were saying to Pilate, "Do not write, 'The King of the Jews'; but that he said, 'I am King of the Jews.'" (22) Pilate answered, "What I have written I have written."

(23) Then the soldiers, when they had crucified Joshua, took his outer garments and made four parts, a part to every soldier and also the tunic; now the tunic was seamless, woven in one piece. (24) So they said to one another, "Let us not tear it, but cast lots for it, to decide whose it shall be"; this was to fulfill the Scripture: "They Divided My Outer Garments Among Them, And For My Clothing They Cast Lots." (25) Therefore the soldiers did these things. But standing by the cross of Joshua were his mother, and his mother's sister, Mary the wife of Clopas, and Mary Magdalene. (26) When Joshua then saw his mother, and the disciple whom he loved standing nearby, he said to his mother, "**Woman, behold, your son!**" (27) Then he said to the disciple, "**Behold, your mother!**" From that hour the disciple took her into his own household. (28) After this, Joshua, knowing that all things had already been accomplished, to fulfill the scripture, said, "I am thirsty." (29) A jar full of sour wine was standing there; so they put a sponge full of the sour wine upon a branch of hyssop and brought it up to his mouth.

(30) Therefore when Joshua had received the sour wine, he said, **"It is finished!"** And he bowed his head and gave up his spirit.

(31) Then the Jews, because it was the day of preparation, so that the bodies would not remain on the cross on the Sabbath (for that Sabbath was a high day), asked Pilate that their legs might be broken, and that they might be taken away. (32) So the soldiers came, and broke the legs of the first man and of the other who was crucified with him; (33) but coming to Joshua, when they saw that he was already dead, they did not break his legs. (34) But one of the soldiers pierced his side with a spear, and immediately blood and water came out. (35) And he who has seen has testified, and his testimony is true; and he knows that he is telling the truth, so that you also may believe. (36) For these things came to pass to fulfill the Scripture, "Not A Bone Of Him Shall Be Broken." (37) And again another Scripture says, "They Shall Look On Him Whom They Pierced."

(38) After these things Joseph of Arimathea, being a disciple of Joshua, but a secret one for fear of the Jews, asked Pilate that he might take away the body of Joshua; and Pilate granted permission. So he came and took away his body. (39) Nicodemus, who had first come to him by night, also came, bringing a mixture of myrrh and aloes, about a hundred pounds weight. (40) So they took the body of Joshua and bound it in linen wrappings with the spices, as is the burial custom of the Jews. (41) Now in the place where he was crucified there was a garden, and in the garden a new tomb in which no one had yet been laid. (42) Therefore because of the Jewish day of preparation, since the tomb was nearby, they laid Joshua there.

(20:1) Now on the first day of the week Mary Magdalene came early to the tomb, while it was still dark, and saw the stone already taken away from the tomb. (2) So she ran and came to Simon Peter and to the other disciple whom Joshua loved, and said to them, "They have taken away the body of the Lord out of the tomb, and we do not know where they have laid it." (3) So Peter and the other disciple went forth, and they were going to the tomb. (4) The two were running together; and the other disciple ran ahead faster than Peter and came to the tomb first; (5) and stooping and looking in, he saw the linen wrappings lying there; but he did not go in. (6) And so Simon Peter also came, following him, and entered the tomb; and he saw the linen wrappings lying there, (7) and the face-cloth which had been on his head, not lying with the linen wrappings, but rolled up in a place by itself. (8) So the other disciple who had first come to the tomb then also entered, and he saw and believed. (9) For as yet they did not understand the scripture, that he must rise again from the dead. (10) So the disciples went away again to their own homes.

(11) But Mary was standing outside the tomb weeping; and so, as she wept, she stooped and looked into the tomb; (12) and she saw two angels in white sitting, one at the head and one at the feet, where the body of Joshua had been lying. (13) And they said to her, "Woman, why are you weeping?" She said to them, "Because they have taken away my Lord's body, and I do not know where they have laid it." (14) When she had said this, she turned around and saw Joshua standing there in a shadow, and did not know that it was Joshua. (15) Joshua said to her, "**Woman, why are you weeping? Whom are you seeking?**" Supposing him to be the gardener, she said to him, "Sir, if you have carried him away, tell me where you have laid him, and I will take him away." (16) Joshua said to her, "**Mary!**" She turned and said to him in Hebrew, "Rabboni!" (which means, Teacher). (17) Joshua said to her, "**Stop clinging to me, for I have not yet ascended** (*gone*) **to the Father; but go to my brethren and say to them, 'I ascend to my Father and your Father, and my God and your God.'**" [*73]

"...my God..." is another very plain confession directly from the mouth of Joshua that he has a Father who is God, contradicting the trinity belief. Again the trinity belief gives the religious leaders power over the people by virtue of their saying you must accept a contradiction – and thus check your own mind in at the door so-to-speak - and instead accept them and their teachings to understand God and to go to heaven.

(18) Mary Magdalene came, announcing to the disciples, "I have seen the Lord," and that he had said these things to her. (19) So when it was evening on that day, the first day of the week, and when the doors were shut where the disciples were, for fear of the religious leaders, Joshua came and stood among them and said to them, "**Peace be with you**." (20) And when he had said this, he showed them both his hands and his side. The disciples then rejoiced when they saw the Lord. (21) So Joshua said to them again, "**Peace be with you; as the Father has sent me, I also send you**." (22) And when he had said this, he breathed on them and said to them, "**Receive the Holy Spirit. (23) "If you forgive the sins of any, their sins have been forgiven them; if you retain the sins of any, they have been retained**." [*74]

*[*74] In this disciples opinion, verses 22 and 23 were likely added and did not happen. The main reason I believe that in regard to verse 22 is this saying in John 16:7, "But I tell you the truth, it is to your advantage that I go away; for if I do not go away, the Helper will not come to you; but if I go, I will send Him to you." In regard to verse 23, it is inconsistent with this teaching on the matter, "For if you forgive others for their transgressions, your heavenly Father will also forgive you. But if you do not forgive others, then your Father will not forgive your transgressions." (Matt. 6:14-15), which teachings is repeated several times in both Matt. 18 and Mark 11 as well as a similar and consistent saying in Luke 17. Furthermore, the Christian clergy/leadership used this supposed saying to wield much power over people as they claimed they had the power to forgive the sins of others who did not sin against them. Only God and he individual we sinned against can forgive us our sins, and if the individual we sinned against will not accept our plea for forgiveness, our heavenly Father will!*

(24) But Thomas, one of the twelve, called Didymus, was not with them when Joshua came. (25) So the other disciples were saying to him, "We have seen the Lord!" But he said to them, "Unless I see in his hands the imprint (*or mark*) of the nails, and put my finger into the place of the nails, and put my hand into his side (*where the spear pierced*), I will not believe." (26) After eight days his disciples were again inside, and Thomas with them. Joshua came, the doors having been shut, and stood among them and said, "**Peace be with you**." (27) Then he said to Thomas, "**Reach here with your finger, and see my hands; and reach here your hand and put it into my side; and do not be unbelieving, but believing**." (28) Thomas answered and said to him, "My Lord and my God!" *75 (29) Joshua said to him, "**Because you have seen me, have you believed? Blessed are they who did not see, and yet believed**."

*75 *One of the few verses that those who believe the trinity doctrine cite to support their belief. Of first importance is that Joshua does not say here, 'I am my Father or God' or anything close to that. A plausible re-enactment of that moment and saying could have Thomas on his knees and looking at Joshua when he says, "My Lord", and bowing his head down and saying, "My God", referring to God and not Joshua. What is for certain is that two or three verses do not win out over the hundreds of verses and sayings of Joshua that plainly support the fact that Joshua and his Father are two separate beings.*

(30) Therefore many other signs Joshua also performed in the presence of the disciples, which are not written in this book; (31) but these have been written so that you may believe that Joshua is the Messiah, the Son of God; and that believing you may have Life in his name.

(21:1) After these things Joshua manifested himself again to the disciples at the Sea of Tiberias, and he manifested himself in this way. (2) Simon Peter, and Thomas called Didymus, and Nathanael of Cana in Galilee, and the sons of Zebedee, and two others of his disciples were together. (3) Simon Peter said to them, "I am going fishing." They said to him, "We will also come with you." They went out and got into the boat; and that night they caught nothing. (4) But when the day was now breaking, Joshua stood on the beach; yet the disciples did not know that it was Joshua. (5) So Joshua yelled to them, "**Children, you do not have any fish, do you?**" They answered him, "No." (6) And he said to them, "**Cast the net on the right-hand side of the boat and you will find a catch.**" So they cast, and then they were not able to haul it in because of the great number of fish. (7) Therefore that disciple whom Joshua loved said to Peter, "It is the Lord." So when Simon Peter heard that it was the Lord, he put his outer garment on (for he was stripped for work), and threw himself into the sea. (8) But the other disciples came in the little boat, for they were not far from the land, but about one hundred yards away, dragging the net full of fish.

(9) So when they got out on the land, they saw a charcoal fire already laid and fish placed on it, and bread. (10) Joshua said to them, "**Bring some of the fish which you have now caught.**" (11) Simon Peter went up and drew the net to land, full of large fish, a hundred and fifty-three; and although there were so many, the net was not torn. (12) Joshua to them, "**Come and have breakfast.**" None of the disciples ventured to question him, "Who are you?" knowing that it was the Lord. (13) Joshua came and took the bread and gave it to them, and the fish likewise. (14) This is now the third time that Joshua was manifested to the disciples, after he was raised from the dead.

(15) So when they had finished breakfast, Joshua said to Simon Peter, "**Simon, son of John, do you love me more than these?**" He said to him, "Yes, Lord; you know that I love you." He said to him, "**Tend my lambs.**" (16) He said to him again a second time, "**Simon, son of John, do you love me?**" He said to

him, "Yes, Lord; you know that I love you." He said to him, "**Feed my sheep**." (17) He said to him the third time, "**Simon, son of John, do you love me?**" Peter was grieved because he said to him the third time, "**Do you love me?**" And he said to him, "Lord, you know all things; you know that I love you." Joshua said to him, "**Tend my sheep.**"[*76] (18) "**Truly, truly, I say to you, when you were younger, you used to dress yourself and walk wherever you wished; but when you grow old, you will stretch out your hands and someone else will gird you, and bring you where you do not wish to go.**" (19) Now this he said, signifying by what kind of death he (*Peter*) would glorify God. And when he had spoken this, he said to him, "**Follow me!**" (20) Peter, turning around, saw the disciple whom Joshua loved following them; the one who also had leaned back on his bosom at the supper and said, "Lord, who is the one who betrays you?" (21) So Peter seeing him said to Joshua, "Lord, and what about this man?" (22) Joshua said to him, "**If I want him to remain until I come, what is that to you? You follow me!**" (23) Therefore this saying went out among the brethren that that disciple would not die; yet Joshua did not say to him that he would not die, but only, "**If I want him to remain until I come, what is that to you?**"

[*76] *Many religious leaders try and use these words of the Master to justify their being shepherds of HIS sheep saying Peter is being made a shepherd here. But of course this would contradict Joshua's teachings in John 10 regarding his being the ONLY Good shepherd who does not fail and who alone **owns the sheep**. Would the Good Shepherd entrust his sheep's souls to a man who denied him three times in a time of weakness? A reasonable reading (meaning it does not contradict his other plain teachings – see John 10:16 & Matt. 23:8-12) would be that Joshua is simply saying feed HIS sheep – meaning repeat HIS words to them (bring them food/grass to eat), like all disciples are supposed to do – and look out for them (tend them) like any good friend (especially a more experienced or mature friend) would look out for his friends and help guide others in dangerous and difficult times and places if he has gone through that experience before. What is certain is that Joshua did not contradict himself and make Peter a Shepherd,*

Teacher or Leader, for only Joshua is those things to his disciples as he teaches plainly elsewhere (see Matt. 23:8-12; John 10:13, for example).

(24) This is the disciple who is testifying to these things and wrote these things, and we know that his testimony is true. (25) And there are also many other things which Joshua did, which if they were written in detail, I suppose that even the world itself would not contain the books that would be written.

END OF THE BOOK OF JOHN

The Life and Words of Joshua* of Nazareth According to Luke:

* Joshua is a more accurate translation of what has been traditionally translated "Jesus"

Basic Book Introduction:
Distinguish between the Author and his Subject

The author is a man named Luke, assumed to be a non-Jew, who lived at the same time and in the same area that Joshua lived, and who probably had encounters with Joshua. Luke was thought to be a physician based primarily on this comment of Paul in the new testament book of Colossians:

Colossians 4:14 "Luke, the beloved physician, sends you his greetings, and also Demas."

Luke opens his book with these words about his reason and methods for writing it:

"(1:1) Inasmuch as many have undertaken to compile an account of the things accomplished among us, (2) just as they were handed down to us by those who from the beginning were eyewitnesses and servants of the word *1, (3) it seemed fitting for me as well, having investigated everything carefully from the beginning, to write it out for you in consecutive order, most excellent Theophilus; (4) so that you may know the exact truth about the things you have been taught."

*1 *Joshua is referred to as "the word" by Luke. See John chapter 1. The scripture itself refers to Joshua of Nazareth as "the word", and the bible authors never use the phrase "the word" in reference to the bible or any book in it - yet most bible people substitute the bible for Joshua – a grave error that nullifies the true Word of God who is Joshua.*

Luke, the assumed author of this book, no doubt had most things correct about Joshua since he "investigated everything carefully". This commentator believes that he accurately wrote down what Joshua said and did based on his own encounters with Joshua, as well as talking to Joshua's other disciples, including the first eleven. However, the reader must understand the distinction between his accurately recording what Joshua said and did versus his having a *perfect understanding* of what Joshua said and did. For example, a person can see a man running down a street in an urgent fashion yelling 'fire'. The person witnessing the man running can accurately identify the time and place and other facts associated with the event, but the witness cannot know for sure **why** the man is running and yelling 'fire'.

In like manner, let the reader understand, all men, including the men who were with Joshua (and including this commentator) - had beliefs, religious baggage so to speak – that hindered them from having a perfect understanding of Joshua and his purpose. They, like us, had minds containing things (particularly religious things) which are not from Joshua, which things they could not reconcile with some of the things Joshua said (one example is Acts 1:6), **even while they accurately recorded what he said and did. Therefore, the reader should place full confidence in Joshua and his Words only, in terms of having as close to a perfect understanding of Joshua as is possible.** This is only reasonable as no one but Joshua could have a perfect understanding of Joshua. While Luke's narrative and commentary (in contrast to Joshua's own words and teachings) is almost certainly accurate in regard to historical details of the circumstances of Joshua's Life, only the Words of Joshua alone should have the reader's full trust in regard to **understanding Joshua and his purposes...revealing the 'why's' regarding Joshua's words and actions.** To assist the reader in this endeavor, Joshua's words are **in bold** in this publishing of Luke's book.

This commentator's comments are *italicized* and either contained in parenthesis or preceded by a superscripted number. Sections of text that are in title case (where the first letter of each word in a phrase or sentence is capitalized e.g. Thus Said the Lord), are quotes of the old testament scripture.

The purpose of this commentator's comments is threefold. First, is to try and define terms according to Joshua's own usage in the four gospels and to do so using simpler or clarified terms or phrases that avoid religious vocabulary. This is necessary for readers with little or no exposure to concepts they have not encountered before or terms or concepts that have been given an incorrect meaning through current religious culture. For example, an important concept – "religious leaders" - has been hidden by using the name of a specific religious sect's leadership, the "Pharisees". The modern reader will have little idea what "Pharisees" were, but they can certainly grasp the concept, "religious leaders", which is exactly what the Pharisees were.

An example of a term that has been modified by current religious culture would be "prophet". This term has come to mean in the current religious culture, a person who foretells future events. The term as Joshua uses it, simply means someone who speaks God's truths.

Second, is to bring to the reader's attention the important teachings of Joshua which are nullified (cancelled out, or made of no effect) by contradictions with other passages in the bible or by contemporary religious teaching. This is not exhaustive, but rather brings to light the contradictions which, in this commentator's opinion, nullify some of the more important teachings of Joshua.

Third, is to 'clear the dirt off his person and sayings', so to speak, for those who want to hear but have been confused or deceived by the myriad of other voices that claim they understand Joshua better than Joshua understands Joshua. For those people who participate in the religious system, perhaps the most commonly used mantra of the bible based religious system's leadership is, "Jesus doesn't mean that...you need us, your educated clergy, to understand what Jesus really meant". This commentator has news for you – Jesus does mean that! No, I don't mean that you turn figurative language into literal language, like when he says, "if your right eye causes you to sin, rip it from your head". Rather, I am referring to his teachings that go against human kind's normal inclination or that challenge some aspect of the way I am living. For example, the simple teaching, "love your enemies". Yes, it does mean that...no, joining a military and killing the 'enemy' cannot be reconciled with "love your enemies". You may not like what Joshua has to say, but let him say it and don't twist his words. After all, if Joshua is who he says he is, we would do well to listen.

Luke Chapter 1 – Provides information about the women who were pregnant with both Joshua and John the Baptist, and covers John's birth.

Luke Chapter 2 – Information about Joshua' birth and events pertaining to it. Includes this account of Joshua's Words when he was only twelve years old:

(2:42) And when he (*Joshua*) became twelve, they (*Joshua's parents and siblings*) went up there according to the custom of the Feast (*religious celebration*); (43) and as they were returning (*Joshua's parents and siblings*), after spending the full number of days, the boy Joshua stayed behind in Jerusalem. But his parents were unaware of it, (44) but supposed him to be in the caravan, and went a day's journey; and they began looking for him among their relatives and acquaintances. (45) When they did not find him, they returned to Jerusalem looking for him. (46) Then, after three days they found him (*Joshua*) in the temple, sitting in the midst of the teachers, both listening to them and asking them questions. (47) And all who heard him were amazed at his understanding and his answers. (48) When they saw him, they were astonished; and his mother said to him, "Son, why have you treated us this way? Behold, your father and I have been anxiously looking for you." (49) And he said to them, **"Why is it that you were looking for me? Did you not know that I had to be in my Father's house?"** (50) But they did not understand the statement which he had made to them. (51) And he left and went down with them and came to Nazareth, and he continued in subjection to them (*to honor and respect them and do what they said*); and his mother treasured all these things in her heart.

Luke Chapter 3 – Introduces John the Baptist's work and his message of feeling remorse over one's sin and thus changing one's behavior. This chapter covers the genealogical history of Joshua of Nazareth, which was important proof to the Jews to prove he could be Messiah.

Luke Chapter 4 – Introduces Joshua of Nazareth. We pick up right in verse 1:

(4:1) Joshua, full of the Holy Spirit, returned from the Jordan river and was led around by the Spirit in the wilderness (2) for forty days, being tempted by the devil (*or Satan, a powerful spiritual being who hates, and thus works against Joshua's Father*). And he ate nothing during those days, and when they had ended, he became hungry. (3) And the devil said to him, "If you are the Son of God, tell this stone to become bread." (4) And Joshua answered him, "**It is written, 'Man Shall Not Live On Bread Alone**.'" (5) And he led him up and showed him all the kingdoms of the world in a moment of time. (6) And Satan said to him, "I will give you all this domain and its glory; for it has been handed over to me, and I give it to whomever I wish. (7) "Therefore if you worship before me, it shall all be yours." (8) Joshua answered him, "**It is written, 'You Shall Worship The Lord Your God And Serve Him Only**.'" (9) And Satan led him to Jerusalem and had him stand on the pinnacle (*top*) of the temple, and said to him, "If you are the Son of God, throw yourself down from here; (10) for it is written, 'He Will Command His Angels Concerning You To Guard You,' (11) and, 'On their Hands They Will Bear You Up, So That You Will Not Strike Your Foot Against A Stone.'" (12) And Joshua answered and said to him, "**It is said, 'You Shall Not Put The Lord Your God To The Test**.'" (13) When Satan had finished every temptation, he left him until an opportune time.

(14) And Joshua returned to Galilee in the power of the Spirit, and news about him spread through all the surrounding area. (15) And he began teaching in their religious buildings and was praised by all. (16) And he came to Nazareth, where he had been brought up; and as was his custom, he entered the religious building on the sabbath (*the Jew's holy day, which the religious believe no work at all should be done on*), and stood up to read. (17) And the book of the prophet (*a person who spoke God's truths*) Isaiah was handed to him. And he opened the book and found the place where it was written, (18) "**The Spirit Of The**

Lord Is Upon Me, Because He Anointed Me To Preach The Gospel To The Poor. He Has Sent Me To Proclaim Release To The Captives, And Recovery Of Sight To The Blind, To Set Free Those Who Are Oppressed, (19) **To Proclaim The Favorable Year Of The Lord**." (20) And he closed the book, gave it back to the attendant and sat down; and the eyes of all in the religious building were fixed on him. (21) And he began to say to them, "**Today this scripture has been fulfilled in your hearing**." (22) And all were speaking well of him, and wondering at the gracious words which were falling from his lips; but they were also saying, "Is this not Joseph's son?" (23) And he said to them, "**No doubt you will quote this proverb to me, 'Physician, heal yourself'. Whatever we heard was done at Capernaum, do here in your hometown as well**.'" (24) And he said, "**Truly I say to you, no prophet** (*a person who speaks God's truths*) **is welcome in his hometown.** (25) "**But I say to you in truth, there were many widows in Israel in the days of Elijah, when the sky was shut up for three years and six months, when a great famine came over all the land;** (26) **and yet Elijah was sent to none of them, but only to Zarephath, in the land of Sidon, to a woman who was a widow.** (27) "**And there were many lepers in Israel in the time of Elisha the prophet** (*a person who spoke God's truths*); **and none of them was cleansed, but only Naaman the Syrian**." (28) And the people in the religious building were filled with rage as they heard these things; (29) and they got up and drove him out of the city, and led him to the brow of the hill on which their city had been built, in order to throw him down the cliff. (30) But passing through their midst, he went his way.

(31) And he came down to Capernaum, a city of Galilee, and he was teaching them on the sabbath; (32) and they were amazed at his teaching, for his message was with authority. (33) In the religious building there was a man possessed by the spirit of an unclean demon (*bad angel*), and he cried out with a loud voice, (34) "Let us alone! What business do we have with each other, Joshua of Nazareth? Have you come to destroy us? I know who you are--the

Holy One of God!" (35) But Joshua rebuked him, saying, "**Be quiet and come out of him!**" And when the demon (*bad angel*) had thrown him down in the midst of the people, he came out of him without doing him any harm. (36) And amazement came upon them all, and they began talking with one another saying, "What is this message? For with authority and power he commands the unclean spirits and they come out." (37) And the report about him was spreading into every people group in the surrounding area.

(38) Then he got up and left the religious building, and entered Simon Peter's home. Now Simon's mother-in-law was suffering from a high fever, and they asked him to help her. (39) And standing over her, he rebuked the fever, and it left her; and she immediately got up and waited on them.

(40) While the sun was setting, all those who had any who were sick with various diseases brought them to him; and laying his hands on each one of them, he was healing them. (41) Demons (*bad angels*) also were coming out of many, shouting, "You are the Son of God!" But rebuking them, he would not allow them to speak, because they knew him to be the Messiah. (42) When day came, Joshua left and went to a secluded place; and the crowds were searching for him, and came to him and tried to keep him from going away from them. (43) But he said to them, "**I must preach the kingdom of God to the other cities also, for I was sent for this purpose.**" (44) So he kept on preaching in the religious buildings of Judea.

(5:1) Now it happened that while the crowd was pressing around him and listening to the word of God (*the words of Joshua*), he was standing by the lake of Gennesaret; (2) and he saw two boats lying at the edge of the lake; but the fishermen had gotten out of them and were washing their nets. (3) And he got into one of the boats, which was Simon Peter's, and asked him to put out a little way from the land. And he sat down and began teaching the people from the boat. (4) When he had finished speaking, he said to Simon, **"Put out into the deep water and let down your nets for a catch."** (5) Simon answered and said, "Master, we worked hard all night and caught nothing, but I will do as you say and let down the nets." (6) When they had done this, they captured a great quantity of fish, and their nets began to break; (7) so they signaled to their partners in the other boat for them to come and help them. And they came and filled both of the boats, so that they began to sink. (8) But when Simon Peter saw that, he fell down at Joshua' feet, saying, "Go away from me Lord, for I am a sinful man!" (9) For amazement had seized him and all his companions because of the catch of fish which they had taken; (10) and so also were James and John, sons of Zebedee, who were partners with Simon. And Joshua said to Simon, **"Do not fear, from now on you will be catching men."** [*2] (11) When they had brought their boats to land, they left everything (*forsook – see Luke 12:33*) and followed him.

[*2]   *This is every disciple's job, not 'evangelists', the falsehood that Paul teaches in Eph. 4:11. Peter, a simple fishermen, would become a disciple of Joshua and in turn would become a fisher of men. And so it is with all disciples. Some fish better than others, but all are to fish as our most basic mission in this life...to introduce people to our Father and help others to see He is their Father too.*

(12) While he was in one of the cities, behold, there was a man covered with leprosy (*a bad skin disease*); and when he saw Joshua, he fell on his face and implored him, saying, "Lord, if you are willing, you can make me clean (*heal me*)." (13) And he stretched out his hand and touched him, saying, **"I am willing; be cleansed** (*or healed*)." And immediately the leprosy left him. (14) And he ordered him to tell no one, **"But go and show yourself to**

the religious leader and make an offering for your cleansing, just as Moses commanded, as a testimony to them" (*that they would understand since it fit into their religious beliefs*). (15) But the news about him was spreading even farther, and large crowds were gathering to hear him and to be healed of their sicknesses. (16) But Joshua himself would often slip away to the wilderness and pray.

(17) One day he was teaching; and there were some religious leaders and lawyers sitting there, who had come from every village of Galilee and Judea and from Jerusalem; and the power of the Lord was present for him to perform healing. (18) And some men were carrying on a bed a man who was paralyzed; and they were trying to bring him in and to set him down in front of him. (19) But not finding any way to bring him in because of the crowd, they went up on the roof and let him down through the tiles with his stretcher, into the middle of the crowd, in front of Joshua. (20) Seeing their faith, he said, "**Friend, your sins are forgiven you**." (21) The bible experts and the religious leaders began to reason, saying, "Who is this man who speaks blasphemies (*bad things against God*)? Who can forgive sins, but God alone?" (22) But Joshua, aware of their reasoning, answered and said to them, "**Why are you reasoning so in your hearts?** (23) "**Which is easier, to say, 'Your sins have been forgiven you,' or to say, 'Get up and walk'?** (24) "**But, so that you may know that the Son of Man** (*Joshua's favorite title for himself*) **has authority on earth to forgive sins**,"--he said to the paralytic--"**I say to you, get up, and pick up your stretcher and go home**." (25) Immediately he got up before them, and picked up what he had been lying on, and went home glorifying God. (26) They were all struck with astonishment and began glorifying God; and they were filled with fear, saying, "We have seen remarkable things today."

(27) After that Joshua went out and noticed a tax collector named Levi (*Matthew*) sitting in the tax booth, and he said to him, "**Follow me**." (28) And he left everything behind (see Luke 12:33), and got up and began to follow him. (29) And Levi gave a

big reception for him in his house; and there was a great crowd of tax collectors and other people who were reclining at the table with them. (30) The religious leaders and their bible experts began grumbling at his disciples, saying, "Why do you eat and drink with the tax collectors and sinners?" (31) And Joshua answered and said to them, "**It is not those who are well who need a physician, but those who are sick.** (32) **"I have not come to call the righteous but sinners to repentance** ('*repentance' means to feel truly sorry about your bad behavior or words, and change*)."

(33) And they said to him, "The disciples of John often fast and offer prayers, the disciples of the religious leaders also do the same, but yours eat and drink." (34) And Joshua said to them, "**You cannot make the friends of the bridegroom** (*the man getting married*) **fast** (*not eat*) **while the bridegroom is with them, can you?** (35) **"But the days will come; and when the bridegroom is taken away from them, then they will fast in those days.**" (36) And he was also telling them a parable (*stories with hidden meanings*): "**No one tears a piece of cloth from a new garment and puts it on an old garment; otherwise he will both tear the new, and the piece from the new will not match the old. (37) "And no one puts new wine into old wineskins; otherwise the new wine will burst the skins and it will be spilled out, and the skins will be ruined. (38) "But new wine must be put into fresh wineskins. (39) "And no one, after drinking old wine wishes for new; for he says, 'The old is good enough.'**" [*3]

[*3] *Here illustrates a contrast between the religious people (the disciples of John the baptist and the followers of the current religious leaders) and customs of his day, and his own disciples/followers. The contrast is simple – Joshua's new message and way is so different than the Jewish religious ways that to try and mix them will bring ruin to both. Furthermore, people who are used to their religion will not want to listen to Joshua since their religion is "good enough". This is particularly relevant for the many 'messianic' sects – those sects which attempt to mix Joshua's teachings with the Hebrew scripture's teachings.*

(6:1) Now it happened that he was passing through some grain fields on a sabbath (*the day the Jews said no work must be done on*); and his disciples were picking the heads of grain, rubbing them in their hands, and eating the grain. (2) But some of the religious leaders said, "Why do you do what is not lawful on the sabbath?" (3) And Joshua answering them said, "**Have you not even read what David did when he was hungry, he and those who were with him, (4) how he entered the house of God, and took and ate the consecrated bread which is not legal for any to eat except the priests alone, and gave it to his companions?**" (5) And he was saying to them, "**The Son of Man** (*Joshua's favorite title for himself*) **is Lord of the sabbath.**" *4

*4 *Joshua decides what to do on the sabbath – he is not ruled by the sabbath but rather is ruler of the sabbath and thus can decide what he and others can do on the day. Joshua teaches it is OK to work on the Jewish sabbath – see John 5:17.*

(6) On another sabbath he entered the religious building and was teaching; and there was a man there whose right hand was withered (*deformed*). (7) The bible experts and the religious leaders were watching him closely to see if he healed on the sabbath, so that they might find reason to accuse him of 'breaking the sabbath'. (8) But Joshua knew what they were thinking, and he said to the man with the withered hand, "**Get up and come forward!**" And he got up and came forward. (9) And Joshua said to them, "**I ask you, is it legal to do good or to do harm on the sabbath, to save a life or to destroy it?**" (10) After looking around at them all, he said to him, "**Stretch out your hand!**" And he did so; and his hand was restored (*healed*). (11) But the religious leaders and bible experts were filled with rage, and discussed together what they might do to Joshua (*how they might destroy him*).

(12) It was at this time that Joshua went off to the mountain to pray, and he spent the whole night in prayer to God. (13) And when day came, he called his disciples to him and chose twelve of them, whom he also named as apostles:*5 (14) Simon, whom he also

named Peter, and Andrew his brother; and James and John; and Philip and Bartholomew; (15) and Matthew and Thomas; James the son of Alphaeus, and Simon who was called the Zealot; (16) Judas the son of James, and Judas Iscariot, who became a traitor. (17) Joshua came down with them and stood on a level place; and there was a large crowd of his disciples, and a great throng (*group*) of people from all Judea and Jerusalem and the coastal region of Tyre and Sidon, (18) who had come to hear him and to be healed of their diseases; and those who were troubled with unclean spirits were being cured. (19) And all the people were trying to touch him, for power was coming from him and healing them all. (20) And turning his gaze toward his disciples, he began to say,

*5 *The most literal translation of the Greek word translated "apostles" is "sent ones". The twelve Joshua originally chose to teach and train were sent directly by him to go bring other people to the Father after he left. All apostles were disciples, but not all disciples are apostles, since to be an apostle you had to have been with Joshua during his first visit to earth – see Acts 2 for the qualifications of an apostle – which qualifications Paul did not possess.*

"Blessed* are you who are poor (*materially poor*)**, for yours is the kingdom of God.**
(21) **"Blessed are you who hunger now, for you shall be satisfied. Blessed are you who weep now, for you shall be glad.**
(22) **"Blessed are you when men hate you, and reject you, and insult you, and call your name evil, for the sake of the Son of Man** (*Joshua's favorite title for himself*)**.**
(23) **"Be glad in that day and leap for joy, for behold, your reward is great in heaven. For in the same way their fathers used to treat the prophets** (*people who spoke God's truths*)**.**

* *Blessed means fortunate or favored by the Father and thus happy about what His future holds.*

(24) **"But woe* to you who are rich** (*materially wealthy*), **for you are receiving your comfort in full.**
(25) **"Woe to you who are well-fed now, for you shall be hungry. Woe to you who laugh now, for you shall mourn and weep.**
(26) **"Woe to you when all men speak well of you, for their fathers used to treat the false prophets** (*those who claimed to speak for God but didn't*) **in the same way.**

* *Woe means guilty before God and thus heading for self-condemnation if we don't change.*

(27) **"But I say to you who hear, love your enemies, do good to those who hate you, (28) bless those who curse you, pray for those who mistreat you. (29) "Whoever hits you on the cheek, offer him the other also; and whoever takes away your coat, do not withhold your shirt from him either.**

(30) **"Give to everyone who asks of you, and whoever takes away what is yours, do not demand it back. (31) "Treat others the same way you want them to treat you. (32) "If you love those who love you, what credit is that to you? For even sinners**[*6] **love those who love them. (33) "If you do good to those who do good to you, what credit is that to you? For even sinners do the same. (34) "If you lend to those from whom you expect to receive, what credit is that to you? Even sinners lend to sinners in order to receive back the same amount.**

[*6] *'Sinners' are those who practice bad things or those who regularly do or say what is wrong or hurtful to others or themselves– they are people who do not listen to their conscious nor to any good moral standard of their culture. An example of sinners loving sinners would be any group of people that has as a basic group dynamic to affirm each other and support each other even when what they believe or do is wrong e.g. the Neo-Nazis or the Pedophilia Club.*

(35) "But love your enemies, and do good, and lend, expecting nothing in return; and your reward will be great, and you will be sons of the Most High; for He Himself is kind to ungrateful and evil men."[7] (36) "Be merciful, just as your Father is merciful. (37) "Do not judge and you will not be judged; and do not condemn, and you will not be condemned; pardon and you will be pardoned. (38) "Give and it will be given to you. They will pour into your lap a good measure--pressed down, shaken together, and running over. For by your standard of measure it will be measured to you in return."

[7] *This teaching contains the great message of Joshua – love all, even your enemies - be kind to them, be eager to forgive them and thus do not seek revenge, retribution or 'justice'. Truly, if the people of the earth would practice this, all conflict would end.*

(39) And he also spoke a parable to them: "A blind man cannot guide a blind man, can he? Will they not both fall into a pit? (40) "A pupil is not above his teacher; but everyone, after he has been fully trained, will be like his teacher. (41) "Why do you look at the speck that is in your brother's eye, but do not notice the log that is in your own eye? (42) "Or how can you say to your brother, 'Brother, let me take out the speck that is in your eye,' when you yourself do not see the log that is in your own eye? You hypocrite (*a person who says what others ought to do or not do, but does not do so themselves*), first take the log out of your own eye, and then you will see clearly to take out the speck that is in your brother's eye. (43) "For there is no good tree which produces bad fruit, nor, on the other hand, a bad tree which produces good fruit. (44) "For each tree is known by its own fruit. For men do not gather figs from thorns, nor do they pick grapes from a briar bush. (45) "The good man out of the good treasure of his heart brings forth what is good; and the evil man out of the evil treasure

brings forth what is evil; for his mouth speaks from that which fills his heart.[8]

[8] *A basic and key truth – that what is in our heart will come out of our mouth and actions. If we love our Father, are grateful to the Life He gives us, and are seeking to love others, then good things will fill our mouths and actions...we will not complain, nor express bitterness or envy or dissatisfaction with our lives. Instead we will speak of the One whom we love and appreciate and we will do what our Master says.*

(46) **"Why do you call me, 'Lord, Lord,' and do not do what I say?** (47) **"Everyone who comes to me and hears my words and acts on them, I will show you whom he is like:** (48) **He is like a man building a house, who dug deep and laid a foundation on the rock; and when a flood occurred, the raging waters burst against that house and could not shake it, because it had been well built.** (49) **"But the one who has heard and has not acted accordingly, is like a man who built a house on the ground without any foundation; and the raging waters burst against it and immediately it collapsed, and the ruin of that house was great."** [9]

[9] *See Matt. 7:22*

(7:1) When Joshua had completed all his teaching in the hearing of the people, he went to Capernaum. (2) And a centurion's (*Roman soldier*) servant, who was highly regarded by him, was sick and about to die. (3) When the centurion heard about Joshua, he sent some Jewish leaders asking him to come and save the life of his servant. (4) When they came to Joshua, they earnestly implored him, saying, "He is worthy for you to grant this to him; (5) for he loves our nation and it was he who built us our religious building." (6) Now Joshua started on his way with them; and when he was not far from the house, the centurion sent friends, saying to him, "Lord, do not trouble yourself further, for I am not worthy for you to come under my roof; (7) for this reason I did not even consider myself worthy to come to you, but just say the word, and my servant will be healed. (8) "For I also am a man placed under authority, with soldiers under me; and I say to this one, 'Go!' and he goes, and to another, 'Come!' and he comes, and to my servant, 'Do this!' and he does it." (9) Now when Joshua heard this, he marveled at him, and turned and said to the crowd that was following him, "**I say to you, not even in Israel have I found such great faith**." (10) When those who had been sent returned to the house, they found the servant in good health.

(11) Soon afterwards he went to a city called Nain; and his disciples were going along with him, accompanied by a large crowd. (12) Now as he approached the gate of the city, a dead man's body was being carried out, the only son of his mother, and she was a widow; and a sizeable crowd from the city was with her. (13) When the Lord saw her, he felt compassion for her, and said to her, "**Do not weep**." (14) And he came up and touched the coffin; and the bearers came to a halt. And he said, "**Young man, I say to you, arise!**" (15) The dead man came back to life, sat up and began to speak. And Joshua gave him back to his mother. (16) Fear gripped them all, and they began glorifying God, saying, "A great prophet (*a person who speaks God's truths*) has arisen among us!" and, "God has visited his people!" (17) This report concerning him went out all over Judea and in all the surrounding area.

(18) The disciples of John reported to him about all these things. (19) Summoning two of his disciples, John sent them to Joshua, saying, "Are you the Expected One, or do we look for someone else?" (20) When the men came to him, they said, "John the Baptist has sent us to you, to ask, 'Are you the Expected One, or do we look for someone else?'" (21) At that very time he cured many people of diseases and various physical problems and evil spirits; and he gave sight to many who were blind. (22) And he answered and said to them, "**Go and report to John what you have seen and heard: the Blind Receive Sight, the lame walk, the lepers are healed, and the deaf hear, the dead are raised up, the Poor Have The Gospel Preached To Them.** (23) **"Blessed is he who does not take offense at me.**"

(24) When the messengers of John had left, he began to speak to the crowds about John, "**What did you go out into the wilderness to see? A reed shaken by the wind?** (25) **"But what did you go out to see? A man dressed in soft clothing? Those who wear expensive cloths and live in luxury are found in royal palaces!** (26) **"But what did you go out to see? A prophet** (*a person who speaks God's truths*)**? Yes, I say to you, and one who is more than a prophet.** (27) **"This is the one about whom it is written, 'Behold, I Send My Messenger Ahead Of You, Who Will Prepare Your Way Before You.'** (28) **"I say to you, among those born of women there is no one greater than John; yet he who is least in the kingdom of God is greater than he.**" *10 (29) When all the people and the tax collectors heard this, they acknowledged God's justice, having been baptized with the baptism of John. (30) But the religious leaders and the lawyers rejected God's purpose for themselves, not having been baptized by John.

*10   *Joshua says that even 'the least' of those people who enter the kingdom of God from that time forward (for the kingdom of God had not yet come until the King – Joshua – had come) through faith in the King, are greater than the greatest of Israel's past prophets. Perhaps because the King and his message are* *greater – if received and lived out – than all the prophets prior to the King's arrival? Love!*

(31) **"To what then shall I compare the men of this generation**[*11]**, and what are they like?** (32) **"They are like children who sit in the market place and call to one another, and they say, 'We played the flute for you, and you did not dance; we sang a sad song, and you did not cry.'** (33) **"For John the Baptist has come eating no bread and drinking no wine, and you say, 'He has a demon** (*bad angel*)**!'** (34) **"The Son of Man has come eating and drinking, and you say, 'Behold, a gluttonous man** (*a person who loves food and thus eats too much*) **and a drunkard, a friend of tax collectors and sinners!'** (35) **"Yet wisdom is vindicated** (*proved right*) **by all her children."**

[*11] *Joshua defines three ages or generations in his teachings: All those alive on the earth prior to his first coming; all those alive on the earth during and after his first coming, prior to his second coming; and all those alive during and after his second coming.*

(36) Now one of the religious leaders was requesting that Joshua have dinner with him, and he entered the religious leader's house and reclined at the table. (37) And there was a woman in the city who was a sinner (*prostitute*); and when she learned that Joshua was reclining at the table in the religious leader's house, she brought an alabaster vial (*expensive*) of perfume, (38) and standing behind him at his feet, weeping, she began to wet his feet with her tears, and kept wiping them with the hair of her head, and kissing his feet and anointing them with the perfume. (39) Now when the religious leader who had invited him saw this, he said to himself, "If this man were a prophet he would know who and what sort of person this woman is who is touching him, that she is a sinner." (40) And Joshua answered him, **"Simon, I have something to say to you."** And he replied, "Say it, Teacher." (41) **"A moneylender had two debtors: one owed him three thousand dollars, and the other thirty dollars.** (42) **"When**

they were unable to repay, he graciously forgave them both. So which of them will love him more?" (43) Simon answered and said, "I suppose the one whom he forgave more." And he said to him, "**You have judged correctly.**" (44) Turning toward the woman, he said to Simon, "**Do you see this woman? I entered your house; you gave me no water for my feet, but she has wet my feet with her tears and wiped them with her hair.** (45) "**You gave me no kiss; but she, since the time I came in, has not ceased to kiss my feet.** (46) "**You did not anoint my head with oil, but she anointed my feet with perfume.** (47) "**For this reason I say to you, her sins, which are many, have been forgiven, for she loved** (*me*) **much; but he who is forgiven little, loves little.**" *12 (48) Then he said to her, "**Your sins have been forgiven.**" (49) Those who were reclining at the table with him began to say to themselves, "Who is this man who even forgives sins?" (50) And he said to the woman, "**Your faith has saved you; go in peace.**"

*12 *An important principle. If we have not experienced the forgiveness of our heavenly Father, then we will not have much love to give to others...if we have never seen our deep and important need to be forgiven by our heavenly Father, then we remain in pride or fear which makes our heart hard and cold. The more we can see the damage and pain our sin has brought, the more grateful we will be to be granted forgiveness from our heavenly Father and those we have wronged and the more love we will be able to express to others.*

(8:1) Soon afterwards, he began going around from one city and village to another, proclaiming and preaching the kingdom of God. The twelve were with him, **(2)** and also some women who had been healed of evil spirits and sicknesses: Mary who was called Magdalene, from whom seven demons (*bad angels*) had gone out, **(3)** and Joanna the wife of Chuza, Herod's steward, and Susanna, and many others who were contributing to their support out of their private means.*13

*13 *Women played an important role in Joshua's mission and are here shown supporting him and his twelve sent ones ("apostles") as they traveled around proclaiming the kingdom of God. Women are equally valuable to men, but they do have different natures and thus different roles to play and different talents and attributes. For example, there is no good substitute for the role of a mother – that is a woman who has children and who loves and values those children above all other thing in this world, and who thus nurtures and raises those children instead of giving them to others to raise while she goes and works for money. And yes, dads are equally important to the proper raising of the children.*

(4) When a large crowd was coming together, and those from the various cities were journeying to him, he spoke by way of a parable: **(5)** "**The sower (*planter*) went out to sow (*plant*) his seed; and as he sowed, some fell beside the road, and it was trampled underfoot and the birds of the air ate it up.** **(6)** "**Other seed fell on rocky soil, and as soon as it grew up, it withered away, because it had no moisture. (7)** "**Other seed fell among the thorns; and the thorns grew up with it and choked it out. (8)** "**Other seed fell into the good soil, and grew up, and produced a crop a hundred times as great.**" As he said these things, he would call out, "**He who has ears to hear, let him hear.**"

(9) His disciples began questioning him as to what this parable meant. **(10)** And he said, "**To you it has been granted to know the mysteries of the kingdom of God, but to the rest it is in parables, so that 'Seeing They May Not See, And Hearing They May Not Understand'.**"*14 **(11)** "**Now the parable is this:**

the seed is the word of God (*the truths of God's Kingdom as spoken by Joshua*). (12) "Those beside the road are those who have heard; then the devil comes and takes away the word from their heart, so that they will not believe and be saved. (13) "Those on the rocky soil are those who, when they hear, receive the word with joy; and these have no firm root; they believe for a while, and in time of temptation or testing, they fall away. (14) "The seed which fell among the thorns, these are the ones who have heard, and as they go on their way they are choked with worries and riches and pleasures of this life, and bring no fruit to maturity. (15) "But the seed in the good soil, these are the ones who have heard the word in an honest and good heart, and hold it fast, and bear fruit through difficult times.

*14 *Here Joshua tells the disciples why he speaks in parables – simple stories with hidden meanings. He does this so that those who are open to his Kingdom (humble in heart, seeing their need) will hear and understand, but those who are against him (proud, not seeing their need) will not understand.*

(16) "Now no one after lighting a lamp covers it over with a container, or puts it under a bed; but rather he puts it on a table, so that those who come in may see the light. (17) "For nothing is hidden that will not become evident, nor anything secret that will not be known and come to light. (18) "So take care how you listen; for whoever has, to him more shall be given; and whoever does not have, even what he thinks he has shall be taken away from him."

(19) And his mother and brothers came to him, and they were unable to get to him because of the crowd. (20) And it was reported to him, "Your mother and your brothers are standing outside, wishing to see you." *15 (21) But Joshua answered and said to them, "**My mother and my brothers are these who hear the word of God and do it.**" *16

*15 *This is yet another passage that shows that Mary, Joshua's earthly mom, had children after she gave birth to Joshua thus contradicting the roman tradition.*
*16 *One of several sayings of Joshua that lay out the new order of who is really a disciples family. Due largely to the christian organizations/'churches' providing a shallow social club as a substitute for actual love and family, most ignore this and remain with their natural family or their 'church family' (a mere shallow organization), refusing to truly love those who Joshua defines as their "mother, brothers and sisters".*

(22) Now on one of those days Joshua and his disciples got into a boat, and he said to them, **"Let us go over to the other side of the lake."** So they launched out. (23) But as they were sailing along he fell asleep; and a fierce gale of wind descended on the lake, and their boat began to be filled with water and to be in danger. (24) They came to Joshua and woke him up, saying, "Master, Master, we are dying!" And he got up and rebuked the wind and the surging waves, and they stopped, and it became calm. (25) And he said to them, **"Where is your faith?"** They were fearful and amazed, saying to one another, "Who then is this, that he commands even the winds and the water, and they obey him?"

(26) Then they sailed to the country of the Gerasenes, which is opposite Galilee. (27) And when he came out onto the land, he was met by a man from the city who was possessed with demons (bad angels); and who had not put on any clothing for a long time, and was not living in a house, but in the tombs. (28) Seeing Joshua, he cried out and fell before him, and said in a loud voice, "What business do we have with each other, Joshua, Son of the Most High God? I beg you, do not torment me." (29) For he had commanded the unclean spirit to come out of the man. For it had seized him many times; and he was bound with chains and shackles and kept under guard, and yet he would break his chains and be driven by the demon into the desert. (30) And Joshua asked him, **"What is your name?"** And he said, "Legion"; for many demons had entered him. (31) They were imploring him not to command them to go away into the abyss. (32) Now there was a herd of many swine (*pigs*) feeding there on the mountain; and the demons implored

Joshua to permit them to enter the swine. And he gave them permission. (33) And the demons came out of the man and entered the swine; and the herd rushed down the steep bank into the lake and was drowned. (34) When the herdsmen saw what had happened, they ran away and reported it in the city and out in the country. (35) The people went out to see what had happened; and they came to Joshua, and found the man from whom the demons had gone out, sitting down at the feet of Joshua, clothed and in his right mind; and they became frightened. (36) Those who had seen it reported to them how the man who was demon-possessed had been made well. (37) And all the people of the country of the Gerasenes and the surrounding area asked Joshua to leave them, for they were gripped with great fear; and he got into a boat and returned. (38) But the man from whom the demons had gone out was begging Joshua that he might accompany him; but he sent him away, saying, (39) "**Return to your house and describe what great things God has done for you.**" So he went away, proclaiming throughout the whole city what great things God, through Joshua, had done for him.

(40) And as Joshua returned, the people welcomed him, for they had all been waiting for him. (41) And there came a man named Jairus, and he was an official of the religious organization; and he fell at Joshua' feet, and began to implore him to come to his house; (42) for he had an only daughter, about twelve years old, and she was very sick. But as he went, the crowds were pressing against him. (43) And a woman who had a hemorrhage (*bleeding condition*) for twelve years, and could not be healed by anyone, (44) came up behind him and touched the fringe of his cloak, and immediately her hemorrhage (*bleeding*) stopped. (45) And Joshua said, "**Who is the one who touched me?**" And while they were all denying it, Peter said, "Master, the people are crowding and pressing in on you." (46) But Joshua said, "**Someone did touch me, for I was aware that power had gone out of me.**" (47) When the woman saw that she had not escaped notice, she came trembling and fell down before him, and declared in the presence of all the people the reason why she had touched him, and how she had been

immediately healed. (48) And he said to her, "**Daughter, your faith has made you well; go in peace**."

(49) While he was still speaking, someone came from the house of Jairus the religious official, saying, "Your daughter has died; do not trouble the teacher anymore." (50) But when Joshua heard this, he said to Jairus, "**Do not be afraid any longer; only believe, and she will be made well**." (51) When he came to the house, he did not allow anyone to enter with him, except Peter and John and James, and the girl's father and mother. (52) Now they were all weeping and lamenting for her; but he said, "**Stop weeping, for she has not died, but is asleep**." (53) And they began laughing at him, knowing that she had died. (54) Joshua, however, went into her room and took her by the hand and said, "**Child, arise!**" (55) And her spirit returned, and she got up immediately; and he gave orders for something to be given her to eat. (56) Her parents were amazed; but he instructed them to tell no one what had happened.

(9:1) And he called the twelve (*sent ones*) together, and gave them power and authority over all the demons and to heal diseases. (2) And he sent them out to proclaim the kingdom of God and to perform healing. (3) And he said to them, "**Take nothing for your journey, neither a staff** (*walking stick*)**, nor a bag, nor bread, nor money; and do not even have two coats apiece.** (4) "**Whatever house you enter, stay there until you leave that city.** (5) "**And as for those who do not receive you, as you go out from that city, shake the dust off your feet as a testimony against them.**" (6) Departing, they began going throughout the villages, preaching the gospel and healing everywhere.

(7) Now Herod the roman ruler heard of all that was happening; and he was greatly perplexed, because it was said by some that John the Baptist had risen from the dead, (8) and by some that Elijah had appeared, and by others that one of the prophets of old had risen again. (9) Herod said, "I myself had John's head cut off; but who is this man about whom I hear such things?" And he kept trying to see him.

(10) When the twelve returned, they gave an account to him of all that they had done. Taking them with him, he withdrew by himself to a city called Bethsaida. (11) But the crowds were aware of this and followed him; and welcoming them, he began speaking to them about the kingdom of God and curing those who had need of healing. (12) Now the day was ending, and the twelve came and said to him, "Send the crowd away, that they may go into the surrounding villages and countryside and find lodging and get something to eat; for here we are in a desolate (*remote*) place." (13) But he said to them, "**You give them something to eat!**" And they said, "We have no more than five loaves of bread and two fish, unless perhaps we go and buy food for all these people." (14) (For there were about five thousand men.) And he said to his disciples, "**Have them sit down to eat in groups of about fifty each.**" (15) They did so, and had them all sit down. (16) Then he took the five loaves and the two fish, and looking up to heaven, he blessed

them, and broke them, and kept giving them to the disciples to set before the people. (17) And they all ate and were satisfied; and the broken pieces which they had left over were picked up, twelve baskets full.

(18) And it happened that while he was praying alone, the disciples were nearby, and he questioned them, saying, "**Who do the people say that I am?**" (19) They answered and said, "John the Baptist, and others say Elijah; but others, that one of the prophets of old has risen again." (20) And he said to them, "**But who do you say that I am?**" And Peter answered and said, "The Messiah of God." (21) But he warned them and instructed them not to tell this to anyone, (22) saying, "**The Son of Man must suffer many things and be rejected by the political and religious leaders and legal experts, and be killed and be raised up on the third day.**"

(23) And he was saying to them all, "**If anyone wishes to come after me, he must deny himself, and take up his cross daily and follow me.**

(24) "**For whoever wishes to save his life** (*in the world*) **will lose it, but whoever loses his life** (*in the world*) **for my sake, he is the one who will save it** (*eternal life*).

(25) "**For what has a man profited if he gains the whole world** (*all the wealth and power the world offers*), **and loses or forfeits himself** (*his soul destroyed*)? (26) "**For whoever is ashamed of me and my words**[*17], **the Son of Man will be ashamed of him when he comes in his glory, and the glory of the Father and of the holy angels.**

[*17] *If we are not ashamed of his person and his words, then we will be proclaiming and speaking his message, words and teachings to others. This act is driven by love and truth, and all true disciples will speak the Master's words to others.*

(27) **"But I say to you truthfully, there are some of those standing here who will not taste death until they see the kingdom of God**." (28) Some eight days after these sayings, he took along Peter and John and James, and went up on the mountain to pray. (29) And while he was praying, the appearance of his face became different, and his clothing became white and gleaming. (30) And behold, two men were talking with him; and they were Moses and Elijah, (31) who, appearing in glory, were speaking of his departure which he was about to accomplish at Jerusalem. (32) Now Peter and his companions had been overcome with sleep; but when they were fully awake, they saw his glory and the two men standing with him. (33) And as these were leaving him, Peter said to Joshua, "Master, it is good for us to be here; let us make three tabernacles (shelters): one for you, and one for Moses, and one for Elijah"--not realizing what he was saying. (34) While he was saying this, a cloud formed and began to overshadow them; and they were afraid as they entered the cloud. (35) Then a voice came out of the cloud, saying, "***This is My Son, My Chosen One; listen to Him!***" *18 (36) And when the voice had spoken, Joshua was found alone. And they kept silent, and reported to no one in those days any of the things which they had seen.

*18 *Sadly, very few listen to the Father's command here, and instead will listen to just about anyone other than Joshua...bible writers, their religious leaders, authors, speakers...anyone but the Light. See John 3:19 for the reason why.*

(37) On the next day, when they came down from the mountain, a large crowd met him. (38) And a man from the crowd shouted, saying, "Teacher, I beg you to look at my son, for he is my only boy, (39) and a spirit seizes him, and he suddenly screams, and it throws him into a convulsion with foaming at the mouth; and only with difficulty does it leave him, injuring him as it leaves. (40) "I begged your disciples to cast it out, and they could not." (41) And Joshua answered and said, "**You unbelieving and perverted generation, how long shall I be with you and put up with you? Bring your son here**." (42) While he was still approaching, the demon slammed him to the ground and threw him

into a convulsion. But Joshua rebuked the unclean spirit, and healed the boy and gave him back to his father. (43) And they were all amazed at the greatness of God. But while everyone was marveling at all that he was doing, he said to his disciples, (44) "**Let these words sink into your ears; for the Son of Man is going to be delivered into the hands of sinful men.**" (45) But they did not understand this statement, and it was concealed from them (*due to their misunderstandings of Messiah's role during his first visit*) so that they would not perceive it; and they were afraid to ask him about this statement.[*19]

[*19] *The first disciples did not understand Joshua's mission because of the false beliefs they held about Messiah, which false beliefs came from the Jewish scripture which tells of a Messiah that is a conquering King destroying Israel's enemies by force. Instead, he was and is the Rescuer and giver of Life. Therefore, it is reasonable to listen only to Joshua himself to understand Joshua perfectly; instead of listening to those who misunderstood him or who 'prophesied' (really invented or made up) what they wanted in a leader.*

(46) An argument started among them as to which of them might be the greatest. (47) But Joshua, knowing what they were thinking in their heart, took a child and stood him by his side, (48) and said to them, "**Whoever receives this child in my name receives me, and whoever receives me receives him who sent me; for the one who is least among all of you, this is the one who is great.**" (49) John answered and said, "Master, we saw someone casting out demons in your name; and we tried to prevent him because he does not follow along with us." (50) But Joshua said to him, "**Do not hinder him; for he who is not against you is for you.**" [*20]

[*20] *This saying should eliminate all competitiveness or envy among disciples, for competitiveness or envy is the manifestation of a heart of pride which destroys love and unity. See John 17.*

(51) When the days were approaching for his ascension (*Joshua returning to his Father*), he was determined to go to Jerusalem;

(52) and he sent messengers on ahead of him, and they went and entered a village of the Samaritans to make arrangements for him. (53) But they did not receive him, because he was traveling toward Jerusalem. (54) When his disciples James and John saw this, they said, "Lord, do you want us to command fire to come down from heaven and consume them?" (55) But Joshua turned and rebuked them, and said, **"You do not know what kind of spirit you are of; (56) for the Son of Man did not come to destroy men's lives, but to save them."** *21 And they went on to another village.

*21 *Joshua's heart/spirit does not change for he reflects his Father, who does not change. Therefore this saying will always be true of Joshua, that he does not come to destroy men's lives, but to save them. Contrast this truth with the spirit expressed in the book of revelation, which falsely attributes to Joshua the spirit of vengeance and destruction...the book of revelation presents a different 'Jesus' than what is presented in these books.*

(57) As they were going along the road, someone said to him, "I will follow you wherever you go." (58) And Joshua said to him, **"The foxes have holes and the birds of the air have nests, but the Son of Man has nowhere to lay his head."** *22 (59) And he said to another, **"Follow Me."** But he said, "Lord, permit me first to go and bury my father." (60) But he said to him, **"Allow the** (*spiritually*) **dead to bury their own** (*physically*) **dead; but as for you, go and proclaim everywhere the kingdom of God."** (61) Another also said, "I will follow you, Lord; but first permit me to say good-bye to those at home." (62) But Joshua said to him, **"No one, after putting his hand to the plow and looking back, is fit for the kingdom of God."**

*22 *A rebuke to all the religious leaders and false prophets who say God wants people to be materially wealthy. If the King's Father wanted people to be materially wealthy, then surely that would include His Son, the appointed King. And yet this King has no material things to his name...no material wealth. Rather, his treasure is in his subjects, we who love our King back and seek to be like him.*

(10:1) Now after this Joshua appointed seventy others, and sent them in pairs ahead of him to every city and place where he himself was going to come. (2) And he was saying to them, **"The harvest is plentiful, but the laborers are few; therefore beseech** (*diligently call upon*) **the Lord of the harvest to send out laborers into his harvest.** (3) **"Go; behold, I send you out as lambs in the midst of wolves.**[*23] (4) **"Carry no money belt, no bag, no shoes; and greet no one on the way.** (5) **"Whatever house you enter, first say, 'Peace be to this house.'** (6) **"If a man of peace is there, your peace will rest on him; but if not, it will return to you.** (7) **"Stay in that house, eating and drinking what they give you; for the laborer is worthy of his wages. Do not keep moving from house to house.** (8) **"Whatever city you enter and they receive you, eat what is set before you;** (9) **and heal those in it who are sick, and say to them, 'The kingdom of God has come near to you.'**

[*23]   *The harvest the Light speaks of is not just 'harmless grain', but rather hostile people who will react negatively to the Light, his message, and his messengers.*

---

(10) **"But whatever city you enter and they do not receive you, go out into its streets and say,** (11) **'Even the dust of your city which clings to our feet we wipe off in protest against you; yet be sure of this, that the kingdom of God has come near.'** (12) **"I say to you, it will be more tolerable in that day** (*of judgment – see Matt. 24*) **for Sodom than for that city.** (13) **"Woe to you, Chorazin! Woe to you, Bethsaida! For if the miracles had been performed in Tyre and Sidon which occurred in you, they would have repented** (*feel truly sorry about your bad behavior and words, and change*) **long ago, sitting in sackcloth** (*very uncomfortable clothing*) **and ashes.** (14) **"But it will be more tolerable for Tyre and Sidon in the judgment than for you.** (15) **"And you, Capernaum, will not be exalted to heaven, will you? You will be brought down to Hell!** [*24]

Words which run counter to the "always be positive, never negative" and "never judge" beliefs so popular in the contemporary US culture. We ought to be careful how we judge others, but we better be judging what is true and false and what is right and wrong according to Joshua or else we surely will be misled or deceived.

(16) "The one who listens to you listens to Me, and the one who rejects you rejects Me; and he who rejects Me rejects the One who sent Me."

(17) The seventy returned with joy, saying, "Lord, even the demons are subject to us in your name." (18) And he said to them, "**I was watching Satan fall from heaven like lightning. (19) "Behold, I have given you authority to tread on serpents and scorpions, and over all the power of the enemy, and nothing will injure you. (20) "Nevertheless do not rejoice in this, that the spirits are subject to you, but rejoice that your names are recorded in heaven."**

(21) At that very time he rejoiced greatly in the Holy Spirit, and said, "**I praise You, O Father, Lord of heaven and earth, that you have hidden these things from the smart and intelligent and have revealed them to little children. Yes, Father, for this way was well-pleasing in your sight.**"[*25] (22) "**All things have been handed over to me by my Father, and no one knows who the Son is except the Father, and who the Father is except the Son, and anyone to whom the Son wills to reveal him.**" (23) Turning to the disciples, he said privately, "**Blessed are the eyes which see the things you see, (24) for I say to you, that many prophets and kings wished to see the things which you see, and did not see them, and to hear the things which you hear, and did not hear them.**"

[*25] *A key teaching of Joshua regarding what kind of people can understand and receive the truths he taught about the kingdom of God. See Matt. 11:25-26. It runs completely against the beliefs and practices of both the religious systems and the educational systems of the world. The religious 'educational' systems declare*

that a person needs advanced degrees and the ability to understand complicated theology in order to understand God. They use complication to hide the simple truth.

(25) And a lawyer stood up and put him to the test, saying, "Teacher, what shall I do to inherit eternal life?" (26) And he said to him, "**What is written in the Law? How does it read to you?**" (27) And he answered, "YOU SHALL LOVE THE LORD YOUR GOD WITH ALL YOUR HEART, AND WITH ALL YOUR SOUL, AND WITH ALL YOUR STRENGTH, AND WITH ALL YOUR MIND; AND YOUR NEIGHBOR AS YOURSELF." (28) And he said to him, "**You have answered correctly; DO THIS AND YOU WILL LIVE.**" (29) But wishing to justify himself, he said to Joshua, "But who is my neighbor?" (30) Joshua replied and said, "**A man was going down from Jerusalem to Jericho, and fell among robbers, and they stripped him and beat him, and went away leaving him half dead. (31) "And by chance a religious man was going down on that road, and when he saw him, he passed by on the other side. (32) "Likewise another religious man from a different sect also, when he came to the place and saw him, passed by on the other side. (33) "But a Samaritan, who was on a journey, came upon him; and when he saw him, he had compassion, (34) and came to him and bandaged up his wounds, pouring oil and wine on them; and he put him on his own horse, and brought him to an inn and took care of him. (35) "On the next day he took out one hundred and fifty dollars and gave them to the innkeeper and said, 'Take care of him; and whatever more you spend, when I return I will repay you.'** (36) Joshua asked the lawyer, "**Which of these three do you think proved to be a neighbor to the man who fell into the robbers' hands?**" (37) And he said, "The one who showed mercy toward him." Then Joshua said to him, "**Go and do the same.**"

(38) Now as they were traveling along, he entered a village; and a woman named Martha welcomed him into her home. (39) She had

a sister called Mary, who was seated at the Lord's feet, listening to his word. (40) But Martha was distracted with all her preparations; and she came up to him and said, "Lord, do you not care that my sister has left me to do all the serving alone? Then tell her to help me." (41) But the Lord answered and said to her, "**Martha, Martha, you are worried and bothered about so many things; (42) but only one thing is necessary, and Mary has chosen the good part, which shall not be taken away from her.**"

(11:1) It happened that while Joshua was praying in a certain place, after he had finished, one of his disciples said to him, "Lord, teach us to pray just as John also taught his disciples." (2) And he said to them, **"When you pray, pray in this manner: 'Father, high above is your name. Your kingdom come. (3) 'Give us each day our daily bread. (4) 'And forgive us our sins, as we ourselves also forgive everyone who is indebted to us. And lead us not into temptation.'"** [26]

[26] *Short, simple, straightforward talking to one's Father – that is prayer as both taught (see Matt. 6:5-6) and modeled by Joshua. Not long or eloquent speeches in front of others which is the practice in most christian religious organizations and which practices contradict Joshua's teachings.*

(5) Then he said to them, **"Suppose one of you has a friend, and goes to him at midnight and says to him, 'Friend, lend me three loaves of bread; (6) for a friend of mine has come to me from a journey, and I have nothing to set before him'; (7) and from inside he answers and says, 'Do not bother me; the door has already been shut and my children and I are in bed; I cannot get up and give you anything.' (8) "I tell you, even though he will not get up and give him anything even when he is his friend, yet because of his persistence he will get up and give him as much as he needs. (9) "So I say to you, ask, and it will be given to you; seek, and you will find; knock, and it will be opened to you. (10) "For everyone who asks, receives; and he who seeks, finds; and to him who knocks, it will be opened. (11) "Now suppose one of you fathers is asked by his son for a fish; he will not give him a snake instead of a fish, will he? (12) "Or if he is asked for an egg, he will not give him a scorpion, will he? (13) "If you then, being evil, know how to give good gifts to your children, how much more will your heavenly Father give the Holy Spirit to those who ask Him?"**

(14) And he was casting out a demon, and it was mute (*a person who cannot speak*); when the demon had gone out, the mute man spoke; and the crowds were amazed. (15) But some of them said, "He casts out demons by Satan, the ruler of the demons." (16) Others, to test him, were demanding of him a sign from heaven. (17) But he knew their thoughts and said to them, **"Any kingdom divided against itself will fail; and a house divided against itself falls.** (18) **"If Satan also is divided against himself, how will his kingdom stand? For you say that I cast out demons by Satan.** (19) **"And if I by Satan cast out demons, by whom do your sons cast them out? So they***27 **will be your judges.** (20) **"But if I cast out demons by the finger of God, then the kingdom of God has come upon you.** (21) **"When a strong man, fully armed, guards his own house, his possessions are undisturbed.** (22) **"But when someone stronger than he attacks him and overpowers him, he takes away from him all his armor on which he had relied and takes his possessions.**

(23) **"He who is not with me is against me; and he who does not gather with me, scatters.***28

*27 *Commentator's opinion - the men's son's will be their dad's judges when they all stand before the King and the son's will say, 'we told our dad's that we cast them out by God but they would not listen and insisted on condemning Joshua'.*

*28 *This statement leaves no neutral ground regarding what a person believes regarding Joshua – you are either positively for him and working for him, or you are negatively against him and working against him. Once you hear Joshua's claims, you must make a choice what you are going to do with him. Many think ignoring him is a third option – this teaching says they are wrong. Most think having some beliefs in their head about him – mere facts - satisfies being "with him", but they are badly mistaken.*

(24) **"When the unclean spirit goes out of a man, it passes through waterless places seeking rest, and not finding any, it says, 'I will return to my house from which I came.'** (25)

"And when it comes, it finds it swept and put in order. (26) **"Then it goes and takes along seven other spirits more evil than itself, and they go in and live there; and the last state of that man becomes worse than the first."** *29

*29 *Commentator's opinion - A man without faith but who understands his fault, struggles and weaknesses, has 'a spirit' which encourages the man's sin struggles. The spirit leaves and the man find's religion, and religion helps him outwardly clean up his life, but inside, the man hasn't changed. When the unclean spirits find the man under outward control (religious rules or laws constraining him), but inwardly more open to evil and hypocrisy, the man's state of pride in his religious status is worse than when he saw his faults and needs.*

(27) While Joshua was saying these things, one of the women in the crowd raised her voice and said to him, "Blessed is the womb that bore you and the breasts at which you nursed." (28) But he said, **"On the contrary, blessed are those who hear the word of God and observe it."** (29) As the crowds were increasing, he began to say, **"This generation is a wicked (*evil*) generation; it seeks for a sign, and yet no sign will be given to it but the sign of Jonah.** (30) **"For just as Jonah became a sign to the Ninevites, so will the Son of Man be to this generation.** (31) **"The Queen of the South will rise up with the men of this generation at the judgment and condemn them, because she came from the ends of the earth to hear the wisdom of Solomon; and behold, someone greater than Solomon is here.** (32) **"The men of Nineveh will stand up with this generation at the judgment and condemn it, because they repented at the preaching of Jonah; and behold, someone greater than Jonah is here.**"*30

*30 *People are willing to say they admire Joshua, yet they are generally not willing to listen to his words – the word of God as given by his Father – and are not willing to do what he says, even though he is greater than the religious leaders and heroes of the past or present whom the people highly exalt.*

(33) "No one, after lighting a lamp, puts it away in a cellar nor under a basket, but on the table, so that those who enter may see the light. (34) "The eye is the lamp of your body; when your eye is clear, your whole body also is full of light; but when it is bad, your body also is full of darkness. (35) "Then watch out that the light in you is not darkness. (36) "If therefore your whole body is full of light, with no dark part in it, it will be wholly illumined, as when the lamp illumines you with its rays."

(37) Now when he had spoken, a religious leader asked him to have lunch with him; and he went in, and reclined at the table. (38) When the religious leader saw it, he was surprised that he had not first ceremonially washed before the meal. (39) But the Lord said to him, "**Now you religious leaders clean the outside of the cup and of the plate; but inside of you, you are full of robbery and wickedness. (40) "You foolish ones, did not he who made the outside make the inside also? (41) "But give that which is within as charity** (*love*)**, and then all things are clean for you. (42) "But woe** (*guilty before God and heading for judgment*) **to you religious leaders! For you pay ten percent of your expensive spices to your religion, and yet disregard justice and the love of God; but these are the things you should have done without neglecting the others.**

(43) "**Woe to you religious leaders! For you love the best seats in the religious buildings and respectful greetings in the market places. (44) "Woe to you! For you are like concealed tombs, and the people who walk over them are unaware of it** (*and thus get unclean by interacting with you*)." (*verses 45-46 inserted after verse 51 below*) (47) "**Woe to you! For you build the tombs of the prophets, and it was your fathers who killed them. (48) "So you are witnesses and approve the deeds of your fathers; because it was they** (*your father's*) **who killed them, and you build their** (*your father's*) **tombs** (*and thereby honor your fathers who killed the*

prophets). (49) **"For this reason also the wisdom of God said, 'I will send to them prophets and one's trained by my Son; and some of them they will kill and some they will persecute** (*do things to harm them*)**, (50) so that the blood of all the prophets, shed since the foundation of the world, may be charged against this generation, (51) from the blood of Abel to the blood of Zechariah, who was killed between the altar and the house of God; yes, I tell you, it shall be charged against this generation.'**

(45) One of the lawyers said to him in reply, "Teacher, when you say this, you insult us too." (46) But he said, **"Woe to you lawyers as well! For you weigh men down with burdens hard to bear, while you yourselves will not even help carry the burdens with one of your fingers. (52) "Woe to you lawyers! For you have taken away the key of knowledge; you yourselves did not enter, and you hindered those who were entering."** *31 (53) When he left there, the bible experts (*lawyers*) and the religious leaders began to be very hostile and to question him closely on many subjects, (54) plotting against him to catch him in something he might say.

---

*31 *Joshua singled out two "professions" or "vocations" for rebuke – religious leaders and lawyers who interpret the law. People in both professions make things complicated so average people cannot understand without their 'help', and they generally don't help people without receiving payment or something in return. They take away the key to knowledge –simplicity – and by so doing, hinder other people who would otherwise be willing to become as a child (simple, straightforward) in order to enter the kingdom of God – see Matt. 18:3.*

(12:1) Under these circumstances, after so many thousands of people had gathered together that they were stepping on one another, he began saying to his disciples first of all, "**Beware of the leaven of the religious leaders, which is hypocrisy** (*two-facedness*). (2) "**But there is nothing covered up that will not be revealed, and hidden that will not be known.** (3) "**Accordingly, whatever you have said in the dark will be heard in the light, and what you have whispered in private will be proclaimed upon the housetops.** (4) "**I say to you, my friends, do not be afraid of those who kill the body and after that have no more that they can do.** (5) "**But I will warn you whom to fear: fear the One who, after your body is dead, has authority to cast into hell; yes, I tell you, fear Him!**"*32

*32 *After warning us about hypocrisy and attempts to hide our evil, the Light provides a back-up or lesser motivation to love. If we are doing poorly with the greatest command – to love our Father with all that is in us - then it is better to abstain from evil due to fear than to commit evil. Note he DOES NOT say "fear the One who...casts into hell", but rather, "who has authority".*

(6) "**Are not five sparrows sold for two cents? Yet not one of them is forgotten before God.** (7) "**Indeed, the very hairs of your head are all numbered. Do not fear; you are more valuable than many sparrows.**"*33

*33 *He follows his setting of the lesser motivation of fear with a reminder that we are valuable to God - in fact more valuable than animals according to this teaching and v.24 below – and thus we should not fear because we are valuable or important to our Father...we who have faith in Joshua are received and beloved sons and daughters!*

(8) "**And I say to you, everyone who speaks about me to people, the Son of Man will speak favorably about him before the angels of God;** (9) **but he who ignores me before men will be ignored before the angels of God.** (10) "**And everyone who speaks a word against the Son of Man,**

it will be forgiven him; but he who blasphemes (*speaks badly of*) against the Holy Spirit, it will not be forgiven him. (11) "When they bring you before the religious leaders and the judges and the authorities, do not worry about how or what you are to speak in your defense, or what you are to say; (12) for the Holy Spirit will teach you in that very hour what you ought to say."**

(13) Someone in the crowd said to him, "Teacher, tell my brother to divide the family inheritance with me." (14) But he said to him, **"Man, who appointed me a financial judge or arbitrator over you?"** (15) Then he said to them, **"Beware, and be on your guard against every form of greed; for not even when one is wealthy does his life consist of his material things."** (16) And he told them a parable, saying, **"The land of a rich man was very productive. (17) "And he began reasoning to himself, saying, 'What shall I do, since I have no place to store my crops?' (18) "Then he said, 'This is what I will do: I will tear down my barns and build larger ones, and there I will store all my grain and my goods. (19) 'And I will say to my soul, "Soul, you have many goods laid up for many years to come; take it easy, eat, drink and be merry."' (20) "But God said to him, 'You fool! This very night your soul is required of you; and now who will own what you have stored up?' (21) "So is the man who stores up treasure for himself, and is not rich toward God."** *34

*34 *How is one "rich toward God"? By storing up one's treasures in heaven by doing what Joshua says, primarily loving other people - see Matt. 6.*

(22) And he said to his disciples, **"For this reason** (*that a person's life does not consist of their material things*) **I say to you, do not worry about your life, as to what you will eat; nor for your body, as to what clothes you will wear. (23) "For life is about more than food, and the body more than clothing. (24) "Consider the birds, for they neither sow nor reap; they have no storeroom nor barn, and yet God**

feeds them; how much more valuable you are than the birds! (25) "And which of you by worrying can add a single hour to his life's span? (26) "If then you cannot do even a very little thing, why do you worry about other matters? (27) "Consider the lilies, how they grow: they neither toil nor spin; but I tell you, not even Solomon in all his glory clothed himself like one of these. (28) "But if God so clothes the grass in the field, which is alive today and tomorrow is thrown into the furnace, how much more will he clothe you? you men of little faith! (29) "And do not wonder what you will eat and what you will drink, and do not keep worrying. (30) "For all these things the people of the world eagerly seek; but your Father knows that you need these things".

(13:1) Now on the same occasion there were some present who reported to Joshua about the Galileans whose blood Pilate had mixed with their sacrifices. (2) And Joshua said to them, "**Do you suppose that these Galileans were greater sinners than all other Galileans because they suffered this fate? (3) "I tell you, no, but unless you repent** (*feel truly sorry about your bad behavior and words, and change*)**, you will all likewise perish. (4) "Or do you suppose that those eighteen on whom the tower in Siloam fell and killed them were worse culprits than all the men who live in Jerusalem?***35 **(5) "I tell you, no, but unless you repent, you will all likewise perish."** (6) And he began telling this parable: "**A man had a fig tree which had been planted in his vineyard; and he came looking for fruit on it and did not find any. (7) "And he said to the vineyard-keeper, 'Behold, for three years I have come looking for fruit on this fig tree without finding any. Cut it down! Why does it even use up the ground?' (8) "And he answered and said to him, 'Please let it alone, sir, for this year too, until I dig around it and put in fertilizer; (9) and if it bears fruit next year, fine; but if not, cut it down.'"**

*35   *This teaching rebukes the "God punishes or kills those who do bad things" belief. See Matt. 5:45. It also teaches that all people ("All the men who live in Jerusalem") have failed to do what God wants to some degree, and thus need to repent, have faith in Joshua and listen to him.*

(10) And he was teaching in one of the religious buildings on the sabbath. (11) And there was a woman who for eighteen years had had a sickness caused by a spirit; and she was bent double, and could not straighten up at all. (12) When Joshua saw her, he called her over and said to her, "**Woman, you are freed from your sickness.**" (13) And he laid his hands on her; and immediately she was made erect again and began glorifying God. (14) But the religious official, indignant because Joshua had healed on the sabbath, began saying to the crowd in response, "There are six days in which work should be done; so come during them and get healed, and not on the sabbath day." (15) But the Lord answered him and

said, "**You hypocrites** (*a person who says what others ought to do or not do, but does not do so themselves*)**, does not each of you on the sabbath untie his ox or his donkey from the stall and lead him away to water him?** (16) **"And this woman, a daughter of Abraham as she is, whom Satan has bound for eighteen long years, should she not have been released from this bond on the sabbath day?"** (17) As he said this, all his opponents were being humiliated; and the entire crowd was rejoicing over all the glorious things being done by him.

(18) So he was saying, "**What is the kingdom of God like, and to what shall I compare it?** (19) **"It is like a mustard seed, which a man took and threw into his own garden; and it grew and became a tree, and THE BIRDS OF THE AIR NESTED IN ITS BRANCHES.**" (20) And again he said, "**To what shall I compare the kingdom of God?** (21) **"It is like leaven, which a woman took and hid in three pints of flour until it was all leavened.**"

(22) And he was passing through from one city and village to another, teaching, and proceeding on his way to Jerusalem. (23) And someone said to him, "Lord, are there just a few who are being saved?" And he said to them, (24) **"Strive** (*or agonize*) **to enter through the narrow door; for many, I tell you, will seek to enter** (*through bible religion*) **and will not be able.** (25) **"Once the head of the house gets up and shuts the door, and you begin to stand outside and knock on the door, saying, 'Lord, open up to us!' then he will answer and say to you, 'I do not know where you are from.'** (26) **"Then you will begin to say, 'We ate and drank in your presence, and you taught in our streets';** (27) **and he will say, 'I tell you, I do not know where you are from; DEPART FROM ME, ALL YOU EVILDOERS.'** (28) **"In that place there will be weeping and great anger when you see Abraham and Isaac and Jacob and all the prophets in the kingdom of God, but yourselves being thrown out.** (29) **"And they will come from east and west and from north and south, and will**

recline at the table in the kingdom of God. **(30) "And behold, some are last** (*in this life*) **who will be first and some are first** (*in this life*) **who will be last."**

(31) Just at that time some religious leaders approached, saying to him, "Go away, and leave here, for Herod wants to kill you." (32) And he said to them, **"Go and tell that fox, 'Behold, I cast out demons and perform cures today and tomorrow, and the third day I reach my goal.' (33) "Nevertheless I must journey on today and tomorrow and the next day; for it cannot be that a prophet would perish outside of Jerusalem. (34) "O Jerusalem, Jerusalem, the city that kills the prophets and stones those sent to her! How often I wanted to gather your children together, just as a hen gathers her chicks under her wings, and you would not have it! (35) "Behold, your house is left to you desolate** (*empty, barren*)**; and I say to you, you will not see me until the time comes when you say, 'BLESSED IS HE WHO COMES IN THE NAME OF THE LORD!'"**

(14:1) It happened that when he went into the house of one of the religious leaders on the sabbath to eat bread, they were watching him closely. (2) And there in front of him was a man suffering from a disease called dropsy. (3) And Joshua answered and spoke to the lawyers and religious leaders, saying, "**Is it lawful to heal on the sabbath, or not?**" (4) But they kept silent. And Joshua took hold of him and healed him, and sent him away. (5) And he said to them, "**Which one of you who has a son or an ox fall into a well, will not immediately pull him out on a sabbath day?**" *36 (6) And they could make no reply to this.

*36 *Joshua's points are clear. First, it is fine to do good work on their sabbath. Second, he points out their hypocrisy - how people will justify their own work on a sabbath as acceptable, even while they tell others it breaks God's law to work on the sabbath. The Jewish 'no work on the sabbath' had a good reason when it was first given by Moses, due to the Jewish people being worked so hard - seven days a week - by the Egyptian rulers at the time. But now the Lord of the sabbath (in fact the King) makes it clear that his followers are not bound by Moses' rules!*

(7) And he began speaking a parable (*short story with lesson*) to the invited guests when he noticed how they had been picking out the places of honor at the table, saying to them, (8) "**When you are invited by someone to a wedding celebration, do not take the place of honor, for someone more distinguished than you may have been invited by him,** (9) **and he who invited you both will come and say to you, 'Give your place to this man,' and then in disgrace you proceed to occupy the last place.** (10) "**But when you are invited, go and recline at the last place, so that when the one who has invited you comes, he may say to you, 'Friend, move up higher'; then you will have honor in the sight of all who are at the table with you.** (11) "**For everyone who exalts himself will be humbled, and he who humbles himself will be exalted.**" *37 (12) And he also went on to say to the one who had invited him, "**When you give a luncheon or a dinner, do not invite your friends or your brothers or your relatives or rich neighbors, otherwise they may also invite you in**

return and that will be your repayment. (13) **"But when you give a reception, invite the poor, the crippled, the lame, the blind,** (14) **and you will be blessed, since they do not have the means to repay you; for you will be repaid at the resurrection of the righteous."** *38

*37   *A key teaching of Joshua which he repeats several times in his teachings – be humble. That is, don't count yourself important, rather don't look at yourself at all and instead live to help and serve others...see others as more important than yourself. This teaching goes completely against human nature as well as goes against the practices and teachings of much of christianity – the "self-esteem" teachings which many christians have adopted from the world.*

*38   *Another key teaching of Joshua is don't look for reward in this life, rather look for reward in the Life to come – "the resurrection of the righteous". Help the helpless and truly needy and don't look for earthly reward, and your treasure will be great in heaven.*

(15) When one of those who were reclining at the table with him heard this, he said to him, "Blessed is everyone who will eat bread in the kingdom of God!" (16) But Joshua said to him, "**A man was giving a big dinner, and he invited many; (17) and at the dinner hour he sent his servant to say to those who had been invited, 'Come; for everything is ready now.'** (18) **"But they all alike began to make excuses. The first one said to him, 'I have bought a piece of land and I need to go out and look at it; please consider me excused.'** (19) **"Another one said, 'I have bought five pairs of oxen, and I am going to try them out; please consider me excused.'** (20) **"Another one said, 'I have married a wife, and for that reason I cannot come.'** (21) **"And the servant came back and reported this to his master. Then the head of the household became angry and said to his servant, 'Go out at once into the streets and lanes of the city and bring in here the poor and crippled and blind and lame.'** (22) **"And the servant said, 'Master, what you commanded has been done, and still there is room.'** (23) **"And the master said to**

the servant, 'Go out into the highways and along the hedges, and compel them to come in, so that my house may be filled. (24) 'For I tell you, none of those men who were invited shall taste of my dinner.'" *39

*39 *The heavenly Father invites all to his blessings, yet most who see themselves as worthy to be invited – typically religious people who put their faith in their bibles and their church going, etc. – will find themselves outside the kingdom since they did not DO what the Son says - "love one another as I have loved you". See the new command in John 13:33-34.*

(25) Now large crowds were going along with Him; and he turned and said to them, (26) **"If anyone comes to me, and does not hate his own father and mother and wife and children and brothers and sisters, yes, and even his own life, he cannot be my disciple.**[*40] (27) **"Whoever does not carry his own cross and come after me cannot be my disciple. (28) "For which one of you, when he wants to build a tower, does not first sit down and calculate the cost to see if he has enough to complete it? (29) "Otherwise, when he has laid a foundation and is not able to finish, all who observe it begin to ridicule him, (30) saying, 'This man began to build and was not able to finish.' (31) "Or what king, when he sets out to meet another king in battle, will not first sit down and consider whether he is strong enough with ten thousand men to encounter the one coming against him with twenty thousand? (32) "Or else, while the other is still far away, he sends a delegation and asks for terms of peace. (33) "So then, none of you can be my disciple who does not give up all that he has** (*the things the world considers important, especially material security*).**[*41] (34) "Therefore, salt is good; but if even salt has become tasteless, with what will it be seasoned? (35) "It is useless either for the soil or for the manure pile; it is thrown out. He who has ears to hear, let him hear."**

*40 *A key part of losing our lives in this world. Joshua knows that the natural family will many times be the thing that prevents individuals from becoming his followers, so he makes it clear here how an individual must disregard their natural family's will and desires, and must instead do what he says. Sadly, when so many people are deceived in terms of what it means to be a follower of Joshua, this teaching has no meaning since people think, 'we are all christians'.*

*41 *A powerful and solemn teaching that is utterly ignored by the vast majority of people who claim to somehow belong to 'christ'. This teaching is perfectly consistent with his "lose our life" teachings. We must not hold onto, seek after, work for, anything the world considers valuable, especially money and material security. Instead, we are to be a people filled with compassion, truth and rightness - living for our Father and Master and being the example the world needs to see. See John 13:34-35.*

(15:1) Now all the tax collectors and the sinners[*42] were coming near him to listen to him. (2) Both the religious leaders and the bible experts began to grumble, saying, "This man receives sinners and eats with them." (3) So he told them this parable, saying, (4) **"What man among you, if he has a hundred sheep and has lost one of them, does not leave the ninety-nine in the open pasture and go after the one which is lost until he finds it? (5) "When he has found it, he lays it on his shoulders, rejoicing. (6) "And when he comes home, he calls together his friends and his neighbors, saying to them, 'Rejoice with me, for I have found my sheep which was lost!' (7) "I tell you that in the same way, there will be more joy in heaven over one sinner who repents** (*feel truly sorry about your bad behavior and words, and change*) **than over ninety-nine righteous persons who need no repentance. (8) "Or what woman, if she has ten silver coins and loses one coin, does not light a lamp and sweep the house and search carefully until she finds it? (9) "When she has found it, she calls together her friends and neighbors, saying, 'Rejoice with me, for I have found the coin which I had lost!' (10) "In the same way, I tell you, there is joy in the presence of the angels of God over one sinner who repents."** [*43]

[*42] *Those people who were aware of their faults and problems – who saw themselves as missing the mark of a good, rightly-lived life and looking for help - typically not people involved in religion, which people generally do not see their need.*

[*43] *A rebuke against pride, and a glimpse into the Father's heart of compassion and desire for people who turn from their pride and come running to Him...when we do, there is rejoicing in heaven!*

(11) And he said, **"A man had two sons. (12) "The younger of them said to his father, 'Father, give me the share of the estate that I am due to inherit.' So he divided his wealth between his two sons. (13) "And not many days later, the**

younger son gathered everything together and went on a journey into a distant country, and there he wasted his inheritance with foolish living. (14) "Now when he had spent everything, a severe famine occurred in that country and he began to be in need of help. (15) "So he went and hired himself out to one of the citizens of that country, and he sent him into his fields to feed pigs. (16) "And he would have gladly filled his stomach with the food that the pigs were eating, and no one was giving anything to him. (17) "But when he came to his senses, he said, 'How many of my father's hired men have more than enough bread, but I am dying here with hunger! (18) 'I will get up and go to my father, and will say to him, "Father, I have sinned against heaven, and in your sight; (19) I am no longer worthy to be called your son; make me as one of your hired men."'

(20) "So he got up and came to his father. But while he was still a long way off, his father saw him and felt compassion for him, and ran and embraced him and kissed him. (21) "And the son said to him, 'Father, I have sinned against heaven and in your sight; I am no longer worthy to be called your son.' (22) "But the father said to his servants, 'Quickly bring out the best robe and put it on him, and put a ring on his hand and sandals on his feet; (23) and bring the fattened calf, kill it, and let us eat and celebrate; (24) for this son of mine was dead and has come to life again; he was lost and has been found!' And they began to celebrate.

(25) "Now his older son was in the field, and when he came and approached the house, he heard music and dancing. (26) "And he summoned one of the servants and began inquiring what these things could be. (27) "And he said to him, 'Your brother has come, and your father has killed the fattened calf because he has received him back safe and sound.' (28) "But the older son became angry and was not willing to go in; and his father came out and

began pleading with him. (29) "But he answered and said to his father, 'Look! For so many years I have been serving you and I have never neglected a command of yours; and yet you have never given me a young goat, so that I might celebrate with my friends; (30) but when this son of yours came, who has wasted your wealth with prostitutes, you killed the fattened calf for him.' (31) "And he said to him, 'Son, you have always been with me, and all that is mine is yours. (32) 'But we had to celebrate and rejoice, for this brother of yours was dead and has begun to live, and was lost and has been found.'" *44

---

*44 *The story of every person ever born and the correct description of the Father that awaits each of us who sees our need. The son was "dead" and "lost" (a person without faith in the Father Joshua reveals and guided by selfish purposes in life) and repented of his ignoring and dishonoring his father, and was made alive and received by his father. A main thing that stands in the way of this story coming to pass much more often in people's lives is religion, which offers empty knowledge instead of faith, and an angry God instead of the genuine, compassionate Father. Other primary things that prevent people from this story coming to pass in their life is no-faith, self-pride and fear. If I don't believe a heavenly Father exists, I cannot run to him. And if we always justify our wrong words and behavior due to pride, we will never see out need to find that Father or to run to him to beg for forgiveness. How about you, dear reader?*

(16:1) Now he was also saying to the disciples (*sons of Light*), **"There was a rich man who had a manager, and this manager was reported to him as wasting his money.** (2) **"And he called him and said to him, 'What is this I hear about you? Give an accounting of your management, for you can no longer be manager.'** (3) **"The manager said to himself, 'What shall I do, since my master is taking the management away from me? I am not strong enough to dig; I am ashamed to beg.** (4) **'I know what I shall do, so that when I am removed from the management people will welcome me into their homes.'** (5) **"And he summoned each one of his master's debtors, and he began saying to the first, 'How much do you owe my master?'** (6) **"And he said, 'A hundred measures of oil.' And he said to him, 'Take your bill, and sit down quickly and write fifty.'** (7) **"Then he said to another, 'And how much do you owe?' And he said, 'A hundred measures of wheat.' he said to him, 'Take your bill, and write eighty.'** (8) **"And his master** (*a son of darkness*) **praised the unrighteous manager because he had acted shrewdly; for the sons of this age** (*sons of darkness*) **are shrewder in relation to their own kind than the sons of light.** (9) **"And I say to you, make friends for yourselves by means of the wealth of unrighteousness, so that when it fails** (*the money*)**, they** (*the righteous in heaven, your friends who have passed to be with the Father*) **will receive you into the eternal dwellings.**

(10) **"He who is faithful in a very little thing is faithful also in much; and he who is unrighteous in a very little thing is unrighteous also in much.** (11) **"Therefore if you have not been faithful in the use of unrighteous wealth, who will entrust the true riches to you?** (12) **"And if you have not been faithful in the use of that which is another's, who will give you that which is your own?** (13) **"No servant can serve two masters; for either he will hate the one and love the other, or else he will be devoted to one and despise the other. You cannot serve God and wealth."** (14) Now the

religious leaders, who loved money, were listening to all these things and were scoffing at him. (15) And he said to them, "**You are those who justify yourselves in the sight of men, but God knows your hearts; for that which is highly esteemed among men** (*in this case, material wealth*) **is detestable in the sight of God.**"[45]

[45] *A person who has a faithful heart will act consistently and not be swayed by the perceived value of the material things he is entrusted with. Those with faith know that their Father thinks that those who highly value material things are failing badly. The same can be said for those who highly value power over others or those who highly value other's opinions of them, etc.*

(16) "**The Law and the Prophets were proclaimed until John; since that time the gospel of the kingdom of God has been preached**[46], **and everyone is forcing his way into it.** (17) "**But it is easier for heaven and earth to pass away than for one stroke of a letter of the Law to fail** (*the law is good and shall not pass - "do not commit adultery" for example - but it is incomplete and imperfect as Joshua showed in Matt. 5*). (18) "**Everyone who divorces his wife and marries another commits adultery** (*"adultery" is a married person having sex with someone other than their spouse*), **and he who marries one who is divorced from a husband commits adultery.**

[46] *Joshua says a major and significant change happened regarding the kingdom of God with John the baptist as the change point. Moses' teachings of the law, and the prophets was proclaimed among the Jews **until** the time of John the Baptist. After John, the "gospel" or good news of the kingdom of God has been preached by the King himself to all who will listen, with a new and different good news message of love and faith-based behavior based on the King's teachings and example. See the new and old garment and wineskin teaching of the King in Luke 5:36 ff. The old message of Moses - "the law" - while good, has faded away in comparison to the new message of love, compassion and humble righteousness. Thus, those who still look to Moses and the Hebrew prophets are in great error, for in so doing, they reject the King and his new and superior Way.*

(19) "Now there was a rich man, and he normally dressed in colorful and fine clothes, joyously living in luxury every day. (20) "And a poor man named Lazarus was laid at his gate, covered with sores, (21) and longing to be fed with the crumbs which were falling from the rich man's table; even the dogs were coming and licking his sores. (22) "Now the poor man died and was carried away by the angels to Abraham's bosom (*a Jewish concept of heaven*); and the rich man also died and was buried. (23) "In Hell the rich man lifted up his eyes, being in torment, and saw Abraham far away and Lazarus with him in comfort. (24) "And he cried out and said, 'Father Abraham, have mercy on me, and send Lazarus so that he may dip the tip of his finger in water and cool off my tongue, for I am in agony in this flame.' (25) "But Abraham said, 'Child, remember that during your life you received your material comfort, and likewise Lazarus was materially poor and experiencing pain; but now he is being comforted here, and you are in agony. (26) 'And besides all this, between us and you there is a great chasm fixed, so that those who wish to come over from here to you will not be able, and that none may cross over from there to us.' (27) "And the rich man said, 'Then I beg you, father, that you send him to my father's house - (28) for I have five brothers - in order that he may warn them, so that they will not also come to this place of torment.' (29) "But Abraham said, 'They have Moses and the Prophets; let them hear them.' (30) "But the rich man said, 'No, father Abraham, but if someone goes to them from the dead, they will repent!' (*feel truly sorry about your bad behavior and words, and change*) (31) "But Abraham said to him, 'If they do not listen to Moses and the Prophets, they will not be persuaded even if someone rises from the dead.'" [47]

---

[47]   *If a Jewish person who says they venerate Moses and the Prophets will not listen to them, but rather does what they want without concern for the words or teachings of Moses and the Prophets, then that person will not listen to even the*

resurrected Messiah. In like manner, if a christian person who says they venerate "the christ" yet does not listen to him, but rather does what they want without concern for his words or teachings, what will be the fate of that person? See Matt. 7:22-23.

(17:1) He said to his disciples, "**It is inevitable that stumbling blocks**[48] **come, but woe to him through whom they come!** (2) **"It would be better for him if a millstone** (*giant donut shaped stone*) **were hung around his neck and he were thrown into the sea, than that he would cause one of these little ones to stumble.** (3) **"Be on your guard! If your brother sins, rebuke him; and if he repents** (*feel truly sorry about the bad behavior and words, and change*), **forgive him.** (4) **"And if he sins against you seven times a day, and returns to you seven times, saying, 'I repent,' forgive him."** (5) The twelve sent ones said to the Lord, "Increase our faith!" (6) And the Lord said, "**If you had faith like a mustard seed, you would say to this mulberry tree, 'Be uprooted and be planted in the sea'; and it would obey you.**

[48] *Stumbling blocks mean things people do to encourage you to sin or fail in doing what Joshua says.*

(7) **"Which of you, having a servant plowing or tending sheep, will say to him when he has come in from the field, 'Come immediately and sit down to eat'?** (8) **"But will he not say to him, 'Prepare something for me to eat, and properly clothe yourself and serve me while I eat and drink; and afterward you may eat and drink'?** (9) **"He does not thank the servant because he did the things which were commanded, does he?** (10) **"So you too, when you do all the things which are commanded you, say, 'We are unworthy servants; we have done only that which we ought to have done.'"** [49]

[49] *This teaching is very foreign to people in contemporary western cultures since it promotes humility in servants...the exact opposite of proud, 'me first' humans. So, likewise, disciples of Joshua have nothing to be proud about since the best we can do is to simply do what we have already been told to do, and thus what we ought to have done. To do otherwise is to promote one's self above the Master who provided us the Light to follow in the first place.*

(11) While he was on the way to Jerusalem, he was passing between Samaria and Galilee. (12) As he entered a village, ten leprous men (*men with a disease thought to be contagious*) who stood at a distance met Him; (13) and they raised their voices, saying, "Joshua, Master, have mercy on us!" (14) When he saw them, he said to them, "**Go and show yourselves to the religious men**." And as they were going, they were cleansed. (15) Now one of them, when he saw that he had been healed, turned back, glorifying God with a loud voice, (16) and he fell on his face at Joshua's feet, giving thanks to him. And he was a Samaritan. (17) Then Joshua answered and said, "**Were there not ten cleansed? But the nine--where are they? (18) "Was no one found who returned to give glory to God, except this foreigner?**" (19) And he said to him, "**Stand up and go; your faith has made you well**."

(20) Now having been questioned by the religious leaders as to when the kingdom of God was coming, Joshua answered them and said, "**The kingdom of God is not coming with signs to be observed; (21) nor will they say, 'Look, here it is!' or, 'There it is!' For behold, the kingdom of God is in your midst** (*the King of the Kingdom is among you!*)." (22) And he said to the disciples, "**The days will come when you will long to see one of the days of the Son of Man, and you will not see it. (23) "They will say to you, 'Look there! Look here!' Do not go away, and do not run after them. (24) "For just like the lightning, when it flashes out of one part of the sky and shines to the other part of the sky, so will the Son of Man be in his day.**"[*50]

[*50] *Contrary to many prophet's-so-called predictions of Joshua's return, he plainly says that his return will be public, very visible and unmistakable.*

(25) "**But first he must suffer many things and be rejected by this generation.**

(26) "And just as it happened in the days of Noah, so it will be also in the days of the Son of Man: (27) they were eating, they were drinking, they were marrying, they were being given in marriage, until the day that Noah entered the ark, and the flood came and destroyed them all. (28) "It was the same as happened in the days of Lot: they were eating, they were drinking, they were buying, they were selling, they were planting, they were building; (29) but on the day that Lot went out from Sodom it rained fire and brimstone from heaven and destroyed them all. (30) "It will be just the same on the day that the Son of Man is revealed. (31) "On that day, the one who is on the housetop and whose goods are in the house must not go down to take them out; and likewise the one who is in the field must not turn back. (32) "Remember Lot's wife. (33) "Whoever seeks to keep his life will lose it, and whoever loses his life will preserve it. (34) "I tell you, on that night there will be two in one bed; one will be taken and the other will be left. (35) "There will be two women grinding at the same place; one will be taken and the other will be left. (36) "Two men will be in the field; one will be taken and the other will be left." (37) And answering they said to him, "Where, Lord?" And he said to them, "Where the body is, there also the vultures will be gathered." *51

---

*51 *Please note that Joshua does NOT say that his Father is causing the natural disasters listed in the above text...he does NOT say that his Father is bringing judgment. People read this into these passages based on their incorrect understanding of God, which misunderstandings are largely based on the authors of the Jewish scriptures view of God.*

(18:1) Now he was telling them a parable to show that at all times they ought to pray and not to lose heart, (2) saying, **"In a certain city there was a judge who did not fear God and did not respect man. (3) "There was a widow in that city, and she kept coming to him, saying, 'Give me legal protection from my opponent.' (4) "For a while he was unwilling; but after a while he said to himself, 'Even though I do not fear God nor respect man, (5) yet because this widow bothers me, I will give her legal protection, otherwise by continually coming she will wear me out.'" (6)** And the Lord said, **"Hear what the unrighteous judge said; (7) now, will not God bring about justice for his elect who cry to him day and night, and will he delay long over them? (8) "I tell you that he will bring about justice for them quickly. However, when the Son of Man comes, will he find faith on the earth?"** *52

*52 *The answer seems to be, 'no, hardly any'. Faith will die among human kind as it collectively comes to believe God does not exist. This does not mean religion will die, for religion will flourish even as it does today...empty souls with mere god beliefs in their minds only. In context, people will no longer cry out to their Father for help due to their lack of faith, even though He does care about their needs. People's lack of faith does not mean the Creator does not exist.*

(9) And he also told this parable to some people who trusted in themselves that they were righteous, and viewed others with contempt: (10) **"Two men went up into the temple to pray, one a religious leader and the other a tax collector. (11) "The religious leader stood and was praying this to himself: 'God, I thank you that I am not like other people: swindlers, unjust, adulterers, or even like this tax collector. (12) 'I fast twice a week; I give my money to the religious organization.' (13) "But the tax collector, standing some distance away, was even unwilling to lift up his eyes to heaven, but was beating his chest, saying, 'God, be merciful to me, the sinner!' (14) "I tell you, the tax collector went to his house accepted by God while the**

religious leader was not; for everyone who exalts himself will be humbled, but he who humbles himself will be exalted." *53

*53 *How does this teaching compare to today's 'self-esteem' teaching? True humility is to know and acknowledge our faults and weaknesses and to take the next step and gain our esteem not based on ourselves but based on our Father's gracious and compassionate love for us!*

(15) And the local women were bringing even their babies to him so that he would touch them, but when the disciples saw it, they began rebuking them. (16) But Joshua called for them, saying, "**Permit the children to come to me, and do not hinder them, for the kingdom of God belongs to such as these. (17) "Truly I say to you, whoever does not receive the kingdom of God like a child will not enter it at all.**" *54

*54 *A regular and key teaching of Joshua since it deals with "entering the kingdom of God". Only those who are as children will enter the kingdom of God. Not scholars. Not those deemed 'intelligent' and 'smart'. No, rather the humble, meek, lowly...those seeking innocence and simplicity and plain answers like, 'a Creator exists; he sent his Son to tell us what he wants; we should listen to him'.*

(18) A ruler questioned him, saying, "Good Teacher, what shall I do to inherit eternal life?" (19) And Joshua said to him, "**Why do you call me good? No one is good except God alone. (20) "You know the commandments, 'DO NOT COMMIT ADULTERY** (*"adultery" is a married person having sex with someone other than their spouse*)**, DO NOT MURDER, DO NOT STEAL, DO NOT BEAR FALSE WITNESS, HONOR YOUR FATHER AND MOTHER.**'" (21) And he said, "All these things I have kept from my youth." (22) When Joshua heard this, he said to him, "**One thing you still lack; sell all that you possess and give it to the poor, and you shall have treasure in heaven; and come, follow me.**" (23) But when he had heard these things, he became very sad, for he was extremely rich. (24) And Joshua looked at him and said, "**How hard it is for those who are**

wealthy to enter the kingdom of God! **(25)** "For it is easier for a camel to go through the eye of a needle than for a rich man to enter the kingdom of God." *[55] **(26)** They who heard it said, "Then who can be saved?" **(27)** But he said, "**The things that are impossible with people are possible with God.**" **(28)** Peter said, "Behold, we have left our own homes and followed you." **(29)** And he said to them, "**Truly I say to you, there is no one who has left house or wife or brothers or parents or children, for the sake of the kingdom of God, (30)** who will not receive many times as much at this time and in the age to come, eternal life.**" *[56]

*[55] *A very unpopular teaching in a world that loves and lives for material wealth and false security it brings. If we are not willing to give up all the material things we have in order to do the Father's will, then we cannot enter the kingdom of God. The way is difficult and narrow, for we must lose our lives in this world in order to find Life Everlasting.*

*[56] *If people are willing to do what Joshua says (and sadly, most are not), then while we lose our natural families, we will become part of a new family, which new family is more valuable than all the material things we ever had. Do not be deceived. This is not some teaching that only has application in certain times and circumstances...rather, it is the normal way of the followers of the Light through the centuries in all places, cultures and times. See Matt. 10.*

(31) Then he took the twelve aside and said to them, "**Behold, we are going up to Jerusalem, and all things which are written through the prophets about the Son of Man will be accomplished. (32)** "For he will be handed over to the gentiles** (*non-Jew or people with no knowledge of Joshua's Father*)**, and will be mocked and mistreated and spit upon, (33) and after they have whipped him, they will kill him; and the third day he will rise again.**" **(34)** But the disciples understood none of these things, and the meaning of this statement was hidden from them, and they did not comprehend the things that were said.

(35) As Joshua was approaching Jericho, a blind man was sitting by the road begging. (36) Now hearing a crowd going by, he began to inquire what this was. (37) They told him that Joshua of Nazareth was passing by. (38) And he called out, saying, "Joshua, Son of David, have mercy on me!" (39) Those who led the way were sternly telling him to be quiet; but he kept crying out all the more, "Son of David, have mercy on me!" (40) And Joshua stopped and commanded that he be brought to him; and when he came near, he questioned him, (41) **"What do you want me to do for you?"** And he said, "Lord, I want to regain my sight!" (42) And Joshua said to him, **"Receive your sight; your faith has made you well."** (43) Immediately he regained his sight and began following him, glorifying God; and when all the people saw it, they gave praise to God.

(19:1) He entered Jericho and was passing through. (2) And there was a man called by the name of Zaccheus; he was a chief tax collector and he was rich. (3) Zaccheus was trying to see who Joshua was, and was unable because of the crowd, for he was short. (4) So he ran on ahead and climbed up into a tree in order to see Joshua, for he was about to pass through that way. (5) When Joshua came to the place, he looked up and said to him, **"Zaccheus, hurry and come down, for today I must stay at your house."** (6) And he hurried and came down and received him gladly. (7) When the people saw it, they all began to grumble, saying, "He has gone to be the guest of a man who is a sinner." (8) Zaccheus stopped and said to the Lord, "Behold, Lord, half of my possessions I will give to the poor, and if I have defrauded anyone of anything, I will give back four times as much." (9) And Joshua said to him, **"Today salvation has come to this house, because he, too, is a son of Abraham.** (10) **"For the Son of Man has come to seek and to save that which was lost."**

(11) While they were listening to these things, Joshua went on to tell a parable, because he was near Jerusalem, and they supposed that the kingdom of God was going to appear immediately. (12) So he said, **"A nobleman went to a distant country to receive a kingdom for himself, and then return.** (13) **"And he called ten of his servants, and gave them about fifteen thousand dollars among them and said to them, 'Do business with this until I come back.'** (14) **"But his citizens hated him and sent a delegation after him, saying, 'We do not want this man to reign over us.'** (15) **"When he returned, after receiving the kingdom, he ordered that these servants, to whom he had given the money, be called to him so that he might know what business they had done.** (16) **"The first appeared, saying, 'Master, your five thousand dollars has made fifty thousand more.'** (17) **"And he said to him, 'Well done, good servant, because you have been faithful in a very little thing, you are to be in authority over ten cities.'** (18) **"The second came, saying, 'Your five thousand dollars, master, has made twenty five thousand**

dollars.' (19) "And he said to him also, 'And you are to be over five cities.' (20) "Another came, saying, 'Master, here is your five thousand, which I kept put away in a piece of clothing; (21) for I was afraid of you, because you are an exacting man; you take up what you did not lay down and reap what you did not sow.' (22) "The master said to him, 'By your own words I will judge you, you worthless servant. Did you know that I am an exacting man, taking up what I did not lay down and reaping what I did not sow? (23) 'Then why did you not put my money in the bank, and having come, I would have collected it with interest?' (24) "Then he said to the bystanders, 'Take the five thousand away from him and give it to the one who has the fifty thousand.' (25) "And they said to him, 'Master, he has fifty thousand already.' (26) "I tell you that to everyone who has, more shall be given, but from the one who does not have, even what he does have shall be taken away. (27) "But these enemies of mine, who did not want me to reign over them, bring them here and slay them in my presence." *57

*57 *The basic principle being taught by the Master is do our sincere best with what is given us, and you shall be rewarded. The lesser, but also true principle is if we squander what we are given and blame the one who gave us what we were given, we will judge ourselves and bring punishment upon ourselves. Try our best and gain much, or be lazy and ungrateful and lose all.*

(28) After he had said these things, he was going on ahead, going up to Jerusalem. (29) When he approached Bethphage and Bethany, near the mount that is called Olivet, he sent two of the disciples, (30) saying, "Go into the village ahead of you; there, as you enter, you will find a colt tied on which no one yet has ever sat; untie it and bring it here. (31) "If anyone asks you, 'Why are you untying it?' you shall say, 'The Lord has need of it.'" (32) So those who were sent went away and found it just as he had told them. (33) As they were untying the colt, its owners said to them, "Why are you untying the

colt?" (34) They said, "The Lord has need of it." (35) They brought it to Joshua, and they threw their coats on the colt and put Joshua on it. (36) As he was going, they were spreading their coats on the road. (37) As soon as he was approaching, near the descent of the Mount of Olives, the whole crowd of the disciples began to praise God joyfully with a loud voice for all the miracles which they had seen, (38) shouting: "BLESSED IS THE KING WHO COMES IN THE NAME OF THE LORD; Peace in heaven and glory in the highest!" (39) Some of the religious leaders in the crowd said to him, "Teacher, rebuke your disciples." (40) But Joshua answered, **"I tell you, if these become silent, the stones will cry out!"** (41) When Joshua approached Jerusalem, he saw the city and wept over it, (42) saying, **"If you had known in this day, even you, the things which make for peace! But now they have been hidden from your eyes. (43) "For the days will come upon you when your enemies will throw up a barricade against you, and surround you and hem you in on every side, (44) and they will level you to the ground and your children within you, and they will not leave in you one stone upon another, because you did not recognize the time of your visitation."**

(45) Joshua entered the temple and began to drive out those who were selling, (46) saying to them, **"It is written, 'AND MY HOUSE SHALL BE A HOUSE OF PRAYER,' but you have made it a ROBBERS' DEN."** (47) And he was teaching daily in the temple; but the religious leaders and the bible experts and the leading men among the people were trying to destroy him, (48) and they could not find anything that they might do, for all the people were hanging onto every word he said.

(20:1) On one of the days while he was teaching the people in the temple and preaching the gospel, the religious leaders, bible experts and political leaders confronted him, (2) and they spoke, saying to him, "Tell us by what authority you are doing these things, or who is the one who gave you this authority?" (3) Joshua answered and said to them, "**I will also ask you a question, and you tell me: (4) "Was the baptism of John from heaven or from men?**" (5) They reasoned among themselves, saying, "If we say, 'From heaven,' he will say, 'Why did you not believe him?' (6) "But if we say, 'From men,' all the people will stone us to death, for they are convinced that John was a prophet." (7) So they answered that they did not know where it came from. (8) And Joshua said to them, "**Nor will I tell you by what authority I do these things**." (9) And he began to tell the people this parable: "**A man planted a vineyard and rented it out to vine-growers, and went on a journey for a long time. (10) "At the harvest time he sent a servant to the vine-growers, so that they would give him some of the produce of the vineyard; but the vine-growers beat him and sent him away empty-handed. (11) "And he proceeded to send another servant; and they beat him also and treated him shamefully and sent him away empty-handed. (12) "And he proceeded to send a third; and this one also they wounded and cast out. (13) "The owner of the vineyard said, 'What shall I do? I will send my beloved son; perhaps they will respect him.' (14) "But when the vine-growers saw him, they reasoned with one another, saying, 'This is the heir; let us kill him so that the inheritance will be ours.' (15) "So they threw him out of the vineyard and killed him. What, then, will the owner of the vineyard do to them? (16) "He will come and destroy these vine-growers and will give the vineyard to others**." When they heard it, they said, "May it never be!" (17) But Joshua looked at them and said, "**What then is this that is written: 'THE STONE WHICH THE BUILDERS REJECTED, THIS BECAME THE CHIEF CORNER stone'? (18) "Everyone who falls on that stone will be broken to pieces; but on whomever it falls, it will scatter him like**

dust." (19) The bible experts and the chief priests tried to lay hands on him that very hour, and they feared the people; for they understood that he spoke this parable against them. (20) So they watched him, and sent spies who pretended to be righteous, in order that they might catch him in some statement, so that they could deliver him to the rule and the authority of the Roman governor. (21) They questioned him, saying, "Teacher, we know that you speak and teach correctly, and you are not partial to any, but teach the way of God in truth. (22) "Is it lawful for us to pay taxes to Caesar, or not?" (23) But he detected their trickery and said to them, (24) "**Show me a coin. Whose likeness and inscription does it have?**" They said, "Caesar's." (25) And he said to them, "**Then render to Caesar the things that are Caesar's, and to God the things that are God's.**" (26) And they were unable to catch him in a saying in the presence of the people; and being amazed at his answer, they became silent.

(27) Now there came to him some of another religious sect (those who say that there is no resurrection), (28) and they questioned him, saying, "Teacher, Moses wrote for us that IF A MAN'S BROTHER DIES, having a wife, AND HE IS CHILDLESS, HIS BROTHER SHOULD MARRY THE WIFE AND RAISE UP CHILDREN TO HIS BROTHER. (29) "Now there were seven brothers; and the first took a wife and died childless; (30) and the second (31) and the third married her; and in the same way all seven died, leaving no children. (32) "Finally the woman died also. (33) "In the resurrection therefore, which one's wife will she be? For all seven had married her." (34) Joshua said to them, "**The sons of this age marry and are given in marriage, (35) but those who are considered worthy to attain to that age and the resurrection from the dead, neither marry nor are given in marriage; (36) for they cannot even die anymore, because they are like angels, and are sons of God, being sons of the resurrection.**"[*58] (37) "**But that the dead are raised, even Moses showed, in the passage about the burning bush, where he calls the Lord THE GOD OF ABRAHAM, AND THE GOD OF ISAAC, AND THE GOD OF**

JACOB. (38) **"Now he is not the God of the dead but of the living; for all live to him."** (39) Some of the bible experts answered and said, "Teacher, you have spoken well." (40) For they did not have courage to question him any longer about anything. (41) Then he said to them, **"How is it that they say the Messiah is David's son?** (42) **"For David himself says in the book of Psalms, 'THE LORD SAID TO MY LORD, "SIT AT MY RIGHT HAND, (43) UNTIL I MAKE YOUR ENEMIES A FOOTSTOOL FOR YOUR FEET."'** (44) **"Therefore David calls him 'Lord,' and how is he his son?"** (45) And while all the people were listening, he said to the disciples, (46) **"Beware of the religious leaders, who like to walk around in different clothing, and love respectful greetings in the market places, and best seats in the religious buildings and places of honor at banquets,** (47) **who devour widows' houses, and for appearance's sake offer long prayers. These will receive greater condemnation."**

[*]58 *Listen to the Light, you sons of the resurrection, and rejoice! Rejoice you were considered worthy (certainly not a 'grace' teaching) and that you will never die again after the resurrection (see John 11:25). We must strive to do good work for our Master so we will be counted worthy. Christianity's grace doctrine derived from Paul's teaching in Eph. 2 seeks to nullify this simple truth - do our best (for which we are accountable) and he will do the rest!*

(21:1) And he looked up and saw the rich putting their gifts into the treasury. (2) And he saw a poor widow putting in two small copper coins. (3) And he said, **"Truly I say to you, this poor widow put in more than all of them; (4) for they all out of their excess wealth put into the offering; but she out of her poverty put in all that she had to live on."** *59

*59   *The wealthy person giving thousands or millions to charity, if done without faith or compassion will amount to nothing in the kingdom of God. This woman had great faith and did not worry about tomorrow, but trusted in her Father.*

(5) And while some were talking about the temple, that it was adorned with beautiful stones and expensive gifts, he said, (6) **"As for these things which you are looking at, the days will come in which there will not be left one stone upon another which will not be torn down."** (7) They questioned him, saying, "Teacher, when therefore will these things happen? And what will be the sign when these things are about to take place?" (8) And he said, **"See to it that you are not misled; for many will come in my name, saying, 'I am He,' and, 'The time is near.' Do not go after them. (9) "When you hear of wars and disturbances, do not be terrified; for these things must take place first, but the end does not follow immediately."** (10) Then he continued by saying to them, **"Nation will rise against nation and government against government, (11) and there will be great earthquakes, and in various places plagues and famines; and there will be fearful things happening in the celestial heavens. (12) "But before all these things, they will lay their hands on you and will persecute you, delivering you to the religious buildings and prisons, bringing you before kings and presidents and governors for my name's sake. (13) "It will lead to an opportunity for your testimony. (14) "So make up your minds not to prepare beforehand to defend yourselves; (15) for I will give you words and wisdom which none of your opponents will be able to resist or refute. (16) "But you will be betrayed even by parents and**

brothers and relatives and friends, and they will put some of you to death, (17) and you will be hated by all because of my name. (18) "Yet not a hair of your head will perish. (19) "By your endurance you will gain your lives.

(In this commentator's opinion, the following is specifically for the people who identify as Jews and their nation of Israel, and the first part was fulfilled with the destruction of Jerusalem in 70 A.D by the Roman general Titus and the resultant dispersion of the Jews.)

(20) "But when you see Jerusalem surrounded by armies, then recognize that her destruction is near. (21) "Then those who are in Judea must flee to the mountains, and those who are in the midst of the city must leave, and those who are in the country must not enter the city; (22) because these are days of vengeance, so that all things which are written regarding Jerusalem (*in the Old Testament*) will be fulfilled. (23) "Woe to those who are pregnant and to those who are nursing babies in those days; for there will be great distress upon the land and wrath to this people; (24) and they will fall by the edge of the sword, and will be led captive into all the nations; and Jerusalem will be trampled underfoot by the Gentiles (*non-Jew or people with no knowledge of Joshua's Father*) until the times of the Gentiles are fulfilled.

(Joshua resumes with a global, non-Jewish view.)

(25) "There will be signs with the sun and moon and stars, and on the earth dismay among the people of nations, who will be not understand the roaring of the sea and the waves, (26) people fainting from fear and the expectation of the things which are coming upon the earth; for the powers of the heavens (*celestial bodies like planets, stars or asteroids*) will be shaken. (27) "Then they will see THE SON OF MAN COMING IN A CLOUD with power and great glory. (28) "But when these things begin to take place,

straighten up and lift up your heads, because your **redemption** (*the completion of being set free from the consequence of your sin*) **is drawing near**."

(29) Then he told them a parable: "**Behold the fig tree and all the trees; (30) as soon as they put forth leaves, you see it and know for yourselves that summer is now near. (31) "So you also, when you see these things happening, recognize that the kingdom of God is near. (32) "Truly I say to you, this generation will not pass away until all things take place. (33) "Heaven and earth will pass away, but my words will not pass away.**[*60] (34) **"Be on guard, so that your hearts will not be weighted down with partying and drunkenness and the worries of life, so that day will not come on you suddenly like a trap; (35) for it will come upon all those who dwell on the face of all the earth. (36) "But keep on the alert at all times, praying that you may have strength to escape all these things that are about to take place, and to stand before the Son of Man."** (37) Now during the day he was teaching in the temple, but at evening he would go out and spend the night on the mount that is called Olivet. (38) And all the people would get up early in the morning to come to him in the temple to listen to him.

[*60] *A significant claim that if true, places his person and words above other people's claims, and sets his words apart from other peoples of history, since who else's words will endure past the end of the earth except one whose words are beyond the physical realm? Thus, his words are not "the bible", but rather the words of the self-proclaimed model for mankind, the Son of Man and Light of the world.*

(22:1) Now the Feast of Unleavened Bread, which is called the Passover, was approaching. (2) The religious leaders and the bible experts were seeking how they might put Joshua to death; for they were afraid of the people supporting Joshua. (3) And Satan entered into Judas who was called Iscariot, belonging to the number of the twelve. (4) And he went away and discussed with the religious leaders and officers how he might betray him to them. (5) They were glad and agreed to give him money. (6) So he consented, and began seeking a good opportunity to betray him to them apart from the crowd.

(7) Then came the first day of Unleavened Bread on which the Passover lamb had to be sacrificed. (8) And Joshua sent Peter and John, saying, "**Go and prepare the Passover for us, so that we may eat it**." (9) They said to him, "Where do you want us to prepare it?" (10) And he said to them, "**When you have entered the city, a man will meet you carrying a pitcher of water; follow him into the house that he enters.** (11) "**And you shall say to the owner of the house, 'The Teacher says to you, "Where is the guest room in which I may eat the Passover with my disciples?"'** (12) "**And he will show you a large, furnished upper room; prepare it there.**" (13) And they left and found everything just as he had told them; and they prepared the Passover. (14) When the hour had come, he reclined at the table, and the apostles with him. (15) And he said to them, "**I have earnestly desired to eat this holiday meal with you before I suffer; (16) for I say to you, I shall never again eat it until it is fulfilled in the kingdom of God.**" (17) And when he had taken a cup and given thanks, he said, "**Take this and share it among yourselves; (18) for I say to you, I will not drink of the fruit of the vine from now on until the kingdom of God comes.**" (19) And when he had taken some bread and given thanks, he broke it and gave it to them, saying, "**This is my body which is given for you; do this in remembrance of me.**" (20) And in the same way he took the cup after they had eaten, saying, "**This cup which is poured out for you is the new covenant in my blood.**"[61] (21) "**But behold,**

**the hand of the one betraying me is with mine on the table.
(22) "For indeed, the Son of Man is going as it has been
determined; but woe to that man by whom he is betrayed!"**
(23) And they began to discuss among themselves which one of
them it might be who was going to do this thing.

*61 *Verse 19 through 20 are clearly metaphors. What he is plainly saying is, "this
bread represents my body (or physical life) which will I will lay down for you
(which he explains elsewhere to pay the ransom; see Matt. 20:28 & Mark 10:45);
and, "this cup represents a new covenant in my blood". The latter is plain and
does not confuse by intimating that the wine/blood is some kind of strange
sacrificial thing, but rather represents a solemn covenant, which covenants have
always commonly been sealed by blood. Joshua nowhere teaches that his
physical death was a sacrifice, contrary to a fundamental tenant of biblianity.*

(24) And there arose also a dispute among them as to which one of
them was regarded to be greatest. (25) And he said to them, **"The
kings of the nations order men around harshly; and those
who have authority over them are called 'Benefactors.'
(26) "But it is not this way with you, but the one who is the
greatest among you must become like the youngest, and
the leader like the servant. (27) "For who is greater, the
one who reclines at the table or the one who serves? Is it
not the one who reclines at the table? But I am among you
as the one who serves. (28) "You are those who have stood
by me in my trials; (29) and just as my Father has granted
me a kingdom, I grant you (30) that you may eat and
drink at my table in my kingdom, and you will sit on
thrones judging the twelve tribes of Israel.***62

*62 *Disciples do what the Master says...we do not lead like the world's leaders.
We lead by example, as servants with love, truth and humility being our wisdom
and way. When we are faithful at doing what our Master says, we will be
rewarded. In the original eleven disciples case, they will be granted the privilege
of judging the people/nation they identified with. It is better still to only identify
with the King and his kingdom.*

(31) **"Simon, Simon, behold, Satan has demanded permission to sift you like wheat;** (32) **but I have prayed for you, that your faith may not fail; and you, when once you have turned again, strengthen your brothers**." (33) But he said to him, "Lord, with you I am ready to go both to prison and to death!" (34) And he said, "**I say to you, Peter, the rooster will not crow today until you have denied three times that you know me**." (35) And he said to them, "**When I sent you out without money belt and bag and sandals, you did not lack anything, did you?**" They said, "No, nothing." (36) And he said to them, "**But now, whoever has a money belt is to take it along, likewise also a bag, and whoever has no sword is to sell his coat and buy one**"*63 (*the following verse tells why*). (37) "**For I tell you that this which is written must be fulfilled in me, 'AND HE WAS NUMBERED WITH TRANSGRESSORS'; for that which refers to me has its fulfillment**." (38) They said, "Lord, look, here are two swords." And he said to them, "**It is enough**."

*63   *No, Joshua is not telling them to fight to protect themselves, for that would contradict his command to love your enemies. He told them to get some swords so they would be considered "transgressors" – those seen as resisting the acknowledged authority - when they came to arrest Joshua. In this case, Joshua is fulfilling an old testament prophesy.*

(39) And he came out and proceeded as was his custom to the Mount of Olives; and the disciples also followed him. (40) When he arrived at the place, he said to them, "**Pray that you may not enter into temptation**." (41) And he withdrew from them about a stone's throw, and he knelt down and began to pray, (42) saying, "**Father, if you are willing, remove this suffering from me; yet not my will, but Yours be done**." (43) Now an angel from heaven appeared to him, strengthening him. (44) And being in agony he was praying very fervently; and his sweat became like drops of blood, falling down upon the ground. (45) When he rose from prayer, he came to the disciples and found them sleeping from

sorrow, (46) and said to them, **"Why are you sleeping? Get up and pray that you may not enter into temptation**."

(47) While he was still speaking, behold, a crowd came, and the one called Judas, one of the twelve, was preceding them; and he approached Joshua to kiss him. (48) But Joshua said to him, **"Judas, are you betraying the Son of Man with a kiss?"** (49) When those who were around him saw what was going to happen, they said, "Lord, shall we strike with the sword?" (50) And one of them struck the servant of the high priest and cut off his right ear. (51) But Joshua answered and said, **"Stop! No more of this**." And he touched his ear and healed him. (52) Then Joshua said to the religious leaders and officers of the temple and political leaders who had come against him, **"Have you come out with swords and clubs as you would against a robber? (53) "While I was with you daily in the temple, you did not lay hands on me; but this hour and the power of darkness are yours**." (54) Having arrested him, they led him away and brought him to the house of the chief religious leader; but Peter was following at a distance. (55) After they had kindled a fire in the middle of the courtyard and had sat down together, Peter was sitting among them. (56) And a servant-girl, seeing him as he sat in the firelight and looking intently at him, said, "This man was with him too." (57) But he denied it, saying, "Woman, I do not know him." (58) A little later, another saw him and said, "You are one of them too!" But Peter said, "Man, I am not!" (59) After about an hour had passed, another man began to insist, saying, "Certainly this man also was with him, for he is a Galilean too." (60) But Peter said, "Man, I do not know what you are talking about." Immediately, while he was still speaking, a rooster crowed. (61) The Lord turned and looked at Peter (as he was led out of the chief religious leader's court). And Peter remembered the word of the Lord, how he had told him, **"Before a rooster crows today, you will deny me three times**." (62) And he went out and wept bitterly.

(63) Now the men who were holding Joshua in custody were mocking him and beating him, (64) and they blindfolded him and

were asking him, saying, "Prophesy, who is the one who hit You?" (65) And they were saying many other things against him, blaspheming. (66) When it was day, the Council of the leaders of the people assembled, including religious, legal and political, and they led him away to their council chamber, saying, (67) "If you are the Messiah, tell us." But he said to them, **"If I tell you, you will not believe; (68) and if I ask a question, you will not answer. (69) "But from now on THE SON OF MAN WILL BE SEATED AT THE RIGHT HAND of the power OF GOD."** (70) And they all said, "Are you the Son of God, then?" And he said to them, **"Yes, I am."** *64 (71) Then they said, "What further need do we have of testimony? For we have heard it ourselves from his own mouth."

*64   *A very simple, clear confession of Joshua of who HE SAYS he is, and please note he did NOT say "I am God" - a very clear rebuke of the irrational religious doctrine of the trinity. Even his enemies in this instance did not claim he was saying he was "God" but rather "the Son of God".*

(23:1) Then the whole body of them got up and brought him before Pilate. (2) And they began to accuse him, saying, "We found this man misleading our nation and forbidding paying taxes to Caesar, and saying that he Himself is Messiah, a King." (3) So Pilate asked him, saying, "Are you the King of the Jews?" And Joshua answered him and said, "**It is as you say**." (4) Then Pilate said to the chief priests and the crowds, "I find no guilt in this man." (5) But they kept on insisting, saying, "He stirs up the people, teaching all over Judea, starting from Galilee even as far as this place." (6) When Pilate heard it, he asked whether the man was a Galilean. (7) And when he learned that he belonged to Herod's jurisdiction, he sent him to Herod, who himself also was in Jerusalem at that time.

(8) Now Herod was very glad when he saw Joshua; for he had wanted to see him for a long time, because he had been hearing about him and was hoping to see some sign performed by him. (9) And he questioned him at some length; but he answered him nothing. (10) And the chief priests and the bible experts were standing there, accusing him vehemently. (11) And Herod with his soldiers, after treating him with contempt and mocking him, dressed him in a handsome robe and sent him back to Pilate. (12) Now Herod and Pilate became friends with one another that very day; for before they had been enemies with each other. (13) Pilate summoned the religious and political leaders and the people, (14) and said to them, "You brought this man to me as one who incites the people to rebellion, and behold, having examined him before you, I have found no guilt in this man regarding the charges which you make against him. (15) "No, nor has Herod, for he sent him back to us; and behold, nothing deserving death has been done by him. (16) "Therefore I will punish him and release him." (17) Now, due to tradition, Pilate was obliged to release to them at the feast one prisoner. (18) But they cried out altogether, saying, "Away with this man, and release for us Barabbas!" (19) (He was one who had been thrown into prison for an insurrection made in the city, and for murder.) (20) Pilate, wanting to release Joshua, addressed them again, (21) but they kept on calling out, saying, "Crucify, crucify Him!" (22) And he said to them the third time,

"Why, what evil has this man done? I have found in him no guilt demanding death; therefore I will punish him and release him." (23) But they were insistent, with loud voices asking that he be crucified. And their voices began to prevail. (24) And Pilate pronounced sentence that their demand be granted. (25) And he released the man they were asking for who had been thrown into prison for insurrection and murder, but he delivered Joshua to their will.

(26) When they led him away, they seized a man, Simon of Cyrene, coming in from the country, and placed on him the cross to carry behind Joshua. (27) And following him was a large crowd of the people, and of women who were mourning and lamenting him. (28) But Joshua turning to them said, "**Daughters of Jerusalem, stop weeping for me, but weep for yourselves and for your children.** (29) **"For behold, the days are coming when they will say, 'Blessed are the barren, and the wombs that never bore, and the breasts that never nursed.'** (30) **"Then they will begin TO SAY TO THE MOUNTAINS, 'FALL ON US,' AND TO THE HILLS, 'COVER US.'** (31) **"For if they do these things when the tree is green, what will happen when it is dry?"** [*65] (32) Two others also, who were criminals, were being led away to be put to death with him.

[*65] *In this commentator's opinion, Joshua foresaw the destruction of Jerusalem in 70 AD and referred to it here. In terms of the last saying regarding a green tree, in this authors opinion it means something like - 'if they do evil things even when they have plenty of food and water and supplies (or 'green') – evil things like participate in or enjoy the wrongful killing of an innocent man who tried to help them – what evils will they do when they have no food or water or supplies (Titus' siege of the city) and fear for their own survival? See history for the ugly answer.*

(33) When they came to the place called The Skull, there they crucified Joshua and the criminals, one on the right and the other on the left. (34) But Joshua was saying, "**Father, forgive them; for they do not know what they are doing.**" [*66] And they cast

lots, dividing up his garments among themselves. (35) And the people stood by, looking on. And even the leaders were sneering at him, saying, "He saved others; let him save himself if this is the Messiah of God, his Chosen One." (36) The soldiers also mocked him, coming up to him, offering him sour wine, (37) and saying, "If you are the King of the Jews, save yourself!" (38) Now there was also an inscription above him, "THIS IS THE KING OF THE JEWS." (39) One of the criminals who were hanged there was hurling abuse at him, saying, "Are you not the Messiah? Save yourself and us!" (40) But the other answered, and rebuking him said, "Do you not even fear God, since you are under the same sentence of condemnation? (41) "And we indeed are suffering justly, for we are receiving what we deserve for our deeds; but this man has done nothing wrong." (42) And he was saying, "Joshua, remember me when you come in your kingdom!" (43) And Joshua said to him, "**Truly I say to you, today you shall be with me in Paradise.**"

*66 *What a remarkable contrast between the 'great rulers of history' who handle even perceived threats to their person (let alone violent and unjust acts against them) or their power with pride, violence and 'retribution'. Instead, look at the representative to mankind – Joshua and his words and actions – compassion granted to those who drove in the nails, giving them the benefit of the doubt. Truly a Man who knew the One to whom he was going. Have greater words of true love ever been spoken given that context?*

(44) It was now about six o'clock in the morning, and darkness fell over the whole land until nine o'clock, (45) because the sun was obscured; and the veil of the temple was torn in two. (46) And Joshua, crying out with a loud voice, said, "**Father, INTO YOUR HANDS I COMMIT MY SPIRIT.**" Having said this, he breathed his last. (47) Now when the centurion saw what had happened, he began praising God, saying, "Certainly this man was innocent." (48) And all the crowds who came together for this spectacle, when they observed what had happened, began to return, beating their breasts. (49) And all his acquaintances and the women who accompanied him from Galilee were standing at a distance, seeing these things.

(50) And a man named Joseph, who was a member of the Council, a good and righteous man (51) (he had not consented to their plan and action), a man from Arimathea, a city of the Jews, who was waiting for the kingdom of God; (52) this man went to Pilate and asked for the body of Joshua. (53) And he took it down and wrapped it in a linen cloth, and laid him in a tomb cut into the rock, where no one had ever lain. (54) It was the preparation day, and the sabbath was about to begin. (55) Now the women who had come with him out of Galilee followed, and saw the tomb and how his body was laid. (56) Then they returned and prepared spices and perfumes. And on the sabbath they rested according to the commandment.

(24:1) But on the first day of the week, at early dawn, they came to the tomb bringing the spices which they had prepared. (2) And they found the stone rolled away from the tomb, (3) but when they entered, they did not find the body of the Lord Joshua. (4) While they were perplexed about this, behold, two men suddenly stood near them in dazzling clothing; (5) and as the women were terrified and bowed their faces to the ground, the men said to them, "Why do you seek the living One among the dead? (6) "He is not here, but he has risen. Remember how he spoke to you while he was still in Galilee, (7) saying that the Son of Man must be delivered into the hands of sinful men, and be crucified, and the third day rise again." (8) And they remembered his words, (9) and returned from the tomb and reported all these things to the eleven and to all the rest. (10) Now they were Mary Magdalene and Joanna and Mary the mother of James; also the other women with them were telling these things to the eleven sent ones. (11) But these words appeared to them as nonsense, and they would not believe them. (12) But Peter got up and ran to the tomb; stooping and looking in, he saw the linen wrappings only; and he went away to his home, marveling at what had happened.

(13) And behold, two of them were going that very day to a village named Emmaus, which was about seven miles from Jerusalem. (14) And they were talking with each other about all these things which had taken place. (15) While they were talking and discussing, Joshua himself approached and began traveling with them. (16) But their eyes were prevented from recognizing him. (17) And he said to them, "**What are these words that you are exchanging with one another as you are walking?**" And they stood still, looking sad. (18) One of them, named Cleopas, answered and said to him, "Are you the only one visiting Jerusalem and unaware of the things which have happened here in these days?" (19) And he said to them, "**What things?**" And they said to him, "The things about Joshua the Nazarene, who was a prophet mighty in deed and word in the sight of God and all the people, (20) and how the religious leaders and our rulers delivered him to the sentence of death, and crucified him. (21) "But we were hoping that it was he who was

Luke   191

going to redeem Israel. Indeed, besides all this, it is the third day since these things happened. (22) "But also some women among us amazed us. When they were at the tomb early in the morning, (23) and did not find his body, they came, saying that they had also seen a vision of angels who said that he was alive. (24) "Some of those who were with us went to the tomb and found it just exactly as the women had said; but him they did not see."

(25) And Joshua said to them, "**O foolish men and slow of heart to believe in all that the prophets have spoken!** (26) **"Was it not necessary for the Messiah to suffer these things and to enter into his glory?**" (27) Then beginning with Moses and with all the prophets, he explained to them the things concerning himself in all the (*Jewish*) scriptures. (28) And they approached the village where they were going, and he acted as though he were going farther. (29) But they urged him, saying, "Stay with us, for it is getting toward evening, and the day is now nearly over." So he went in to stay with them. (30) When he had reclined at the table with them, he took the bread and blessed it, and breaking it, he began giving it to them. (31) Then their eyes were opened and they recognized him; and he vanished from their sight. (32) They said to one another, "Were not our hearts burning within us while he was speaking to us on the road, while he was explaining the scriptures to us?" (33) And they got up that very hour and returned to Jerusalem, and found gathered together the eleven and those who were with them, (34) saying, "The Lord has really risen and has appeared to Simon." (35) They began to relate their experiences on the road and how he was recognized by them in the breaking of the bread.

(36) While they were telling these things, Joshua himself stood in their midst and said to them, "**Peace be to you**." (37) But they were startled and frightened and thought that they were seeing a spirit. (38) And he said to them, "**Why are you troubled, and why do doubts arise in your hearts? (39) "See my hands and my feet, that it is I myself; touch me and see, for a spirit does not have flesh and bones as you see that I**

have." (40) And when he had said this, he showed them his hands and his feet. (41) While they still could not believe it because of their joy and amazement, he said to them, "**Have you anything here to eat?**" (42) They gave him a piece of a broiled fish; (43) and he took it and ate it before them. (44) Now he said to them, "**These are my words which I spoke to you while I was still with you, that all things which are written about me in the Law of Moses and the Prophets and the Psalms must be fulfilled.**" (45) Then he opened their minds to understand the scriptures, (46) and he said to them, "**Thus it is written, that the Messiah would suffer and rise again from the dead the third day, (47) and that repentance** (*feel truly sorry about your bad behavior and words, and change*) **for forgiveness of sins would be proclaimed in his name to all the nations, beginning from Jerusalem. (48) "You are witnesses of these things. (49) "And behold, I am sending forth the promise of my Father upon you; but you are to stay in the city until you are clothed with power from on high.**"

(50) And he led them out as far as Bethany, and he lifted up his hands and blessed them. (51) While he was blessing them, he parted from them and was carried up into the sky. (52) And they, after worshiping him, returned to Jerusalem with great joy, (53) and were continually in the temple praising God. [67]

[67] *Luke will pick up this narrative and finish it in the first book of Acts, which he authored.*

END OF THE BOOK OF LUKE

The Life and Words of Joshua* of Nazareth According to Mark:

* Joshua is a more accurate translation of what has been traditionally translated 'Jesus'

Basic Book Introduction:
Distinguish between the Author and his Subject

The author is a man named Mark who lived at the same time and in the same area that Joshua lived. Mark is thought to be the nephew of Simon Peter who was one of the twelve whom Joshua chose to teach and train for over three years. If Mark was Peter's nephew, then he would likely have had regular contact with Joshua.

Mark no doubt had most things correct about Joshua since he had access to both Joshua himself, as well as the original twelve disciples, especially Peter. This commentator believes that he accurately wrote down what Joshua said and did (John 14:26). However, the reader must understand the distinction between his accurately recording what Joshua said and did versus his having a *perfect understanding* of what Joshua said and did. For example, a person can see a man running down a street in an urgent fashion yelling 'fire'. The person witnessing the man running can accurately identify the time and place and other facts associated with the event, but the witness cannot know for sure **why** the man is running and yelling 'fire'.

In like manner, let the reader understand, all men, including the men who were with Joshua (and including this commentator) - had beliefs, religious baggage so to speak – that hindered them from having a perfect understanding of Joshua and his purpose. They, like us, had minds containing things (particularly religious things) which are not from Joshua, which things they could not reconcile with some of the things Joshua said (one example is Acts 1:6), **even while they accurately recorded what he said and did. Therefore, the reader should place full confidence in**

Joshua and his Words only, in terms of having as close to a perfect understanding of Joshua as is possible. This is only reasonable as no one but Joshua could have a perfect understanding of Joshua. While Mark's narrative and commentary (in contrast to Joshua's own words and teachings) is almost certainly accurate in regard to historical details of the circumstances of Joshua's Life, only the Words of Joshua alone should have the reader's full trust in regard to **understanding Joshua and his purposes...revealing the 'why's' regarding Joshua's words and actions**. To assist the reader in this endeavor, Joshua's words are **in bold** in this publishing of Mark's book.

This commentator's comments are *italicized* and either contained in parenthesis or preceded by a superscripted number. Sections of text that are in title case (where the first letter of each word in a phrase or sentence is capitalized e.g. Thus Said the Lord), are quotes of the old testament scripture.

The purpose of this commentator's comments is threefold. First, is to try and define terms according to Joshua's own usage in the four gospels and to do so using simpler or clarified terms or phrases that avoid religious vocabulary. This is necessary for readers with little or no exposure to concepts they have not encountered before or terms or concepts that have been given an incorrect meaning through current religious culture. For example, an important concept – "religious leaders" - has been hidden by using the name of a specific religious sect's leadership, the "Pharisees". The modern reader will have little idea what "Pharisees" were, but they can certainly grasp the concept, "religious leaders", which is exactly what the Pharisees were.

An example of a term that has been modified by current religious culture would be "prophet". This term has come to mean in the current religious culture, a person who foretells future events. The term as Joshua uses it, simply means someone who speaks God's truths.

Second, is to bring to the reader's attention the important teachings of Joshua which are nullified (cancelled out, or made of no effect) by contradictions with other passages in the bible or by contemporary religious teaching. This is not exhaustive, but rather brings to light the contradictions which, in this commentator's opinion, nullify some of the more important teachings of Joshua.

Third, is to 'clear the dirt off his person and sayings', so to speak, for those who want to hear but have been confused or deceived by the myriad of other voices that claim they understand Joshua better than Joshua understands Joshua. For those people who participate in the religious system, perhaps the most commonly used mantra of the bible based religious system's leadership is, "Jesus doesn't mean that...you need us, your educated clergy, to understand what Jesus really meant". This commentator has news for you – Jesus does mean that! No, I don't mean that you turn figurative language into literal language, like when he says, "if your right eye causes you to sin, rip it from your head". Rather, I am referring to his teachings that go against human kind's normal inclination or that challenge some aspect of the way I am living. For example, the simple teaching, "love your enemies". Yes, it does mean that...no, joining a military and killing the 'enemy' cannot be reconciled with "love your enemies". You may not like what Joshua has to say, but let him say it and don't twist his words. After all, if Joshua is who he says he is, we would do well to listen.

This book opens with Mark writing a brief summary of Joshua coming to the Jewish people as Messiah, and John the baptists' role of introducing Messiah to the people of Israel. We begin at the beginning of the book.

(1:1) The beginning of the gospel of Messiah Joshua, the Son of God. (2) As it is written in Isaiah the prophet (*a person who spoke God's truths*): "Behold, I Send My Messenger Ahead Of You, Who Will Prepare Your Way; (3) The Voice Of One Crying In The Wilderness, 'Make Ready The Way Of The Lord, Make his Paths Straight.'" (4) John the Baptist appeared in the wilderness preaching a baptism of repentance for the forgiveness of sins. (5) And all the country of Judea was going out to him, and all the people of Jerusalem; and they were being baptized by him in the Jordan River, confessing their sins. (6) John was clothed with camel's hair and wore a leather belt around his waist, and his diet was locusts and wild honey. (7) And he was preaching, and saying, "After me One is coming who is mightier than I, and I am not fit to stoop down and untie the strings of his sandals. (8) "I baptized you with water; but he will baptize you with the Holy Spirit."

(9) In those days Joshua came from Nazareth in Galilee and was baptized by John in the Jordan river. (10) Immediately coming up out of the water, he saw the heavens opening, and the Spirit like a dove descending upon him; (11) and a voice came out of the heavens: "***You are My beloved Son, in you I am well-pleased.***"

(12) Immediately the Spirit led Joshua to go out into the wilderness. (13) And he was in the wilderness forty days being tempted by Satan (*a powerful spiritual being who is against Joshua and his Father*); and he was with the wild beasts, and the angels were ministering to him.

(14) Now after John had been taken into custody, Joshua came into Galilee, preaching the gospel (*good news*) of God, (15) and saying, **"The time is fulfilled, and the kingdom of God is at hand; repent** (*feel truly sorry about your bad behavior and words, and change*) **and believe in the good news."** [*1] (16) As Joshua was going along by the Sea of Galilee, he saw Simon and Andrew, the brother of Simon, casting a net in the sea; for they were fishermen.

(17) And Joshua said to them, "**Follow me, and I will make you fishers of men.**" *2 (18) Immediately they left their nets and followed him. (19) Going on a little farther, he saw James the son of Zebedee, and John his brother, who were also in the boat mending the nets. (20) Immediately he called them; and they left their father Zebedee in the boat with the hired servants, and went away to follow him. (21) They went into Capernaum; and immediately on the Sabbath (*a day the Jew's kept religious rituals on*) he entered the religious building and began to teach. (22) They were amazed at his teaching; for he was teaching them as one having authority, and not as the bible experts.

*1 *Contrary to many people's view of Joshua, his message does include the need for "repentance", which means to understand the cost of our sin – primarily the sin of unbelief or un-faith and its associated behavior - and be filled with remorse and seek to change. He asks us to "believe in the good news", which good news is summed up in John 3:16-18 and is centered on Joshua.*

*2 *Did Joshua say he would make them 'christians'? No, Joshua focused on the primary work of a disciple and used an illustration they could well understand. All disciples (including simple fishermen) are to be fishers of men, that is we **try to bring people to our Father**, which Father we love with all our heart, soul, mind and strength – for if we do love Him that way, how could we behave any differently?*

(23) Just then there was a man in their religious building with an unclean spirit; and he cried out, (24) saying, "What business do we have with each other, Joshua of Nazareth? Have you come to destroy us? I know who you are--the Holy One of God!" (25) And Joshua rebuked him, saying, "**Be quiet, and come out of him!**" (26) Throwing him into convulsions, the unclean spirit cried out with a loud voice and came out of him. (27) They were all amazed, so that they debated among themselves, saying, "What is this? A new teaching with authority! He commands even the unclean spirits, and they obey him." (28) Immediately the news about him spread everywhere into all the surrounding area of Galilee.

(29) And immediately after they came out of the religious building, they came into the house of Simon and Andrew, with James and John. (30) Now Simon's mother-in-law was lying sick with a fever; and immediately they spoke to Joshua about her. (31) And he came to her and raised her up, taking her by the hand, and the fever left her, and she waited on them. (32) When evening came, after the sun had set, they began bringing to him all who were ill and those who were demon-possessed. (33) And it seemed the whole city had gathered at the door. (34) And he healed many who were ill with various diseases, and cast out many demons (*bad angels*); and he was not permitting the demons to speak, because they knew who he was.

(35) In the early morning, while it was still dark, Joshua got up, left the house, and went away to a secluded place, and was praying there. (36) Simon and his companions searched for him; (37) they found him, and said to him, "Everyone is looking for you." (38) He said to them, "**Let us go somewhere else to the towns nearby, so that I may preach there also; for that is what I came for.**" *3 (39) And he went into their religious buildings throughout all Galilee, preaching and casting out the demons (*bad angels*). (40) And a leper (*a person with a bad skin disease*) came to Joshua, beseeching him and falling on his knees before him, and saying, "If you are willing, you can heal me." (41) Moved with compassion, Joshua stretched out his hand and touched him, and said to him, "**I am willing; be healed.**" (42) Immediately the leprosy left him and he was healed (*or cleansed*). (43) And Joshua sternly warned him and immediately sent him away, (44) and he said to him, "**See that you say nothing to anyone; but go, show yourself to the priest and offer for your cleansing what Moses commanded, as a testimony to them.**" (45) But he went out and began to proclaim it freely and to spread the news around, to such an extent that Joshua could no longer publicly enter a city, but stayed out in unpopulated areas; and they were coming to him from everywhere.

*3   *What did Joshua come to do? He tells us plainly right here – to bring the message he received from his Father. He **did not** come to die as a sacrifice, as christianity would have you believe. Joshua nowhere says he will be a "sacrifice" for anyone. Rather, he said he would pay a ransom to set people free – see Matt. 20:28. His core message was, 'believe me and what I say for I do represent the Creator'.*

(2:1) When he had come back to Capernaum several days afterward, it was heard that he was at home. (2) And many were gathered together, so that there was no longer room, not even near the door; and he was speaking the word to them. (3) And they came, bringing to him a paralytic (*someone who could not move his legs*), carried by four men. (4) Being unable to get to him because of the crowd, they removed the roof above Joshua; and when they had dug an opening, they let down the mat on which the paralytic was lying. (5) And Joshua seeing their faith said to the paralytic, "**Son, your sins are forgiven**." *4 (6) But some of the bible experts were sitting there and reasoning in their hearts, (7) "Why does this man speak that way? He is blaspheming (*saying bad things about God*); for who can forgive sins but God alone?" (8) Immediately Joshua, aware in his spirit that they were reasoning that way within themselves, said to them, "**Why are you reasoning about these things in your hearts?** (9) "**Which is easier, to say to the paralytic, 'Your sins are forgiven'; or to say, 'Get up, and pick up your mat and walk'?** (10) "**But so that you may know that the Son of Man** (*Joshua's favorite title for himself*) **has authority on earth to forgive sins**"--he said to the paralytic, (11) "**I say to you, get up, pick up your mat and go home**." (12) And he got up and immediately picked up the mat and went out in the sight of everyone, so that they were all amazed and were glorifying God, saying, "We have never seen anything like this."

*4 *As humans, I would suggest this is our greatest need. We fail, we hurt others through our insensitive, prideful or selfish words and behavior. We need forgiveness from our Father who created us and loves us. Don't let the sad and lost psychologists tell you differently. Ask for forgiveness from those we sin against, and ask for forgiveness from the One who loves them.*

(13) And he went out again by the seashore; and all the people were coming to him, and he was teaching them. (14) As he passed by, he saw Levi the son of Alphaeus sitting in the tax booth, and he said to him, "**Follow me!**" *5 And he got up and followed him. (15) And it happened that he was reclining at the table in his house, and many

tax collectors and sinners (*people considered morally bad*) were dining with Joshua and his disciples; for there were many of them, and they were following him. (16) When the bible experts and the religious leaders saw that he was eating with the sinners and tax collectors, they said to his disciples, "Why is he eating and drinking with tax collectors and sinners?" (17) And hearing this, Joshua said to them, "**It is not those who are healthy who need a doctor, but those who are sick; I did not come to call the righteous** (*those with faith who are listening to God and trying to do what he says*), **but sinners** (*those without faith and who live to please primarily themselves*)."

*5 *Did Joshua go to the graduates of some theological seminary? Did he go to the graduation of some religious sect's training program? No, he did not. Joshua is looking at people's heart only, not the things of the flesh that men value.*

(18) John's disciples and the religious leaders were fasting; and they came and said to him, "Why do John's disciples and the disciples of the religious leaders fast, but your disciples do not fast?" (19) And Joshua said to them, "**While the bridegroom** (*the man getting married*) **is with them, the friends of the bridegroom cannot fast** (*not eating, often an act of sadness*)**, can they? So long as they have the bridegroom with them, they cannot fast.** (20) "**But the days will come when the bridegroom is taken away from them, and then they will fast.** (21) "**No one sews a patch of unshrunk cloth on an old garment; otherwise the patch pulls away from it, the new from the old, and a worse tear results.** (22) "**No one puts new wine into old wineskins; otherwise the wine will burst the skins, and the wine is lost and the skins as well; but one puts new wine into fresh wineskins."** *6

*6 *The context is a contrast between the old religious ways of John and the religious establishment at that time, versus the new spiritual Way of Joshua. Joshua is saying the old way of Moses-based religion (religious law) is incompatible with the new Way of following Joshua (love & truth). See Luke 5:36 & Luke 16:16.*

(23) And it happened that he was passing through the grain fields on the sabbath, and his disciples began to make their way along while picking the heads of grain. (24) The religious leaders were saying to him, "Look, why are they doing what is not lawful on the Sabbath?" (25) And he said to them, "**Have you never read what David did when he was in need and he and his companions became hungry; (26) how he entered the house of God in the time of Abiathar the high priest, and ate the consecrated bread, which is not lawful for anyone to eat except the priests, and he also gave it to those who were with him?**" (27) Joshua said to them, "**The sabbath was made for man** (*as a time to rest*)**, and not man for the sabbath** (*to be ruled by a day*)**. (28) "So the Son of Man** (*Joshua's favorite title for himself*) **is Lord even of the sabbath.**" [7]

[7]   *The many bible/christian sects that observe sabbath do so against this teaching of Joshua. Joshua plainly states that the sabbath was given by Moses so that people could rest, NOT for people to have to obey religious law. The context the sabbath rose out of was the Egyptian's harsh treatment of the Jews in forcing them to build their temples. If you need rest one day out of seven, then take the rest so your body can heal/rest – if you don't need it, God doesn't care if you don't take it, the Lord of the sabbath says so!*

(3:1) He entered again into a religious building; and a man was there whose hand was withered (*deformed*). (2) The religious leaders were watching him to see if he would heal him on the Sabbath, so that they might accuse him. (3) He said to the man with the withered hand, "Get up and come forward!" (4) And Joshua said to the religious leaders, "**Is it lawful to do good or to do harm on the sabbath, to save a life or to kill?**" But they kept silent. (5) After looking around at them with anger, grieved at their hardness of heart, he said to the man, "**Stretch out your hand.**" And he stretched it out, and his hand was restored. (6) The religious leaders went out and immediately began conspiring with a political group against him, as to how they might destroy Him.*8

*8 *Probably more than anything else, Joshua's rebuking the religious people's main ritual of 'keeping the sabbath' was what angered them the most. It is the same today for disciples who rebuke the christians for 'going to church' instead of doing what Joshua says which is to love (selfless behavior motivated by compassion; to care for, take care of, want to be with) one another.*

(7) Joshua withdrew to the sea with his disciples; and a great multitude from Galilee followed; and also from Judea, (8) and from Jerusalem, and from Idumea, and beyond the Jordan, and the vicinity of Tyre and Sidon, a great number of people heard of all that he was doing and came to him. (9) And he told his disciples that a boat should stand ready for him because of the crowd, so that they would not crowd him; (10) for he had healed many, with the result that all those who had sickness and injuries pressed around him in order to touch him. (11) Whenever those people with unclean spirits saw him, they would fall down before him and shout, "You are the Son of God!" (12) And he earnestly warned them not to tell who he was.

(13) And he went up on the mountain and summoned those whom he himself wanted, and they came to him. (14) And he appointed twelve, so that they would be with him and that he could send them (*'apostle' is the Greek word meaning "one who is sent away"*) out to preach, (15) and to have authority to cast out the demons (*bad*

angels). (16) And he appointed the twelve: Simon (to whom he gave the name Peter), (17) and James, the son of Zebedee, and John the brother of James (to them he gave the name Boanerges, which means, "Sons of Thunder"); (18) and Andrew, and Philip, and Bartholomew, and Matthew, and Thomas, and James the son of Alphaeus, and Thaddaeus, and Simon the Zealot; (19) and Judas Iscariot, who would later betray him. (20) And he came home, and the crowd gathered again, to such an extent that they could not even eat a meal. (21) When his natural family (*his mom and natural brothers, see verse 31 below*) heard of this, they went out to take custody of him; for they were saying, "He has lost his mind."

(22) The bible experts who came down from Jerusalem were saying, "He is possessed by Satan," and "He casts out the demons by the ruler of the demons." (23) And he called them to himself and began speaking to them in parables (*stories with hidden meanings*), **"How can Satan cast out Satan? (24) "If a kingdom is divided against itself, that kingdom cannot stand. (25) "If a house is divided against itself, that house will not be able to stand. (26) "If Satan has risen up against himself and is divided, he cannot stand, but he is finished! (27) "But no one can enter the strong man's house and take his property unless he first ties up the strong man, and then he will take the stuff in his house. (28) "Truly I say to you, all sins shall be forgiven the sons of men, and whatever blasphemies** (*speaking evil of someone, especially regarding God*) **they speak; (29) but whoever blasphemes against the Holy Spirit never has forgiveness, but is guilty of an eternal sin**"-- (30) because they were saying, "Joshua had an unclean spirit." [9]

[9] *The religious people attributed an evil spirit to what was actually the Father's Spirit in Joshua. Thus, blasphemy against the Holy Spirit is to speak evil of the Holy Spirit [or the Father's Spirit] as he enables someone to speak the Truths of Joshua. The sin is eternal because it can prevent people from having faith in – and loving back – their Father.*

(31) Then his mother and his brothers arrived, and standing outside they sent word to him and called him. (32) A crowd was sitting around him, and they said to him, "Behold, your mother and your brothers are outside looking for you." (33) Answering them, Joshua said, "**Who are my mother and my brothers?**" (34) Looking about at those who were sitting around him, he said, "**Behold my mother and my brothers!** (35) "**For whoever does the will of God, he is my brother and sister and mother.**" *10

*10   *Joshua here defines what his family is. It is not the natural family of blood or law (see verse 31), but rather a group of people bound by faith in Joshua's Father doing what Joshua says starting with the new command – see John 13:34-35. Sadly, manifestations of this family are extremely rare in the US at this time and instead religious social clubs or organizations that are called "the church" are substituted for Joshua's family.*

(4:1) He began to teach again by the sea. And such a very large crowd gathered to him that he got into a boat in the sea and sat down; and the whole crowd was by the sea on the land. (2) And he was teaching them many things in parables, and was saying to them in his teaching, (3) "**Listen to this! Behold, the sower** (*planter or farmer*) **went out to sow** (*plant seed*); (4) **as he was sowing, some seed fell beside the road, and the birds came and ate it up.** (5) "**Other seed fell on the rocky ground where it did not have much soil; and it sprang up quickly because it had no depth of soil.** (6) "**And after the sun had risen, it was burned; and because it had no root, it withered away.** (7) "**Other seed fell among the thorns, and the thorns came up and choked it, and it yielded no crop.** (8) "**Other seeds fell into the good soil, and as they grew up and increased, they yielded a crop and produced thirty, sixty, and a hundred times more.**" (9) And he was saying, "**He who has ears to hear, let him hear.**"

(10) As soon as he was alone, his followers, along with the twelve, began asking him about the parables. (11) And he was saying to them, "**To you has been given the mystery of the kingdom of God, but those who are outside get everything in parables,** (12) **so that While Seeing, They May See And Not Perceive, And While Hearing, They May Hear And Not Understand, If They Did They Might Return And Be Forgiven.**" (13) And he said to them, "**Do you not understand this parable? How will you understand all the parables?** (14) "**The sower sows the word** (*of God, God's truths through Joshua*). (15) "**These are the ones who are beside the road where the word is sown; and when they hear, immediately Satan comes and takes away the word which has been sown in them.** (16) "**In a similar way these are the ones on whom seed was sown on the rocky places, who, when they hear the word, immediately receive it with joy;** (17) **and they have no firm root in themselves, but are only temporary; then, when hard times occur or people reject or are mean to them because of the word, immediately they fall away.**

(18) "And others are the ones on whom seed was sown among the thorns; these are the ones who have heard the word, (19) but the worries of the world, and the deceitfulness of riches, and the desires for other things (*of this world*) enter in and choke the word, and it becomes unfruitful. (20) "And there are the ones on whom seed was sown on the good soil; and they hear the word and accept it and bear fruit, thirty, sixty, and a hundred times."

(21) And he was saying to them, "A lamp is not brought to be put under a basket, is it, or under a bed? Is it not brought to be put on the table? (22) "For nothing is hidden, except to be revealed; nor has anything been secret, but that it would come to light. (23) "If anyone has ears to hear, let him hear." (24) And he was saying to them, "Take care what you listen to. By your standard of measure it will be measured to you; and more will be given you besides. (25) "For whoever has (*spiritual life*), to him more shall be given; and whoever does not have, even what he has (*things of the world*) shall be taken away from him." (26) And he was saying, "The kingdom of God is like a man who casts seed upon the soil; (27) and he goes to bed at night and gets up by day, and the seed sprouts and grows--how, he himself does not know. (28) "The soil produces crops by itself; first the blade, then the head, then the mature grain in the head. (29) "But when the crop permits, he immediately cuts it, because the harvest has come." *11

*11 *As a farmer may not understand the all processes of a plant's growth, yet he farms and gains from his efforts - so shall the man who works for the King. He may not understand all of the workings of spiritual life, but if he perseveres in his efforts and sows the seed of Joshua's words (NOT the scripture or the bible), he will enjoy a harvest someday.*

(30) And he said, "How shall we picture the kingdom of God, or by what parable shall we present it? (31) "It is like a mustard seed, which, when sown upon the soil, though it

is smaller than all the seeds that are upon the soil, (32) **yet when it is sown, it grows up and becomes larger than all the garden plants and forms large branches; so that The Birds Of The Air Can Nest Under Its Shade.**" (33) With many such parables he was speaking the word to them, so far as they were able to hear it; (34) and he did not speak to them without a parable; but he was explaining everything privately to his own disciples.

(35) On that day, when evening came, he said to them, "**Let us go over to the other side**." (36) Leaving the crowd, they took him along with them in the boat, just as he was; and other boats were with him. (37) And there arose a fierce gale of wind, and the waves were breaking over the boat so much that the boat was already filling up. (38) Joshua himself was in the stern (*back of the boat*), asleep on the cushion; and they woke him and said to him, "Teacher, do you not care that we are about to drown?" (39) And he got up and rebuked the wind and said to the sea, "**Hush, be still.**" And the wind died down and it became perfectly calm. (40) And he said to them, "**Why are you afraid? Do you still have no faith?**" [12] (41) They became very much afraid and said to one another, "Who then is this, that even the wind and the sea obey him?"

[12] *Fear and faith are each other's 'enemies'...they fight for predominance in a person. If we have faith in a particular area, we will not be afraid. We want to reach the place where our faith overcomes all our fears and then we will be like the Master, and death itself will hold no fear over us for our faith assures us we will be going to be with our wonderful Father!*

(5:1) They came to the other side of the sea, into the country of the Gerasenes. (2) When he got out of the boat, immediately a man from the tombs with an unclean (*evil*) spirit met him, (3) and he had his dwelling among the tombs. And no one was able to bind (*tie*) him anymore, even with a chain; (4) because he had often been bound with shackles and chains, and the chains had been torn apart by him and the shackles broken in pieces, and no one was strong enough to subdue him. (5) Constantly, night and day, he was screaming among the tombs and in the mountains, and gashing himself with stones. (6) Seeing Joshua from a distance, he ran up and bowed down before him; (7) and shouting with a loud voice, he said, "What business do we have with each other, Joshua, Son of the Most High God? I implore you by God, do not torment me!" (8) For Joshua had been saying to him, "**Come out of the man, you unclean spirit!**" (9) And Joshua was asking him, "**What is your name?**" And he said to him, "My name is Legion; for we are many." (10) And Legion began to implore Joshua earnestly not to send them out of the country. (11) Now there was a large herd of swine (*pigs*) feeding nearby on the mountain. (12) The demons implored him, saying, "Send us into the swine so that we may enter them." (13) Joshua gave them permission. And coming out, the unclean spirits entered the swine; and the herd rushed down the steep bank into the sea, about two thousand of them; and they were drowned in the sea.

(14) Their herdsmen ran away and reported it in the city and in the country. And the people came to see what it was that had happened. (15) They came to Joshua and observed the man who had been demon-possessed sitting down, clothed and in his right mind, the very man who had had the "legion"; and they became frightened. (16) Those who had seen it described to them how it had happened to the demon-possessed man, and all about the pigs. (17) And they began to implore (*ask strongly*) Joshua to leave their region. (18) As he was getting into the boat, the man who had been demon-possessed was imploring him that he might accompany him. (19) And he did not let him, but he said to him, "**Go back to your people and report to them what great things the Lord has**

done for you, and how he had mercy on you." (20) And he went away and began to proclaim in Decapolis what great things Joshua had done for him; and everyone was amazed.

(21) When Joshua had crossed over again in the boat to the other side, a large crowd gathered around him; and so he stayed by the seashore. (22) One of the religious officials named Jairus came up, and on seeing him, fell at his feet (23) and implored him earnestly, saying, "My little daughter is at the point of death; please come and lay your hands on her, so that she will get well and live." (24) And he went off with him; and a large crowd was following him and pressing in on him.

(25) A woman who had had a blood hemorrhage (*bleeding*) for twelve years, (26) and had endured much at the hands of many physicians, and had spent all that she had and was not helped at all, but rather had grown worse-- (27) after hearing about Joshua, she came up in the crowd behind him and touched his cloak. (28) For she thought, "If I just touch his clothes, I will get well." (29) Immediately her blood hemorrhage stopped; and she felt in her body that she was healed of her affliction. (30) Immediately Joshua, perceiving in himself that the power proceeding from him had gone out, turned around in the crowd and said, "**Who touched my clothes?**" (31) And his disciples said to him, "You see the crowd pressing in on you, and you ask, 'Who touched me?'" (32) And he looked around to see the woman who had done this. (33) But the woman fearing and trembling, aware of what had happened to her, came and fell down before him and told him the whole truth. (34) And he said to her, "**Daughter, your faith has made you well; go in peace and be healed of your illness.**" [13]

[13] *Most bible people want a formula of "if you have faith, you will be physically healed" from this event and saying of Joshua. If their belief is correct, then any person who has some physical problem will be healed if they have faith in Joshua. Does this happen in reality? No, it does not. Therefore, perhaps the saying should be understood in a different way? Perhaps Joshua's miracles had one primary purpose – to validate who Joshua is? And perhaps this purpose was*

accomplished during Joshua's first visit? That should seem to be a reasonable explanation since all disciples of Joshua are not healed!

(35) While he was still speaking, they came from the house of the religious official, saying, "Your daughter has died; why trouble the Teacher anymore?" (36) But Joshua, overhearing what was being spoken, said to the religious official, "**Do not be afraid any longer, only believe**." (37) And he allowed no one to accompany him, except Peter and James and John the brother of James. (38) They came to the house of the religious official; and he saw a commotion, and people loudly weeping and wailing. (39) And entering in, he said to them, "**Why make a commotion and weep? The child has not died, but is asleep**." [*14] (40) So they began laughing at him. But putting them all out, he took along the child's father and mother and his own companions, and entered the room where the child was. (41) Taking the child by the hand, he said to her, "**Little girl, I say to you, get up!**" (42) Immediately the girl got up and began to walk, for she was twelve years old. And immediately they were completely astounded. (43) And he gave them strict orders that no one should know about this, and he said that something should be given her to eat.

[*14] *Joshua here teaches that physical death is merely like sleep, in that the child's soul has not perished, but rather her body is merely in a state of sleep-like inactivity. He might have said this to try and prevent people from treating the girl badly once he raised her since many had the belief that a dead body was 'unclean'.*

(6:1) Joshua went out from there and came into his hometown; and his disciples followed him. (2) When the Sabbath came, he began to teach in the religious building; and the many listeners were astonished, saying, "Where did this man get these things, and what is this wisdom given to him, and such miracles as these performed by his hands? (3) "Is not this the carpenter, the son of Mary, and brother of James and Joses and Judas and Simon? Are not his sisters here with us?" And they took offense at him. (4) Joshua said to them, "**A prophet** (*a person who speaks God's truths*) **is not without honor except in his hometown and among his own relatives and in his own household.**" (5) And he could do no miracle there except that he laid his hands on a few sick people and healed them. (6) And he marveled at their unbelief.[*15]

[*15]   *Verse 3 is more proof that Joshua's mom had more children after Joshua was born. Also, many use accounts like this to justify 'going to church' since 'Joshua went to the synagogue'. Well, what happened to him most of the time when he went to their religious buildings and spoke the truth? What happened here was typical. He went to their buildings and meetings to enlighten them – not to participate in, or validate, their religion – and as happened here, he was regularly cast out.*

And he was going around the villages teaching. (7) And he summoned the twelve and began to send them out in pairs, and gave them authority over the unclean spirits; (8) and he instructed them that they should take nothing for their journey, except a mere staff--no bread, no bag, no money in their belt-- (9) but to wear sandals; and he added, "**Do not put on two coats.**" (10) And he said to them, "**Wherever you enter a house, stay there until you leave town.** (11) "**Any place that does not receive you or listen to you, as you go out from there, shake the dust off the soles of your feet for a testimony against them.**" (12) They went out and preached that men should repent (*feel truly sorry about your bad behavior and words, and change*). (13) And they were casting out many demons and were anointing with oil many sick people and healing them.[*16]

Joshua granted his first twelve disciples the power to work these miracles to validate his own person and message. The physical healings were a one-time granting of the privilege of affirming who Joshua was and who he represented. When Joshua went back to the Father, the miracles ceased – see John 9. Please also note that there is a cost implied when someone rejects the message of Joshua – the rejection will be recounted at the final judgment where "He who rejects me and does not receive my sayings, has one who judges him; the word I spoke is what will judge him at the last day." (John 12:48)

(14) And King Herod heard of it, for Joshua's name had become well known; and people were saying, "John the Baptist has risen from the dead, and that is why these miraculous powers are at work in him." (15) But others were saying, "He is Elijah." And others were saying, "He is a prophet (*a person who speaks God's truths*), like one of the prophets of old." (16) But when Herod heard of it, he kept saying, "John, whom I beheaded, has risen!" (17) For Herod himself had sent and had John arrested and bound in prison on account of Herodias, the wife of his brother Philip, because he had married her. (18) For John had been saying to Herod, "It is not lawful for you to have your brother's wife." (19) Herodias had a grudge against him and wanted to put him to death and could not do so; (20) for Herod was afraid of John, knowing that he was a righteous and holy man, and he kept him safe. And when he heard him, he was very perplexed; but he used to enjoy listening to him.

(21) A strategic day came when Herod on his birthday gave a banquet for his managers and military commanders and the leading men of Galilee; (22) and when the daughter of Herodias herself came in and danced, she pleased Herod and his dinner guests; and the king said to the girl, "Ask me for whatever you want and I will give it to you." (23) And he swore to her, "Whatever you ask of me, I will give it to you; up to half of my kingdom." (24) And she went out and said to her mother, "What shall I ask for?" And she said, "The head of John the Baptist." (25) Immediately she came in a hurry to the king and asked, saying, "I want you to give me at once the head of John the Baptist on a platter." (26) And although the king was very sorry, yet because of his oaths and because of his

dinner guests, he was unwilling to refuse her. (27) Immediately the king sent an executioner and commanded him to bring back his head. And he went and had him beheaded in the prison, (28) and brought his head on a platter, and gave it to the girl; and the girl gave it to her mother. (29) When his disciples heard about this, they came and took away his body and laid it in a tomb.

(30) The twelve gathered together with Joshua; and they reported to him all that they had done and taught.

(31) And he said to them, "**Come away by yourselves to a private place and rest a while**." (For there were many people coming and going, and they did not even have time to eat.) (32) They went away in the boat to a secluded place by themselves. (33) The people saw them going, and many recognized them and ran there together on foot from all the cities, and got there ahead of them. (34) When Joshua went ashore, he saw a large crowd, and he felt compassion for them because they were like sheep without a shepherd; and he began to teach them many things. (35) When it was already quite late, his disciples came to him and said, "This place is desolate (*has no place to get food or shelter*) and it is already quite late; (36) send them away so that they may go into the surrounding countryside and villages and buy themselves something to eat." (37) But he answered them, "**You give them something to eat!**" And they said to him, "Shall we go and spend hundreds of dollars on bread and give them something to eat?" (38) And he said to them, "**How many loaves do you have? Go look!**" And when they found out, they said, "Five, and two fish." (39) And he commanded them all to sit down by groups on the green grass. (40) They sat down in groups of hundreds and of fifties. (41) And he took the five loaves and the two fish, and looking up toward heaven, he blessed the food and broke the loaves and he kept giving them to the disciples to set before them; and he divided up the two fish among them all. (42) They all ate and were satisfied, (43) and they picked up twelve full baskets of the broken pieces, and also of the fish. (44) There were five thousand men who ate the loaves.

Mark   215

(45) Immediately Joshua made his disciples get into the boat and go ahead of him to the other side to Bethsaida, while he himself was sending the crowd away. (46) After bidding them farewell, he left for the mountain to pray. (47) When it was evening, the boat was in the middle of the sea, and he was alone on the land. (48) Seeing them straining at the oars, for the wind was against them, at about the fourth watch of the night he came to them, walking on the sea; and he intended to pass by them. (49) But when they saw him walking on the sea, they supposed that it was a ghost, and cried out; (50) for they all saw him and were terrified. But immediately he spoke with them and said to them, "**Take courage; it is I, do not be afraid.**" (51) Then he got into the boat with them, and the wind stopped; and they were utterly astonished, (52) for they had not gained any insight from the incident of the loaves, for their hearts were hard. (53) When they had crossed over they came to land at Gennesaret, and moored to the shore. (54) When they got out of the boat, immediately the people recognized him, (55) and ran about that whole country and began to carry here and there on their mats those who were sick, to the place they heard he was. (56) Wherever he entered villages, or cities, or countryside, they were laying the sick in the market places, and imploring him that they might just touch the fringe of his coat; and as many as touched it were being cured.

(7:1) The religious leaders and some of the bible experts gathered around him when they had come from Jerusalem, (2) and had seen that some of his disciples were eating their bread with impure hands, that is, unwashed. (3) [For the religious leaders and all the Jews do not eat unless they carefully wash their hands a certain way, thus observing the religious traditions of the elders; (4) and when they come back from shopping, they do not eat unless they cleanse themselves a certain way; and there are many other things which they have received in order to observe, such as the washing of cups and pitchers and copper pots.] (5) The religious leaders and the bible experts asked him, "Why do your disciples not walk according to the tradition of the elders, but eat their bread with impure hands?" (6) And he said to them, "**Rightly did Isaiah prophesy of you hypocrites** (*a person who says what others ought to do or not do, but does not do so themselves*)**, as it is written: 'This People Honors Me With Their Lips, But Their Heart Is Far Away From Me.** (7) **'But In Vain Do They Worship Me, Teaching As Doctrines** (*teachings or beliefs they say are from God*) **The Precepts** (*commandments*) **Of Men.'** (8) **"Neglecting the commandment of God, you hold to the tradition of men."** (9) He was also saying to them, "**You are experts at setting aside the commandment of God in order to keep your tradition** (*the teachings and practices of their religion*)**.** (10) **"For Moses said, 'Honor Your Father And Your Mother'; and, 'He Who Speaks Evil Of Father Or Mother, Is To Be Put To Death';** (11) **but you say, 'If a man says to his father or his mother, whatever I have that could have been used to help you, I am giving to God** (*really to their religious organization*)**,'** (12) **you no longer permit him to do anything for his father or his mother;** (13) **thus invalidating** (*canceling or making of no effect*) **the word of God** (*honor your dad and mom*) **by your tradition which you have handed down; and you do many things such as that."** [17]

---

[17] *The basic teaching of Joshua here is this - beware substituting something that God does not want for something he does. In other words, be very careful not to invalidate what God wants with one's religion. While this example was given*

2,000 year ago, it is evident little has changed. *The religious systems of men specialize in invalidating Joshua's teachings with their traditions. Perhaps the greatest tradition which invalidates his commands is to substitute a book (the bible) for the person of Joshua, and men as leaders (pastors, ministers, priests, etc.) in the place of Joshua. Perhaps the other tradition which nullifies his teachings is the tradition of 'going to church' in place of actually caring for one another as Family – which would actually be loving one another.*

(14) After he called the crowd to him again, he began saying to them, "**Listen to me, all of you, and understand: (15) there is nothing outside the man which can defile him** (*make him spiritually dirty, or unacceptable to God*) **if it goes into him; but the things which proceed out of the man are what defile the man** (*make him spiritually dirty, or unacceptable to God*). (16) "If anyone has ears to hear, let him hear.**" (17) When he had left the crowd and entered the house, his disciples questioned him about the parable. (18) And he said to them, "**Are you so lacking in understanding also? Do you not understand that whatever goes into the man from outside** (*food or drink*) **cannot defile him, (19) because it does not go into his heart, but into his stomach, and is eliminated?"** (Thus Joshua declared that no food that is eaten can make a person dirty or unacceptable to God.) **(20)** And he was saying, "**That which proceeds out of the man, that is what defiles the man.**"[18]

[18] *Joshua's point in versus 14 through 23 could not be clearer – that eating certain types of food is not what makes a person unclean before God, but rather what comes out of a person heart (words and behavior) is what makes a person unclean. And yet, many hundreds of bible sects and perhaps millions of individuals reject this plain teaching of the Light in favor of listening to Moses. So they falsely believe that God is concerned (pleased or displeased) about what people eat – what a sad and petty god people create. It is no coincidence that this rebuke of Moses was spoken right after the 'tradition of men' warning.*

(21) "**For from within, out of the heart** (*"heart", meaning the center of men's will and soul*) **of men, proceed...**

evil thoughts (*thinking about the things below (see Matt. 5), or anything that is not morally pure or good but especially harming others for your own gain, pleasure or vengeance*),

fornications (*touching another person in a sexual way before being married*),

thefts (*stealing*),

murders,

adulteries (*once you are married, touching another person in a sexual way who is not your spouse*),

(22) deeds of coveting (*trying to gain more things than you need or lying to get material things*)

(23) and wickedness (*wanting to hurt other people, having malice, un-forgiveness*),

as well as deceit (*being less than perfectly honest and truthful in order to selfishly gain things*),

sensuality (*speaking, dressing or behaving in such a way to encourage or promote yourself sexually*),

envy (*to be wrongfully jealous of another person, or to want to be like another person for the wrong reasons*)

slander (*to speak falsehoods or twist facts about another person with the intent to harm them or their reputation*),

pride (*to think you are more valuable than others*)

and foolishness (*senseless, reckless, careless, un-thinking, joking-insincerity*).

(23) **"All these evil things proceed from within** (*start from the heart*) **and defile the man** (*make him spiritually dirty or unacceptable to God*)." [19]

[19] *Here Joshua lists a number of things which are wrong for people to commit or engage in. It is a good list for understanding Joshua's moral teachings and what we should avoid to be clean before God. As we look at our lives, how are we doing with staying clean before our heavenly Father? We should examine ourselves regularly without self-deceit or self-denial or self-deception.*

(24) Joshua got up and went away from there to the region of Tyre. And when he had entered a house, he wanted no one to know of it; yet he could not escape notice. (25) But after hearing of him, a woman whose little daughter had an unclean spirit immediately came and fell at his feet. (26) Now the woman was a Gentile (*non-Jew or person with no knowledge of Joshua's Father*), of the Syrophoenician race. And she kept asking him to cast the demon out of her daughter. (27) And he was saying to her, "**Let the children be satisfied first, for it is not good to take the children's bread and throw it to the little dogs.**" (28) But she answered and said to him, "Yes, Lord, but even the dogs under the table feed on the children's crumbs." (29) And he said to her, "**Because of this answer go; the demon** (*bad angel*) **has gone out of your daughter.**" (30) And going back to her home, she found the child healed, lying on the bed, the demon having left.[*20]

[*20] *Joshua gave the woman a simple test of humility, which the woman passed and thus had her faith rewarded. Note she was not of Israel. God doesn't care what nationality or race or ethnic group a person was born into – physical attributes we cannot control. Rather, he cares about the things we can control, our choices, words and actions.*

(31) Again he went out from the region of Tyre, and came through Sidon to the Sea of Galilee, within the region of Decapolis. (32) They brought to him one who was deaf and spoke with difficulty, and they implored him to lay his hand on him. (33) Joshua took him aside from the crowd, by himself, and put his fingers into his ears, and after spitting, he touched his tongue with the saliva; (34) and looking up to heaven with a deep sigh, he said to him, "**Be opened!**" (35) And his ears were opened, and the impediment of his tongue was removed, and he began speaking plainly. (36) And he gave them orders not to tell anyone; but the more he ordered them, the more widely they continued to proclaim it. (37) They were utterly astonished, saying, "He has done all things well; he makes even the deaf to hear and the mute to speak."

(8:1) In those days, when there was again a large crowd and they had nothing to eat, Joshua called his disciples and said to them, (2) **"I feel compassion for the people because they have remained with me now three days and have nothing to eat. (3) "If I send them away hungry to their houses, they will faint on the way; and some of them have come from a great distance."** (4) And his disciples answered him, "Where will anyone be able to find enough bread here in this desolate place to satisfy these people?" (5) And he was asking them, **"How many loaves do you have?"** And they said, "Seven." (6) And he directed the people to sit down on the ground; and taking the seven loaves, he gave thanks and broke them, and started giving them to his disciples to serve to them, and they served them to the people. (7) They also had a few small fish; and after he had blessed them, he ordered these to be served as well. (8) And they ate and were satisfied; and they picked up seven large baskets full of what was left over of the broken pieces. (9) About four thousand men were there; and he sent them away.

(10) And immediately he entered the boat with his disciples and came to the district of Dalmanutha. (11) The religious leaders came out and began to argue with him, seeking from him a sign from heaven, to test him. (12) Sighing deeply in his spirit, he said, **"Why does this generation[*21] seek for a sign? Truly I say to you, no sign will be given to this generation."**

[*21] *Joshua defines three basic ages or generations in his teachings. The first generation is all those living on the earth prior to his first coming. The second is those living on the earth during and after his first coming, prior to his second coming. The third is all those living during and after his second coming. This saying would apply to the second generation.*

(13) Leaving them, he again embarked and went away to the other side. (14) And they had forgotten to take bread, and did not have more than one loaf in the boat with them. (15) And he was giving orders to them, saying, **"Watch out! Beware of the leaven (or yeast) of the religious leaders and the leaven of Herod."**

(16) They began to discuss with one another the fact that they had no bread. (17) And Joshua, aware of this, said to them, **"Why do you discuss the fact that you have no bread? Do you not yet see or understand? Do you have a hardened heart? (18) "Having Eyes, Do You Not See? And Having Ears, Do You Not Hear? And do you not remember, (19) when I broke the five loaves for the five thousand, how many baskets full of broken pieces you picked up?"** They said to him, "Twelve." (20) **"When I broke the seven for the four thousand, how many large baskets full of broken pieces did you pick up?"** And they said to him, "Seven." (21) And he was saying to them, **"Do you not yet understand?"** (*see Matt. 16:5-12, esp. 12*)

(22) And they came to Bethsaida. And they brought a blind man to Joshua and implored him to touch him. (23) Taking the blind man by the hand, he brought him out of the village; and after spitting on his eyes and laying his hands on him, he asked him, **"Do you see anything?"** (24) And he looked up and said, "I see men, for I see them like trees, walking around." (25) Then again he laid his hands on his eyes; and he looked intently and was restored, and began to see everything clearly. (26) And he sent him to his home, saying, **"Do not even enter the village."**

(27) Joshua went out, along with his disciples, to the villages of Caesarea Philippi; and on the way he questioned his disciples, saying to them, **"Who do people say that I am?"** (28) They told him, saying, "John the Baptist; and others say Elijah; but others, one of the prophets (*a person who spoke God's truths*)." (29) And he continued by questioning them, **"But who do you say that I am?"** Peter answered and said to him, **"You are the Messiah."** (30) And he warned them to tell no one about him. (31) And he began to teach them that the Son of Man must suffer many things and be rejected by the politicians and religious leaders and the bible experts, and be killed, and after three days rise again. (32) And he was stating the matter plainly. And Peter took him aside and began to rebuke him. (33) But turning around and seeing his disciples, he

rebuked Peter and said, **"Get behind me, Satan; for you are not setting your mind on God's interests, but man's."** *22

*22   *This commentator does not take this saying of Joshua to mean that Peter was possessed by Satan for a brief moment, but rather that Peter spoke Satan's desire that Joshua not complete his work to pay the ransom – see Luke 10:45 & Matt. 20:28.*

(34) And he summoned the crowd with his disciples, and said to them, **"If anyone wishes to come after me, he must deny himself, and take up his cross and follow me. (35) "For whoever wishes to save his life** (*in this world*) **will lose it** (*Life Everlasting*)**, but whoever loses his life for my sake and the gospel's will save it. (36) "For what does it profit a man to gain the whole world, and forfeit** (*give away*) **his soul? (37) "For what will a man give in exchange for his soul? (38) "For whoever is ashamed of me and my words in this adulterous** (*un-faithful*) **and sinful generation, the Son of Man** (*Joshua's favorite title for himself*) **will also be ashamed of him when he comes in the glory of his Father with the holy angels."** *23

*23   *Joshua in these words says what is required to come after him or follow him. It requires a person to stop trying to be successful in this world and instead seek to turn away from what the people of the earth consider valuable and successful. If we don't, we will lose our soul, meaning our soul will be bankrupt in this life, and destroyed at some point after the death of our body. Finally, to ignore him – to seldom tell others who my Master is and what he wants – means we are ashamed of him and the cost will be great. Please, dear reader, consider these words carefully for they are eternally important for each of us.*

(9:1) And Joshua was saying to them, "**Truly I say to you, there are some of those who are standing here who will not taste death until they see the kingdom of God after it has come with power**." (2) Six days later, Joshua took with him Peter and James and John, and brought them up on a high mountain by themselves. And he was transfigured (*his appearance changed*) before them; (3) and his garments (*clothes*) became radiant (*glowed, gave off light*) and exceedingly white, as no launderer on earth can whiten them. (4) Elijah appeared to them along with Moses; and they were talking with Joshua. (5) Peter said to Joshua, "Teacher, it is good for us to be here; let us make three tabernacles, one for you, and one for Moses, and one for Elijah." (6) For he did not know what to answer; for they (*Peter, James and John*) became terrified. (7) Then a cloud formed, overshadowing them, and a voice came out of the cloud, "*__This is my beloved Son, listen to him!__*" (8) All at once they looked around and saw no one with them anymore, except Joshua alone.*24

*24 *The saying in the first verse regarding seeing the kingdom of God come, was fulfilled in the following verses when they saw the Son, the King, in his future state of power. The Father's voice from heaven confirmed who Joshua was and the Designer gave what He desires of mankind – to* <u>listen to his beloved Son</u>. *Not the bible or the scripture or apostle so-and-so or all the past or current religious leaders, pastors or popes, monsignors or ministers, scholars or popular authors, etc. – but rather, His "beloved Son". Will* **his voice** *be the only voice you base your life on?*

(9) As they were coming down from the mountain, he gave them orders not to relate to anyone what they had seen, until the Son of Man rose from the dead. (10) They seized upon that statement, discussing with one another what rising from the dead meant. (11) They asked him, saying, "Why is it that the bible experts say that Elijah must come first?" (12) And he said to them, "**Elijah does first come and restore all things. And yet how is it written of the Son of Man that he will suffer many things and be treated with contempt?** (13) "**But I say to you that Elijah has indeed come, and they did to him whatever they**

wished (*speaking of John the baptist*)**, just as it is written of him**."

(14) When they came back to the disciples, they saw a large crowd around them, and some bible experts arguing with them. (15) Immediately, when the entire crowd saw him, they were amazed and began running up to greet him. (16) And he asked them, **"What are you discussing with them?"** (17) And one of the crowd answered him, "Teacher, I brought you my son, possessed with a spirit which makes him mute; (18) and whenever it seizes him, it slams him to the ground and he foams at the mouth, and grinds his teeth and stiffens out. I told your disciples to cast it out, and they could not do it." (19) And he answered them and said, **"O unbelieving generation, how long shall I be with you? How long shall I put up with you? Bring him to me!"** (20) They brought the boy to him. When he saw him, immediately the spirit threw him into a convulsion, and falling to the ground, he began rolling around and foaming at the mouth. (21) And he asked his father, **"How long has this been happening to him?"** And he said, "From childhood. (22) "It has often thrown him both into the fire and into the water to destroy him. But if you can do anything, take pity on us and help us!" (23) And Joshua said to him, **"'If you can?' All things are possible to him who has faith**." (24) Immediately the boy's father cried out and said, **"I do have faith; help my unbelief**." (25) When Joshua saw that a crowd was rapidly gathering, he rebuked the unclean spirit, saying to it, **"You deaf and mute spirit, I command you, come out of him and do not enter him again**." (26) After crying out and throwing him into terrible convulsions, it came out; and the boy became so much like a corpse that most of them said, "He is dead!" (27) But Joshua took him by the hand and raised him; and he got up. (28) When he came into the house, his disciples began questioning him privately, "Why could we not drive it out?" (29) And he said to them, **"This kind cannot come out by anything but prayer**."
*25

Many take the last saying in this section as another formula. What he was saying to his disciples was in essence, 'For you who have less faith than I, you need to pray more to help you gain the faith necessary to help me more effectively during this first visit of mine'.

(30) From there they went out and began to go through Galilee, and he did not want anyone to know about it. (31) For he was teaching his disciples and telling them, **"The Son of Man is to be delivered into the hands of men, and they will kill him; and when he has been killed, he will rise three days later."** (32) But they did not understand this statement, and they were afraid to ask him.

(33) They came to Capernaum; and when he was in the house, he began to question them, **"What were you discussing on the way?"** (34) But they kept silent, for on the way they had discussed with one another which of them was the greatest. (35) Sitting down, he called the twelve and said to them, **"If anyone wants to be first, he shall be last of all and servant of all."**[*26] (36) Taking a child, he set him before them, and taking him in his arms, he said to them, (37) **"Whoever receives one child like this in my name receives me; and whoever receives me does not receive me, but him who sent me."** [*27]

*26 *A basic teaching of Joshua repeated several times, and lived out all the time. The disciple of Joshua will want to serve others in all times, places and circumstances. While we do have different talents, we should all have servant attitudes as we practice those talents and thus help others.*

*27 *To receive a disciple of Joshua is to receive the heavenly Father - to reject a disciple is to reject the heavenly Father.*

(38) John said to him, "Teacher, we saw someone casting out demons in your name, and we tried to prevent him because he was not following us." (39) But Joshua said, **"Do not hinder him, for there is no one who will perform a miracle in my name, and be able soon afterward to speak evil of me.**

(40) "For he who is not against us is for us."[*28] **(41)** "For whoever gives you a cup of water to drink because of your name as followers of me, truly I say to you, he will not lose his reward.**

[*28] *This saying is meant to keep peace between various Families of disciples. Just because another Family might have some minor differences of understandings of how to live out Joshua's teachings does not make them "against " another Family. If a person or persons know that we are followers of the Light and they understand what that means and they are not against us, we need to consider them for us. Unfortunately, people no longer know what a Family of disciples is so this saying has little application today as Families of disciples will generally be hated by those who say they are part of his church. In other words, a Family of disciples will be considered "against" the church since we speak against its teachings & practices.*

(42) "Whoever causes one of these little ones who believe to stumble (*sin*), it would be better for him if, with a heavy millstone (*huge donut shaped rock*) hung around his neck, he had been cast into the sea. **(43)** "If your hand causes you to stumble (*sin*), cut it off; it is better for you to enter Life crippled, than, having your two hands, to go into hell, into the unquenchable fire, **(45)** "If your foot causes you to stumble, cut it off; it is better for you to enter Life lame, than, having your two feet, to be cast into hell, **(47)** "If your eye causes you to stumble, throw it out; it is better for you to enter the kingdom of God with one eye, than, having two eyes, to be cast into hell,**[*29]** **(48)** where Their Worm Does Not Die, And The Fire Is Not Quenched. **(49)** "For everyone will be salted with fire. **(50)** "Salt is good; but if the salt becomes unsalty, with what will you make it salty again? Have salt in yourselves, and be at peace with one another."**

[*29] *Joshua teaches we must be very serious about our sin, especially sins that cause or encourage others to sin, especially causing or encouraging children to sin. The concept of "sin" (failing a moral standard) is going away in a US culture*

that is teaching that anything goes as long as it does not directly harm another person – a God-less and low standard that will destroy people's lives. It might work if humans were basically good and selfless, but we are not, thus it is doomed to failure.

(10:1) Getting up, he went from there to the region of Judea and beyond the Jordan; crowds gathered around him again, and, according to his custom, he once more began to teach them. (2) Some religious leaders came up to Joshua, testing him, and began to question him whether it was lawful for a man to divorce a wife. (3) And he answered and said to them, "**What did Moses** (*Not God!*) **command you?**" (4) They said, "Moses permitted a man To Write A Certificate Of Divorce And Send her Away." (5) But Joshua said to them, "**Because of your hardness of heart he** (*Moses, not God!*) **wrote you this commandment. (6) "But from the beginning of creation, God Made Them Male And Female. (7) "For This Reason A Man Shall Leave His Father And Mother, (8) And The Two Shall Become One Flesh; so they are no longer two, but one flesh. (9) "What therefore God has joined together, let no man separate.**" (10) In the house the disciples began questioning him about this again. (11) And he said to them, "**Whoever divorces his wife and marries another woman commits adultery** (*"adultery" is a married person having sex with someone other than their spouse*) **against her; (12) and if she herself divorces her husband and marries another man, she is committing adultery.**" [*30]

[*30] *Joshua makes clear a teaching of man (Moses) versus the intent of God. Moses, not God, allowed divorce. Therefore, this teaching of Moses was not inspired by God, as Paul would have you believe. Marriage – the joining of one man and one woman - was created by God and God did not allow for divorce. Joshua defines the concept of committed love (marriage) as between one man and one woman – male and female - for life. All other joining together types (more than one wife, a man and a man, etc.) are thus illegitimate in God's eyes – see Matt. 19. To wrongfully break that commitment against your spouse is to commit adultery against them.*

(13) And they were bringing children to him so that he might touch them; but the disciples told them to stop. (14) But when Joshua saw this, he was upset and said to them, "**Permit the children to come to me; do not hinder** (*prevent*) **them; for the kingdom of God belongs to such as these. (15) "Truly I say to you,**

whoever does not receive the kingdom of God like a child will not enter it at all." [*31] (16) And Joshua took the children in his arms and began blessing them, laying his hands on them.

[*31] *Do children want to do bible studies to understand God? Do children want to understand the Greek and Hebrew to understand God? Do children want to go to seminary to understand God? Does having child-like faith include all of the intellectual works that men say are required to 'know God' or 'know Him better'? No, it does not. "Those things which are highly valued among men are as garbage to God." – see Luke 16:15. The best way to know God is to know Joshua, and that merely requires reading his words with a simple and sincere heart – and for adults, mixed with faith.*

(17) As he was setting out on a journey, a man ran up to him and knelt before him, and asked him, "Good Teacher, what shall I do to inherit eternal life?" (18) And Joshua said to him, **"Why do you call me good? No one is good except God alone.** (19) **"You know the commandments, 'Do Not Murder, Do Not Commit Adultery, Do Not Steal, Do Not Bear False Witness, Do not defraud, Honor Your Father And Mother.'"** (20) And he said to him, "Teacher, I have kept all these things from my youth up." (21) Looking at him, Joshua felt compassion for him and said to him, **"One thing you lack: go and sell all you possess and give to the poor, and you will have treasure in heaven; and come, follow me."** (22) But at these words the man was saddened, and he went away grieving, for he was one who owned much property. (23) And Joshua, looking around, said to his disciples, **"How hard it will be for those who are wealthy to enter the kingdom of God!"** (24) The disciples were amazed at his words. But Joshua answered again and said to them, **"Children, how hard it is to enter the kingdom of God!** (25) **"It is easier for a camel to go through the eye of a needle than for a rich man to enter the kingdom of God."** (26) They were even more astonished and said to him, "Then who can be saved?" (27) Looking at them, Joshua said, **"With people it is impossible** (*to save themselves*), **but not with God; for all things are possible with God."** (28) Peter

began to say to him, "Behold, we have left everything (*forsaken all*) and followed you." (29) Joshua said, **"Truly I say to you, there is no one who has left house or brothers or sisters or mother or father or children** (*see Matt. 10:34-39; Luke 14:26-33*) **or farms, for my sake and for the gospel's sake,** (30) **but that he will receive a hundred times as much now in the present age, houses and brothers and sisters and mothers and children** (*see Matt. 12:46-50*) **and farms, along with persecutions; and in the age to come, eternal life.** (31) **"But many who are first will be last, and the last, first."** *32

*32 *What a key and amazing teaching of the Light! Materially wealthy people will not enter the kingdom of God – that is people who build up material things for themselves and don't share and/or give away what they have. Peter's reaction in verse 28 leaves no doubt that Joshua meant what he said – to be his follower we must turn away from the material life. The life of following the Life is described clearly in verses 29-31 – a radical change away from a former way of living – away from the material way and blood or legal relatives – to a new non-material way and a new family. While having to leave houses or farms might be more common during certain times and places, the changing of who is our family will never change in any time or place – it is a normal part of following Joshua.*

(32) They were on the road going up to Jerusalem, and Joshua was walking on ahead of them; and they were amazed, and those who followed were fearful. And again he took the twelve aside and began to tell them what was going to happen to him, (33) saying, **"Behold, we are going up to Jerusalem, and the Son of Man** (*Joshua's favorite title for himself*) **will be delivered to the religious leaders and the bible experts; and they will condemn him to death and will hand him over to the Gentiles** (*non-Jew or people with no knowledge of Joshua's Father*). (34) **"They will mock him and spit on him, and whip him and kill him, and three days later he will rise again."**

(35) James and John, the two sons of Zebedee, came up to Joshua, saying, "Teacher, we want you to do for us whatever we ask of you."

(36) And he said to them, "**What do you want me to do for you?**" (37) They said to him, "Grant that we may sit, one on your right and one on your left, in your glory." (38) But Joshua said to them, "**You do not know what you are asking. Are you able to drink the cup** (*of suffering*) **that I drink, or to be baptized with the baptism** (*pain*) **with which I am baptized?**" (39) They said to him, "We are able." And Joshua said to them, "**The cup that I drink you shall drink; and you shall be baptized with the baptism with which I am baptized. (40) "But to sit on my right or on my left, this is not mine to give; but it is for those for whom it has been prepared by my Father.**" *33 (41) Hearing this, the other ten began to feel angry with James and John. (42) Calling them to himself, Joshua said to them, "**You know that those who are recognized as rulers** (*leaders*) **of the Gentiles** (*non-Jew or people with no knowledge of Joshua's Father*) **lord it over them; and their great men exercise authority over them. (43) "But it is not to be this way among you, for whoever wishes to become great among you shall be your servant; (44) and whoever wishes to be first among you shall be servant of all. (45) "For even the Son of Man did not come to be served, but to serve, and to give his life a ransom** (*not a sacrifice!*) **for many.**" *34

*33 *A saying contrary to the trinity doctrine. If Joshua and His Father are the same being, how could he make such a clear distinction between his Father's will and his own? Such clear statements should win over unclear statements.*

*34 *Joshua never once refers to the purpose of his death as a "sacrifice", and he does speak to the 'why' of his death several times, as he does here. A ransom is not at all the same as a sacrifice. A ransom is a payment of some kind by one person to an evil person who is holding yet another person captive – the payment of the ransom has the intent of gaining the freedom of the person held captive. A sacrifice, on the other hand and in the context of the bible, is a person offering the life of an animal in order to gain forgiveness for their guilt by appeasing a god who requires the death of that sacrificial animal – the spilling of its blood - in order to forgive the guilty person. Again,* **Joshua never – not once – describes his death as a sacrifice***.*

(46) Then they came to Jericho. And as Joshua was leaving Jericho with his disciples and a large crowd, a blind beggar named Bartimaeus, the son of Timaeus, was sitting by the road. (47) When he heard that it was Joshua the Nazarene, he began to cry out and say, "Joshua, Son of David, have mercy on me!" (48) Many were sternly telling him to be quiet, but he kept crying out all the more, "Son of David, have mercy on me!" (49) And Joshua stopped and said, "**Call him here**." So they called the blind man, saying to him, "Take courage, stand up! He is calling for you." (50) Throwing aside his coat, he jumped up and came to Joshua. (51) And answering him, Joshua said, "**What do you want me to do for you?**" And the blind man said to him, "Rabbi, I want to regain my sight!" (52) And Joshua said to him, "**Go; your faith has made you well**." Immediately he regained his sight and began following him on the road.

(11:1) As they approached Jerusalem, at Bethphage and Bethany, near the Mount of Olives, Joshua sent two of his disciples, (2) and said to them, **"Go into the village opposite you, and immediately as you enter it, you will find a colt** (*young horse*) **tied there, on which no one yet has ever sat; untie it and bring it here.** (3) **"If anyone says to you, 'Why are you doing this?' you say, 'The Lord has need of it'; and immediately he will send it back here."** (4) They went away and found a colt tied at the door, outside in the street; and they untied it. (5) Some of the bystanders were saying to them, "What are you doing, untying the colt?" (6) They spoke to them just as Joshua had told them, and they gave them permission. (7) They brought the colt to Joshua and put their coats on it; and he sat on it. (8) And many spread their coats in the road, and others spread leafy branches which they had cut from the fields. (9) Those who went in front and those who followed were shouting: "Hosanna! Blessed Is He Who Comes In The Name Of The Lord; (10) Blessed is the coming kingdom of our father David; Hosanna in the highest!"

(11) Joshua entered Jerusalem and came into the temple; and after looking around at everything, he left for Bethany with the twelve, since it was already late. (12) On the next day, when they had left Bethany, he became hungry. (13) Seeing at a distance a fig tree in leaf, he went to see if perhaps he would find anything on it; and when he came to it, he found nothing but leaves, for it was not the season for figs. (14) He said to it, **"May no one ever eat fruit from you again!"** And his disciples were listening.*35

*35   *The disciples may have been listening, but not carefully. It is highly unlikely that Joshua cursed a fig tree. This behavior is very inconsistent with both his teachings and his normal behavior as portrayed elsewhere in the four gospels.*

(15) Then they came to Jerusalem. And he entered the temple and began to drive out those who were buying and selling in the temple, and overturned the tables of the money changers and the seats of those who were selling doves; (16) and he would not permit anyone

to carry merchandise through the temple. (17) And he began to teach and say to them, **"Is it not written, 'My House Shall Be Called A House Of Prayer For All The Nations'? But you have made it a Robbers' Den.**"*36 (18) The religious leaders and the bible experts heard this, and began seeking how to destroy him; for they were afraid of him, for the whole crowd was astonished at his teaching.

*36 *Please note that Joshua did not say, 'Does not my Father say, 'My house ....'. Rather he points to their scripture, which they say represents God's thoughts. Joshua points out their hypocrisy based on their own professed standard of their scripture. This does not mean he validated that a building was his Father's house. Rather he was rebuking a hypocritical religious practice.*

(19) When evening came, they would go out of the city. (20) As they were passing by in the morning, they saw the fig tree withered from the roots up. (21) Being reminded, Peter said to him, "Master, look, the fig tree which you cursed has withered." (22) And Joshua answered saying to them, **"Have faith in God. (23) "Truly I say to you, whoever says to this mountain, 'Be taken up and cast into the sea,' and does not doubt in his heart, but believes that what he says is going to happen, it will be granted him. (24) "Therefore I say to you, all things for which you pray and ask, believe that you have received them, and they will be granted you. (25) "Whenever you pray, forgive, if you have anything against anyone, so that your Father who is in heaven will also forgive you your transgressions. (26) "But if you do not forgive, neither will your Father who is in heaven forgive your transgressions.**"*37

*37 *A clear teaching repeated in several places in the gospels. If I have a heart of bitterness or un-forgiveness or wishing harm against another person, then my Father will not forgive my sins. This does not mean we trust people who have consistently sought our harm. But it does mean that we do not think badly of them and wish them well when the opportunity arises – love those who make*

*themselves your enemies means act kindly towards them and do not desire harm
upon them.*

(27) They came again to Jerusalem. And as he was walking in the
temple, the religious leaders and the bible experts and the elders
came to him, (28) and began saying to him, "By what authority are
you doing these things, or who gave you this authority to do these
things?" (29) And Joshua said to them, "**I will ask you one
question, and you answer me, and then I will tell you by
what authority I do these things. (30) "Was the baptism
of John from heaven, or from men? Answer me.**" (31) They
began reasoning among themselves, saying, "If we say, 'From
heaven,' he will say, 'Then why did you not believe him?' (32) "But
shall we say, 'From men'?"--they were afraid of the people, for
everyone considered John to have been a real prophet (*a person
who spoke God's truths*). (33) Answering Joshua, they said, "We
do not know." And Joshua said to them, "**Nor will I tell you by
what authority I do these things**."

(12:1) And he began to speak to them in parables: "**A man Planted A Vineyard And Put A Wall Around It, And Dug A Container Under The Wine Press And Built A Tower, and rented it out to vine-growers and went on a journey.** (2) "**At the harvest time he sent a servant to the vine-growers, in order to receive some of the produce of the vineyard from the vine-growers.** (3) "**They took him, and beat him and sent him away empty-handed.** (4) "**Again he sent them another servant, and they wounded him in the head, and treated him shamefully.** (5) "**And he sent another, and that one they killed; and so with many others, beating some and killing others.** (6) "**He had one more to send, a beloved son; he sent him last of all to them, saying, 'They will respect my son.'** (7) "**But those vine-growers said to one another, 'This is the heir; come, let us kill him, and the inheritance will be ours!'** (8) "**They took him, and killed him and threw him out of the vineyard.** (9) "**What will the owner of the vineyard do? He will come and destroy the vine-growers, and will give the vineyard to others.** (10) "**Have you not even read this scripture: 'THE STONE WHICH THE BUILDERS REJECTED, THIS BECAME THE CHIEF CORNER stone;** (11) **THIS CAME ABOUT FROM THE LORD, AND IT IS MARVELOUS IN OUR EYES'?**" (12) And they were seeking to seize him, and yet they feared the people, for they understood that he spoke the parable against them. And so they left him and went away.

(13) Then they sent some of the religious leaders and those of a certain political sect to him in order to trap him in a statement. (14) They came and said to him, "Teacher, we know that you are truthful and defer to no one; for you are not partial to any, but teach the way of God in truth. Is it lawful to pay a poll-tax to Caesar, or not? (15) "Shall we pay or shall we not pay?" But he, knowing their hypocrisy (*two-facedness*), said to them, "**Why are you testing me? Bring me a coin to look at.**" (16) They brought one. And he said to them, "**Whose likeness and inscription is this?**" And they said to him, "Caesar's." (17) And Joshua said to them, "**Give to Caesar**

the things that are Caesar's, and to God the things that are God's." And they were amazed at him.*38

*38 *Religious people who say, 'don't pay taxes to the government or IRS for it is wrong for these reasons...', go against Joshua's plain teaching here. Just pay your taxes – give some money to those who depend upon money, but give your heart and life to your Father.*

(18) Another scripture based sect (*who say that there is no resurrection*) came to Joshua, and began questioning him, saying, (19) "Teacher, Moses wrote for us that If A Man's Brother Dies and leaves behind a wife And Leaves No Child, His Brother Should Marry The Wife And Raise Up Children To His Brother. (20) "There were seven brothers; and the first took a wife, and died leaving no children. (21) "The second one married her, and died leaving behind no children; and the third likewise; (22) and so all seven left no children. Last of all the woman died also. (23) "In the resurrection, when they rise again, which one's wife will she be? For all seven had married her." (24) Joshua said to them, "**Is this not the reason you are mistaken, that you do not understand the scriptures or the power of God? (25) "For when they rise from the dead, they neither marry nor are given in marriage, but are like angels in heaven. (26) "But regarding the fact that the dead rise again** (*continue to exist after death*)**, have you not read in the book of Moses, in the passage about the burning bush, how God spoke to him, saying, 'I AM** (*present, not past tense*) **THE GOD OF ABRAHAM** (*who died long ago*)**, AND THE GOD OF ISAAC** (*who died long ago*)**, and the God of Jacob** (*who died long ago*)**'? (27) "He is not the God of the dead, but of the living; you are greatly mistaken.**"

(28) One of the bible experts came and heard them arguing, and recognizing that Joshua had answered them well, asked him, "What commandment is the foremost of all?" (29) Joshua answered, "**The foremost is, 'Hear, O Israel! The Lord Our God Is One Lord; (30) And You Shall Love The Lord Your God With**

All Your Heart, And With All Your Soul, And With All Your Mind, And With All Your Strength.' (31) "The second is this, 'You Shall Love Your Neighbor As Yourself.' There is no other commandment greater than these**." (32) The bible expert said to him, "Right, teacher; you have truly stated that He Is One, And There Is No One Else Besides Him; (33) And To Love Him With All The Heart And With All The Understanding And With All The Strength, And To Love One's Neighbor As Himself, is much more than all burnt offerings and sacrifices." *39 (34) When Joshua saw that he had answered rightly, he said to him, "**You are not far from the kingdom of God**." After that, no one would venture to ask him any more questions.

*39 *Joshua validates the man's answer. Please note that to love our heavenly Father and our neighbor is what God wants – He does not want offerings and sacrifices – a clear rebuke to the old testament or Hebrew sacrificial religious system which system was created by men, not God. See also Matt. 12:7.*

(35) And Joshua began to say, as he taught in the temple, "**How is it that the bible experts say that the Messiah is the son of David? (36) "David himself said in the Holy Spirit, 'The Lord Said To <u>My Lord</u>, "Sit At My Right Hand, Until I Put Your Enemies Beneath Your Feet."' (37) "David himself calls him 'Lord'; so in what sense is he his son?**" And the large crowd enjoyed listening to him. (38) In his teaching he was saying: "**Beware of the religious leaders and bible experts who like to walk around in fancy or religious clothing, and like respectful greetings in the market places, (39) and the best seats in the religious buildings and places of honor at weddings, (40) who devour widows' houses, and for appearance's sake offer long prayers; these will receive greater condemnation**." *40

*40 *Sadly, many will condemn themselves with their words and behavior. But the greater condemnation is reserved for those people who say they represent God – religious leaders and their followers - but who do not do what Joshua says e.g. practice love, humility, righteousness, compassion, etc.*

(41) And he sat down opposite the treasury, and began observing how the people were putting money into the treasury; and many rich people were putting in large sums. (42) A poor widow came and put in two small copper coins, which amount to a cent. (43) Calling his disciples to him, he said to them, "**Truly I say to you, this poor widow put in more than all the rich people; (44) for they all put in out of their surplus** (*'disposable income', that which they did not need for food, clothing or shelter*)**, but she, out of her poverty, put in all she owned, all she had to live on**." [*41]

[*41] *Faith, love and a little material giving is far greater than little or no faith, little love and much material giving.*

(13:1) As he was going out of the temple, one of his disciples said to him, "Teacher, behold what wonderful stones and what wonderful buildings!" (2) And Joshua said to him, "**Do you see these great buildings? Not one stone will be left upon another, all will not be torn down.**" (3) As he was sitting on the Mount of Olives opposite the temple, Peter and James and John and Andrew were questioning him privately, (4) "Tell us, when will these things be, and what will be the sign when all these things are going to be fulfilled?" (5) And Joshua began to say to them, "**See to it that no one misleads you. (6) "Many will come in my name, saying, 'I am He!' and will mislead** (*or deceive*) **many. (7) "When you hear of wars and rumors of wars, do not be frightened; those things must take place; but that is not yet the end. (8) "For nation will rise up against nation** (*political entities*)**, and kingdom against kingdom** (*religious entities, like Islam against Christianity; or private corporations*)**; there will be earthquakes in various places; there will also be famines** (*large areas where food is not available*)**. These things are <u>merely the beginning</u> of birth pangs.**[*42]

[*42] *So, the things mentioned by Joshua are just the* **beginning** *of birth pangs, and as any mother knows, those pangs can go on for some time – a mother can be in labor for many hours compared to the first birth pangs.*

---

(9) "**But be on your guard; for they will deliver you to the courts, and you will be whipped in the religious buildings, and you will stand before governors and kings for my sake, as a testimony to them. (10) "The gospel must first be preached to all the nations. (11) "When they arrest you and hand you over, do not worry beforehand about what you are to say, but say whatever is given you in that hour; for it is not you who speak, but it is the Holy Spirit. (12) "Brother will betray brother to death, and a father his child; and children will rise up against parents and have them put to death. (13) "You will be <u>hated by all because of my name</u>, but the one who endures to the end, he will be saved.**[*43]

Verses 12-13: What a strange picture for the average American christian or biblian, who simply cannot understand being hated by anyone, let alone their blood relatives, for their faith in Joshua as evidenced by living out and repeating HIS teachings. These saying of Joshua are typically brushed aside as 'not applying to us at this time and place'. That is false, as Joshua teaches the same thing in several places (see Matt. 10 for example) where the context cannot be forced into some time frame or special circumstance. Being rejected by those who reject Joshua is the natural or normal occurrence in all times and cultures for the disciple of Joshua (see John 18).

(In this commentator's opinion, the following is specifically for the people and nation of Israel and could well have happened in 70AD when the Roman general Titus destroyed Jerusalem and scattered the Jewish people, effectively destroying their nation; or he could just be speaking to Jewish disciples in this context of the end of the age.)

(14) **"But when you see the ABOMINATION OF DESOLATION standing where it should not be (let the reader understand), then those who are in Judea must flee to the mountains. (15) "The one who is on the housetop must not go down, or go in to get anything out of his house; (16) and the one who is in the field must not turn back to get his coat. (17) "But woe to those who are pregnant and to those who are nursing babies in those days! (18) "But pray that it may not happen in the winter.**

(Joshua resumes with a global view.)

(19) **"For those days will be a time of tribulation such as has not occurred since the beginning of the creation which God created until now, and never will. (20) "Unless the Lord had shortened those days, no life would have been saved; but for the sake of the elect, whom he chose, he shortened the days. (21) "And then if anyone says to you, 'Behold, here is the Messiah'; or, 'Behold, he is there'; do not believe him; (22) for false Messiahs and false prophets**

(people who claim to speak for God but don't) **will arise, and will show signs and wonders, in order to lead astray, if possible, the elect.** (23) **"But take heed; behold, I have told you everything in advance.**[*44]

[*44] *His warning was clear and timeless, for he has told us "everything" in advance. No new prophesies are needed to understand the basics about the future, and yet religious leaders claiming some association with Joshua exist by the tens of thousands profiting off their predictions and subsequent book sales, prophesy conferences, memberships, TV and radio broadcasts, etc.*

(24) **"But in those days, after that tribulation, The Sun Will Be Darkened And The Moon Will Not Give Its Light,** (25) **And The Stars Will Be Falling from heaven, and the powers that are in the heavens** *(celestial bodies like planets or asteroids)* **will be shaken.** (26) **"Then they will see The Son Of Man Coming In Clouds with great power and glory.** (27) **"And then he will send forth the angels, and will gather together his elect from the four winds, from the farthest end of the earth to the farthest end of heaven.**[*45]

[*45] *Please note during both events (vs 19-22 & 24-25), those who chose to follow Joshua will be present – "no life would have been saved but for the sake of the elect"; and, "and will gather together his elect from the...farthest end of the earth". God does not cause these events but He foresaw them and such events motivate people to acknowledge their need of their heavenly Father.*

(28) **"Now learn the parable from the fig tree: when its branch has already become tender and puts forth its leaves, you know that summer is near.** (29) **"Even so, you too, when you see these things happening, recognize that he is near, right at the door.** (30) **"Truly I say to you, this generation**[*46] **will not pass away until all these things take place.** (31) **"Heaven and earth will pass away, but my words**[*47] **will not pass away.** (32) **"But of that day or hour no one knows, not even the angels in heaven, nor the Son, but the Father alone.**[*48] (33) **"Take heed, keep on the alert;**

for you do not know when the appointed time will come. (34) "It is like a man away on a journey, who upon leaving his house and putting his servants in charge, assigning to each one his task, also commanded the doorkeeper to stay on the alert. (35) "Therefore, be on the alert--for you do not know when the master of the house is coming, whether in the evening, at midnight, or when the rooster crows, or in the morning-- (36) in case he should come suddenly and find you asleep. (37) "What I say to you I say to all, 'Be on the alert!'"

*46   *Joshua indirectly speaks of three ages or generations in his teachings. The first generation was all those alive on the earth prior to his first coming. The second generation was/is all those alive on the earth during and after his first coming, prior to his second coming. The third generation will be all those alive during and after his second coming. He speaks to the middle or second generation in this saying.*

*47   *Sadly, many who are deceived will say "my words" mean Paul's words and Jude's words and Moses words, etc. No, "my words" mean "my words", and no one else's. Only Joshua's words will not pass away. Thus, his words or concepts alone perfectly reflect the realities of the eternal realm and the mind of the Father - not all the other author's in the bible or anyone one else living or dead. While others can write true things, only Joshua and his words deserve our faith.*

*48   *A clear proof against the trinity doctrine. None of the few 'pro-trinity' sayings cited by those who accept the contradictory doctrine, even come close to the tight, 'no other understanding possible' nature of this saying - two beings, a Father and Son.*

(14:1) Now the Passover and Unleavened Bread (*religious observance days for the Jews*) were two days away; and the religious leaders and the bible experts were seeking how to seize Joshua secretly and kill him; (2) for they were saying, "Not during the festival, otherwise there might be a riot of the people." (3) While he was in Bethany at the home of Simon the leper, and reclining at the table, there came a woman with an alabaster vial of very costly perfume; and she broke the vial and poured it over his head. (4) But some were indignantly remarking to one another, "Why has this perfume been wasted? (5) "For this perfume might have been sold for over two thousand dollars, and the money given to the poor." And they were scolding her. (6) But Joshua said, "**Let her alone; why do you bother her? She has done a good deed to me. (7) "For you always have the poor with you, and whenever you wish you can do good to them; but you do not always have me.***49 (8) "**She has done what she could; she has anointed my body beforehand for the burial. (9) "Truly I say to you, wherever the gospel is preached in the whole world, what this woman has done will also be spoken of in memory of her.**"

*49   *Helping the poor is good, but not as the primary task as a disciple of Joshua. The primary task for Joshua's followers is to acknowledge him for who he says he is, and do what he says...and the primary thing he says to do is love others and live and speak his words of truth and light to the people who make up the dark world - thus bringing his Father's message of Love, Life and Hope.*

(10) Then Judas Iscariot, who was one of the twelve, went off to the religious leaders in order to betray Joshua to them. (11) They were glad when they heard this, and promised to give him money. And he began seeking how to betray him at an opportune time. (12) On the first day of the Jewish feast of Unleavened Bread, when the Passover lamb was being sacrificed, his disciples said to him, "Where do you want us to go and prepare for you to eat the Passover?" (13) And he sent two of his disciples and said to them, "**Go into the city, and a man will meet you carrying a pitcher of water; follow him; (14) and wherever he**

enters, say to the owner of the house, 'The Teacher says, "Where is my guest room in which I may eat the passover with my disciples?"' *50 **(15) "And he himself will show you a large upper room furnished and ready; prepare for us there."** (16) The disciples went out and came to the city, and found it just as he had told them; and they prepared the holiday meal.

*50 *Many who love things Hebrew will seek to use this saying to say that Joshua was advocating keeping the Jewish religious rituals. That is like saying a christian coach - who coaches Jewish boys and who agrees to attend a player's bar mitzvah (a Jewish ritual of coming of age) - is advocating that all people ought to partake in the bar mitzvah ritual. No, rather the coach understands how important the ritual is to the players and he graciously attends so as not unnecessarily offend. Joshua is the Son of Man-kind, the Son of the Creator of the human race - not the Son of a Jewish God. If he came to another people other than the Jews, he would not unnecessarily offend people who would otherwise listen to him, and he would have respected religious practices that would not contradict or substitute his teachings in order to have the opportunity to guide them to the greater truths. Joshua's important teachings offend so there is no need to offend on relatively unimportant matters.*

(17) When it was evening he came with the twelve. (18) As they were reclining at the table and eating, Joshua said, **"Truly I say to you that one of you will betray me--one who is eating with me."** (19) They began to be grieved and to say to him one by one, "Surely not I?" (20) And he said to them, **"It is one of the twelve, one who dips with me in the bowl. (21) "For the Son of Man is to go just as it is written of him; but woe to that man by whom the Son of Man is betrayed! It would have been good for that man if he had not been born."**

(22) While they were eating, he took some bread, and after a blessing he broke it, and gave it to them, and said, **"Take it; this is as my body."** (23) And when he had taken a cup and given thanks, he gave it to them, and they all drank from it. (24) And he said to them, **"This is as my blood of the covenant, which is poured out for many. (25) "Truly I say to you, I will never**

again drink of the fruit of the vine until that day when I drink it new in the kingdom of God." *51 (26) After singing a song, they went out to the Mount of Olives.

*51 *This saying in Mark might be the best and clearest recording of this saying of Joshua. Joshua simply says that the wine metaphorically represents his blood which blood will literally be used to seal the new covenant the Father made with mankind. What covenant? "This is my beloved Son – listen to him" and if you do so you can be assured you will be welcomed Home.*

(27) And Joshua said to them, **"You will all fall away, because it is written, 'I Will Strike Down The Shepherd, And The Sheep Shall Be Scattered.' (28) "But after I have been raised, I will go ahead of you to Galilee."** (29) But Peter said to him, "Even though all may fall away, yet I will not." (30) And Joshua said to him, **"Truly I say to you, that this very night, before a rooster crows twice, you yourself will deny me three times."** (31) But Peter kept saying insistently, "Even if I have to die with You, I will not deny you!" And they all were saying the same thing also.

(32) They came to a place named Gethsemane; and he said to his disciples, **"Sit here until I have prayed."** (33) And he took with him Peter and James and John, and began to be very distressed and troubled. (34) And he said to them, **"My soul is deeply grieved to the point of death; remain here and keep watch."** (35) And he went a little beyond them, and fell to the ground and began to pray that if it were possible, the hour might pass him by. (36) And he was saying, **"Abba! Father! All things are possible for You; remove this cup from me; yet not what I will, but what you will."** (37) And he came and found them sleeping, and said to Peter, **"Simon, are you asleep? Could you not keep watch for one hour? (38) "Keep watching and praying that you may not come into temptation; the spirit is willing, but the flesh is weak."** (39) Again he went away and prayed, saying the same words. (40) And again he came and found them sleeping, for their eyes were very heavy; and they did not know what to

answer him. (41) And he came the third time, and said to them, **"Are you still sleeping and resting? It is enough; the hour has come; behold, the Son of Man is being betrayed into the hands of sinners. (42) "Get up, let us be going; behold, the one who betrays me is at hand!"** (43) Immediately while he was still speaking, Judas, one of the twelve, came up accompanied by a crowd with swords and clubs, who were from the religious leaders and the bible experts and the elders. (44) Now he who was betraying him (*Judas*) had given them a signal, saying, "Whomever I kiss, he is the one; seize him and lead him away under guard." (45) After coming, Judas immediately went to him, saying, "Rabbi!" and kissed him. (46) They laid hands on him and seized him. (47) But one of those who stood by drew his sword, and struck the servant of the high priest and cut off his ear. (48) And Joshua said to them, **"Have you come out with swords and clubs to arrest me, as you would against a robber? (49) "Every day I was with you in the temple teaching, and you did not seize me; but this has taken place to fulfill the scriptures."** *52 (50) And they all (*Joshua's disciples*) left him and fled. (51) A young man was following him, wearing nothing but a linen sheet over his naked body; and they seized him. (52) But he pulled free of the linen sheet and escaped naked (*perhaps this is a reference to the author, Mark?*).

*52   *Joshua used all he could to point the people to his Father. In this case, he is appealing to his Jewish listener's reverence of their scriptures in order to validate who he was – the promised Messiah. The Jewish scripture did contain some prophetic truths about Messiah – as well as a good bit of human wisdom - even while most of the Jewish scripture presents a clouded or wrong view of the heavenly Father through sinful men's eyes and thoughts. Just because, for example, 2 percent of the Jewish scriptures contain accurate prophesy about Messiah or thoughts that match the Father's Way, does not mean the other 98 percent is from God.*

(53) They led Joshua away to the high priest; and all the religious leaders and the elders and the bible experts gathered together. (54) Peter had followed him at a distance, right into the courtyard of the

highest religious leader; and he was sitting with the officers and warming himself at the fire. (55) Now the religious leaders and the whole Council kept trying to obtain testimony against Joshua to put him to death, and they were not finding any. (56) For many were giving false testimony against him, but their testimony was not consistent. (57) Some stood up and began to give false testimony against him, saying, (58) "We heard him say, 'I will destroy this temple made with hands, and in three days I will build another made without hands.'" (59) Not even in this respect was their testimony consistent. (60) The chief religious leader stood up and came forward and questioned Joshua, saying, "Do you not answer? What is it that these men are testifying against you?" (61) But he kept silent and did not answer. Again the chief religious leader was questioning him, and saying to him, "Are you the Messiah, the Son of God?" (62) And Joshua said, "**I am** [*53]**; and you shall see The Son of Man Sitting At The Right Hand Of Power, And Coming With The Clouds Of Heaven**." (63) Tearing his clothes, the chief religious leader said, "What further need do we have of witnesses? (64) "You have heard the blasphemy (*speaking bad things against God*); how does it seem to you?" And they all condemned him to be deserving of death. (65) Some began to spit at him, and to blindfold him, and to beat him with their fists, and to say to him, "Prophesy!" And the officers received him with slaps in the face.

[*53] *A clear profession of who Joshua of Nazareth claimed to be. Not merely a great moral teacher. Not merely a great man. Not God Himself, but rather the unique Son and messenger – and most accurate representation - of the living Creator of the human race.*

(66) As Peter was below in the courtyard, one of the servant-girls of the chief religious leader came, (67) and seeing Peter warming himself, she looked at him and said, "You also were with Joshua the Nazarene." (68) But he denied it, saying, "I neither know nor understand what you are talking about." And he went out onto the porch. (69) The servant-girl saw him, and began once more to say to the bystanders, "This is one of them!" (70) But again he denied

it. And after a little while the bystanders were again saying to Peter, "Surely you are one of them, for you are a Galilean too." (71) But he began to curse and swear, "I do not know this man you are talking about!" (72) Immediately a rooster crowed a second time. And Peter remembered how Joshua had made the remark to him, **"Before a rooster crows twice, you will deny me three times**." And he began to weep.

(15:1) Early in the morning the religious leaders with the politicians and bible experts and the whole Council, immediately held a consultation; and binding Joshua, they led him away and delivered him to the Roman governor, Pilate. (2) Pilate questioned him, "Are you the King of the Jews?" And he answered him, "**It is as you say**." (3) The religious leaders began to accuse him harshly. (4) Then Pilate questioned him again, saying, "Do you not answer? See how many charges they bring against you!" (5) But Joshua made no further answer; so Pilate was amazed.

(6) Now at the feast Pilate used to release for them any one prisoner whom they requested. (7) The man named Barabbas had been imprisoned with the insurrectionists who had committed murder in the insurrection (*an "insurrection" was an event where a group of people were fighting against Roman rule*). (8) The crowd went up and began asking him to do as he had been accustomed to do for them. (9) Pilate answered them, saying, "Do you want me to release for you the King of the Jews?" (10) For he was aware that the religious leaders had handed him over because of envy. (11) But the religious leaders stirred up the crowd to ask him to release Barabbas for them instead. (12) Answering again, Pilate said to them, "Then what shall I do with him whom you call the King of the Jews?" (13) They shouted back, "Crucify Him!" (14) But Pilate said to them, "Why, what evil has he done?" But they shouted all the more, "Crucify Him!" (15) Wishing to satisfy the crowd, Pilate released Barabbas for them, and after having Joshua whipped, he handed him over to be crucified.

(16) The soldiers took him away into the Roman palace (*that is, the Praetorium*), and they called together the whole Roman cohort. (17) They dressed Joshua up in purple, and after twisting a crown of thorns, they put it on him; (18) and they began to mock him, "Hail, King of the Jews!" (19) They kept beating his head with a reed, and spitting on him, and kneeling and bowing before him. (20) After they had mocked him, they took the purple robe off him and put his own garments on him. And they led him out to crucify him. (21) They pressed into service a passer-by coming from the

country, Simon of Cyrene (the father of Alexander and Rufus), to bear his cross. (22) Then they brought him to the place Golgotha, which is translated, Place of a Skull. (23) They tried to give him wine mixed with myrrh; but he did not take it. (24) And they crucified him, and divided up his garments among themselves, casting lots for them to decide what each man should take. (25) It was the third hour when they crucified him. (26) The writing above his head of the charge against him read, "THE KING OF THE JEWS." (27) They crucified two robbers with him, one on his right and one on his left.

(29) Those passing by were hurling abuse at him, wagging their heads, and saying, "Ha! You who are going to destroy the temple and rebuild it in three days, (30) save yourself, and come down from the cross!" (31) In the same way the religious leaders also, along with the bible experts, were mocking him among themselves and saying, "He saved others; he cannot save himself. (32) "Let this Messiah, the King of Israel, now come down from the cross, so that we may see and believe!" Those who were crucified with him were also insulting him.

(33) When the sixth hour came, darkness fell over the whole land until the ninth hour. (34) At the ninth hour Joshua cried out with a loud voice, "**Eloi, Eloi, Lama Sabachthani?**" which is translated, "**My God, My God, Why Have You Forsaken Me?**" [*54] (35) When some of the bystanders heard it, they began saying, "Behold, he is calling for Elijah." (36) Someone ran and filled a sponge with sour wine, put it on a reed, and gave him a drink, saying, "Let us see whether Elijah will come to take him down." (37) And Joshua uttered a loud cry, and breathed his last. (38) And the veil (*large curtain*) of the temple was torn in two from top to bottom. (39) When the centurion, who was standing right in front of him, saw the way he breathed his last, he said, "Truly this man was the Son of God!"

[*54] *Another saying that clearly contradicts the trinity doctrine – how could 'the Most High God' have a God?*

(40) There were also some women looking on from a distance, among whom were Mary Magdalene, and Mary the mother of James the Less and Joses, and Salome. (41) When he was in Galilee, they used to follow him and serve him; and there were many other women who came up with him to Jerusalem. (42) When evening had already come, because it was the preparation day, that is, the day before the Sabbath, (43) Joseph of Arimathea came, a prominent member of the Council, who himself was waiting for the kingdom of God; and he gathered up courage and went in before Pilate, and asked for the body of Joshua. (44) Pilate wondered if he was dead by this time, and summoning the centurion, he questioned him as to whether he was already dead. (45) And getting this information from the centurion, he granted the body to Joseph. (46) Joseph bought a linen cloth, took him down, wrapped him in the linen cloth and laid him in a tomb which had been hewn out in the rock; and he rolled a stone against the entrance of the tomb. (47) Mary Magdalene and Mary the mother of Joses were looking on to see where he was laid.

(16:1) When the sabbath was over, Mary Magdalene, and Mary the mother of James, and Salome, bought spices, so that they might come and anoint him. (2) Very early on the first day of the week, they came to the tomb when the sun had risen. (3) They were saying to one another, "Who will roll away the stone for us from the entrance of the tomb?" (4) Looking up, they saw that the stone had been rolled away, although it was extremely large. (5) Entering the tomb, they saw a young man sitting at the right, wearing a white robe; and they were amazed. (6) And he said to them, "Do not be amazed; you are looking for Joshua the Nazarene, who has been crucified. He has risen; he is not here; behold, here is the place where they laid him. (7) "But go, tell his disciples and Peter, 'He is going ahead of you to Galilee; there you will see him, just as he told you.'" (8) They went out and fled from the tomb, for trembling and astonishment had gripped them; and they said nothing to anyone, for they were afraid.

[*55] (9) Now after he had risen early on the first day of the week, he first appeared to Mary Magdalene, from whom he had cast out seven demons. (10) She went and reported to those who had been with him, while they were mourning and weeping. (11) When they heard that he was alive and had been seen by her, they refused to believe it. (12) After that, he appeared in a different form to two of them while they were walking along on their way to the country. (13) They went away and reported it to the others, but they did not believe them either. (14) Afterward he appeared to the eleven themselves as they were reclining at the table; and he reproached them for their unbelief and hardness of heart, because they had not believed those who had seen him after he had risen. (15) And he said to them, "**Go into all the world and preach the gospel to all creation**".

[*55] *Most bible translators agree that the material after verse 8 was added at some point after the original book that Mark wrote. Verses 9 through 15 contain things which are repeated in the other three gospels, and thus this author has printed them. This author has chosen to omit altogether verses 16 through 20, as those verses contain alleged sayings of Joshua, most of which – in context - run contrary to some other of his teachings. The reader is free to read them elsewhere.*

END OF THE BOOK OF MARK

The Life and Words of Joshua* of Nazareth According to Matthew:

* Joshua is a more accurate translation of what has been traditionally translated "Jesus"

Basic Book Introduction:
Distinguish between the Author and his Subject

The author is Joshua's disciple (or student) Matthew, a former tax collector who left his former life to follow Joshua. He lived and traveled with Joshua for over three years as Joshua brought his message to the world, starting with the people of Israel.

Matthew no doubt had most things correct about Joshua since he was with him and taught by him for over three years. This commentator believes that he accurately remembered and wrote down what Joshua said and did (John 14:26). However, the reader must understand the distinction between his accurately recording what Joshua said and did versus his having a *perfect understanding* of what Joshua said and did. For example, a person can see a man running down a street in an urgent fashion yelling 'fire'. The person witnessing the man running can accurately identify the time and place and other facts associated with the event, but the witness cannot know for sure **why** the man is running and yelling 'fire'.

In like manner, let the reader understand, all men, including the men who were with Joshua (and including this commentator) - had beliefs, religious baggage so to speak – that hindered them from having a perfect understanding of Joshua and his purpose. They, like us, had minds containing things (particularly religious things) which are not from Joshua, which things they could not reconcile with some of the things Joshua said (one example is Acts 1:6), **even while they accurately recorded what he said and did. Therefore, the reader should place full confidence in**

256

Joshua and his Words only, in terms of having as close to a perfect understanding of Joshua as is possible. This is only reasonable as no one but Joshua could have a perfect understanding of Joshua. While Matthew's narrative and commentary (in contrast to Joshua's own words and teachings) is almost certainly accurate in regard to historical details of the circumstances of Joshua's Life, only the Words of Joshua alone should have the reader's full trust in regard to **understanding Joshua and his purposes...revealing the 'why's' regarding Joshua's words and actions**. To assist the reader in this endeavor, Joshua's words are **in bold** in this publishing of Matthew's book.

This commentator's comments are *italicized* and either contained in parenthesis or preceded by a superscripted number. Sections of text that are in title case (where the first letter of each word in a phrase or sentence is capitalized e.g. The Gospel of Luke According to Luke), are quotes of the Old Testament scripture.

The purpose of this commentator's comments is threefold. First, is to try and define terms according to Joshua's own usage in the four gospels and to do so using simpler or clarified terms or phrases that avoid religious vocabulary. This is necessary for readers with little or no exposure to concepts they have not encountered before or terms or concepts that have been given an incorrect meaning through current religious culture. For example, an important concept – "religious leaders" - has been hidden by using the name of a specific religious sect's leadership, the "Pharisees". The modern reader will have little idea what "Pharisees" were, but they can certainly grasp the concept, "religious leaders", which is exactly what the Pharisees were.

An example of a term that has been modified by current religious culture would be "prophet". This term has come to mean in the current religious culture, a person who foretells future events. The term as Joshua uses it, simply means someone who speaks God's truths.

Second, is to bring to the reader's attention the important teachings of Joshua which are nullified (cancelled out, or made of no effect) by contradictions with other passages in the bible or by contemporary religious teaching. This is not exhaustive, but rather brings to light the contradictions which, in this commentator's opinion, nullify some of the more important teachings of Joshua.

Third, is to 'clear the dirt off his person and sayings', so to speak, for those who want to hear but have been confused or deceived by the myriad of other voices that claim they understand Joshua better than Joshua understands Joshua. For those people who participate in the religious system, perhaps the most commonly used mantra of the bible based religious system's leadership is, "Jesus doesn't mean that...you need us, your educated clergy, to understand what Jesus really meant". This commentator has news for you – Jesus does mean that! No, I don't mean that you turn figurative language into literal language, like when he says, "if your right eye causes you to sin, rip it from your head". Rather, I am referring to his teachings that go against human kind's normal inclination or that challenge some aspect of the way I am living. For example, the simple teaching, "love your enemies". Yes, it does mean that...and no, joining a military and killing the 'enemy' cannot be reconciled with "love your enemies". You may not like what Joshua has to say, but let him say it and don't twist his words. After all, if Joshua is who he says he is, we would do well to listen.

The Book of Matthew: Opening Chapters Summary

Matthew Chapter 1 – Provides Joshua's genealogy (physical birth lineage or 'family tree') and information about Joshua' earthly parents and his birth.

Matthew Chapter 2 – Provides information about Joshua' birth and events pertaining to it.

Matthew Chapter 3 – Introduces John the Baptist and his message of being remorseful over one's sin and thus changing one's behavior. John introduces Joshua to those people of Israel who were seeking after the promised leader of God, known as the messiah.

Text:

We pick up at verse 13:

(3:13) Then Joshua arrived from Galilee at the Jordan coming to John, to be baptized (*dunked under water, representing a spiritual cleansing*) by him. (14) But John tried to prevent him, saying, "I have need to be baptized by you, and do you come to me?" (15) But Joshua answering said to him, "**Permit it at this time; for in this way it is fitting for us to fulfill all righteousness** (*that which is right*)." Then he permitted him. (16) After being baptized, Joshua came up immediately from the water; and behold, the heavens were opened, and he saw the Spirit of God descending as a dove and lighting on him, (17) and behold, a voice out of the heavens said, "**This is my beloved Son, in whom I am well-pleased**."

(4:1) Then Joshua was led up by the Spirit into the wilderness to be tempted by Satan (*a powerful spiritual being who is against Joshua' Father and His Father's Kingdom*). (2) And after he had fasted (*didn't eat*) forty days and forty nights, he was very hungry. (3) And the tempter (*Satan*) came and said to him, "If You are the Son of God, command that these stones become bread." (4) But he answered and said, "**It is written, 'Man Shall Not Live On Bread Alone, But On Every Word That Comes Out Of The Mouth Of God.**'" (5) Then Satan took him into the holy city (*Jerusalem*) and had him stand on the highest point of the temple, (6) and said to him, "If You are the Son of God, throw Yourself down; for it is written, 'He Will Command His Angels Concerning You'; and 'On Their Hands They Will Bear You Up, So That You Will Not Strike Your Foot Against A Stone.'" (7) Joshua said to him, "**On the other hand, it is written, 'You Shall Not Put The Lord Your God To The Test.**'" (8) Again, the devil took him to a very high mountain and showed him all the kingdoms of the world and their glory; (9) and he said to him, "All these things I will give you, if you fall down and worship me." (10) Then Joshua said to him, "**Go, Satan! For it is written, 'You Shall Worship The Lord Your God, And Serve Him Only.**'" (11) Then the devil left him; and behold, angels came and began to help to him. Now when Joshua heard that John had been taken into custody (*arrested by the Roman governor*), he withdrew (12) into Galilee; (13) and leaving Nazareth (*the area where he grew up*), he came and settled in Capernaum, which is by the sea, in the region of Zebulun and Naphtali. (14) This was to fulfill what was spoken through Isaiah the prophet (*a "prophet is a person who speaks God's truths*): (15) "The Land Of Zebulun And The Land Of Naphtali, By The Way Of The Sea, Beyond The Jordan, Galilee Of The Gentiles (*non-Jews or people with no knowledge of Joshua's Father*) -- (16) "The People Who Were Sitting In Darkness Saw A Great Light, And Those Who Were Sitting In The Land And Shadow Of Death, Upon Them A Light Dawned." (17) From that time Joshua began to preach and say, "**Repent** (*feel truly sorry about your bad behavior and words, and change*), **for the kingdom of heaven is at hand**."

(18) Now as Joshua was walking by the Sea of Galilee, he saw two brothers, Simon who was called Peter, and Andrew his brother, throwing a net into the sea; for they were fishermen. (19) And he said to them, "**Follow me, and I will make you fishers of men.**"*1 (20) Immediately they left their nets and followed him. (21) Going on from there he saw two other brothers, James the son of Zebedee, and John his brother, in the boat with Zebedee their father, mending their nets; and he called them. (22) Immediately they left the boat and their father, and followed him. (23) Joshua was going throughout all Galilee, teaching in their religious buildings and proclaiming the gospel (*good news*) of the kingdom, and healing every kind of disease and every kind of sickness among the people. (24) The news about him spread throughout all Syria; and they brought to him all who were ill, those suffering with various diseases and pains, demoniacs (*those possessed or influenced by bad angels*), epileptics, paralytics (*those who could not move their legs*); and he healed them. (25) Large crowds followed him from Galilee and the Decapolis and Jerusalem and Judea and from beyond the Jordan.

*1 *In Eph. 4:11, Paul wrongly sets up classes of leadership, only one of which could be described as fishing for men, 'evangelists', thus nullifying this teaching of Joshua. All disciples of Joshua are to be fishers of men, which mean's telling others to listen to and follow Joshua.*

(5:1) When Joshua saw the crowds, he went up on the mountain; and after he sat down, His disciples (*his students*) came to him. (2) He opened His mouth and began to teach them, saying,

(3) **"Blessed**[*2] **are the poor in spirit, for theirs is the kingdom of heaven.**
(4) **"Blessed are those who mourn, for they shall be comforted.**
(5) **"Blessed are the gentle, for they shall inherit the earth.**
(6) **"Blessed are those who hunger and thirst for righteousness** (*the desire to do what is right as God defines it*)**, for they shall be satisfied.**
(7) **"Blessed are the merciful** (*eager to grant forgiveness*)**, for they shall receive mercy.**
(8) **"Blessed are the pure in heart, for they shall see God.**
(9) **"Blessed are the peacemakers, for they shall be called sons of God.**
(10) **"Blessed are those who have been persecuted** (*treated badly by others*) **for the sake of righteousness** (*doing what is right*)**, for theirs is the kingdom of heaven.**
(11) **"Blessed are you when people insult you and persecute you, and falsely say all kinds of evil against you <u>because of me</u>.**[*3] (12) **"Rejoice and be glad, for your reward in heaven is great; for in the same way they persecuted the prophets** (*those who spoke God's truth*) **who were before you.**

[*2] *Blessed means fortunate or to be rewarded by the Father and thus glad about what your future holds.*

[*3] *Fortunate are the followers of Joshua when they are insulted, persecuted and slandered, not because of their religious label – being a christian or wearing strange clothes or religious rituals or practices – but rather because they speak the Light's truths and behave as he says we ought to behave, which is what he means when he says, "because of ME". A Muslim hating a christian because of their label or outward religious stuff, is NOT what Joshua is speaking of here. It is NOT our label that matters, but rather what we speak (e.g. Joshua is the Son of God) and how we behave (e.g. not affirming people when they want us to).*

(13) "**You are the salt of the earth; but if the salt has become tasteless, how can it be made salty again? It is no longer good for anything, except to be thrown out and trampled underfoot by men.** (14) "**You are the light of the world. A city set on a hill cannot be hidden;** (15) **nor does anyone light a lamp and put it under a basket, but on the table, and it gives light to all who are in the house.** (16) "**Let your light shine before men in such a way that they may see the good things you do** (*help others*) **and glorify your Father who is in heaven.**"*4

*4 *Verses 13 – 16 ought to be understood in light of verse 11. If we are not helping others AND openly confessing our motivation for doing so (our love for our Father, Master and neighbor), then we are good for nothing but to be ignored or mocked by people. "...in such a way..." means we are sincere, seeking not to promote ourselves and thus acting humbly.*

(17) "**Do not think that I came to abolish** (*make of no effect or to cancel*) **the Law or the Prophets** (*God's truths contained in some portions of the Jewish scripture*)**; I did not come to abolish but to fulfill** (*that which was unfulfilled or imperfect in Moses' law*). (18) "**For truly I say to you, until heaven and earth pass away, not the smallest letter or stroke shall pass from the Law until all is accomplished.** (19) "**Whoever then annuls** (*says a person does not have to keep it*) **one of the least of these commandments** (*those he is about to teach in verses 21 and following*)**, and teaches others to do the same, shall be called least in the kingdom of heaven; but whoever keeps and teaches them, he shall be called great in the kingdom of heaven.** (20) "**For I say to you that unless your righteousness is greater than that of the bible experts and religious leaders** (*at that time, those keeping Moses' law*)**, you will not enter the kingdom of heaven.**"*5

*5 *This section of Joshua's teachings are regularly used by people to reject Joshua as Master and instead look to Moses and the Hebrew scripture. One of the things Joshua came for was to perfect and fulfill the imperfect teachings of Moses.*

Because a moral teachings is imperfect does not mean it is not good. For example, 'Do not commit adultery' is a good moral rule, but it does not prevent husband's hearts from lusting after women. Listen to Joshua in the following teachings and hear him perfect the imperfect teachings of Moses. Of course if something is imperfect, then it does not represent a direct communication from a Perfect Being.

(21) **"You have heard that the ancients** (*those alive at Moses' time*) **were told** (*by Moses*), **'You Shall Not Commit Murder'** (*Moses in Exod. 20:13*) **and 'Whoever commits murder shall be liable to the court.'** (22) **"But I say to you that everyone who is angry with his brother shall be guilty before the court; and whoever says to his brother, 'You good-for-nothing,' shall be guilty before the supreme court; and whoever says, 'You fool,' shall be guilty enough to go into the fiery hell** (*a place of painful punishment and destruction*). (23) **"Therefore if you are presenting your offering** (*religious gift*) **at the altar** (*a table in the Jews religious building*), **and there remember that your brother has something against you, (24) leave your offering there before the altar and go; first be reconciled to your brother, and then come and present your offering. (25) "Make friends quickly with your opponent at law while you are with him on the way, so that your opponent may not hand you over to the judge and the judge to the officer, and you be thrown into prison. (26) "Truly I say to you, you will not come out of there until you have paid up the last cent.**

(27) **"You have heard that it was said, 'You Shall Not Commit Adultery'** (*Moses in Exod. 20:14*) (*"adultery" is a married person having sex with someone other than their spouse*); (28) **but I say to you that everyone who looks at a woman with lust for her has already committed adultery with her in his heart. (29) "If your right eye makes you stumble, tear it out and throw it from you; for it is better for you to lose one of the parts of your body, than for your whole body to be thrown into hell. (30) "If your right hand**

makes you stumble, cut it off and throw it from you; for it is better for you to lose one of the parts of your body, than for your whole body to go into hell.

(31) "It was said, 'Whoever Sends His Wife Away, Let Him Give Her A Certificate Of Divorce' (*Moses in Deut. 24:1-3*); (32) but I say to you that everyone who divorces his wife, except for the reason of unchastity (*the wife had sex before being married and did not tell her husband to be*), makes her commit adultery; and whoever marries a divorced woman commits adultery.

(33) "Again, you have heard that the ancients were told, 'You Shall Not Make False Promises, But Shall Fulfill Your Promises To The Lord.' (*Moses in Num. 30:2*) (34) "But I say to you, make no oath (*promise*) at all, either by heaven, for it is the throne of God, (35) or by the earth, for it is the footstool of His feet, or by Jerusalem, for it is THE CITY OF THE GREAT KING. (36) "Nor shall you make an oath by your head, for you cannot make one hair white or black. (37) "But let your statement be, 'Yes, yes' or 'No, no'; anything beyond these is of evil.*6

*6 *In 1 Tim. 2:7, Paul says, "I am telling the truth, I am not lying". While not making an oath, it does break the spirit of let your yes be yes and no be no. Just do what we say, and don't say what we don't mean – keep our word.*

(38) "You have heard that it was said, 'An Eye For An Eye, And A Tooth For A Tooth.' (*Moses in Exod. 21:23-24*) (39) "But I say to you, do not resist an evil person; but whoever slaps you on your right cheek, turn the other to him also. (40) "If anyone wants to sue you and take your shirt, let him have your coat also. (41) "Whoever forces you to go one mile (*to carry their stuff*), go with him two. (42) "Give to him who asks of you, and do not turn away from him who wants to borrow from you.*7

This anti-retaliatory teaching of Joshua rebukes Moses' revenge principle - thus proving that teaching of Moses was not from God. If humans lived by this, would there be any conflict? For the reason why people reject this teaching of Joshua, see the end of John chapter 3, "men love the darkness rather than the light".

(43) "**You have heard that it was said, 'YOU SHALL LOVE YOUR NEIGHBOR and hate your enemy.'** (*Moses in Lev. 19:18 and Num. 31:1, 14-18*) (44) "**But I say to you, love** (*'love' means to be kind to others motivated by a heart of compassion for them*) **your enemies and pray for those who persecute** (*harm your person or property*) **you,** (45) **so that you may be sons of your Father who is in heaven; for he causes His life giving sun to rise on the evil and the good, and sends life giving rain on the righteous and the unrighteous.***8 (46) "**For if you love those who love you, what reward do you have? Do not even people you consider bad do the same?** (47) "**If you greet only your brothers, what more are you doing than others? Do not even those with no knowledge about my Father do the same?** (48) "**Therefore you are to be perfect, as your heavenly Father is perfect.**

8 The Hebrew scriptures (the old testament) are filled with behavior and teachings which contradict the all-important teaching of Joshua of "love your enemies". Several examples would be 1 Sam. 15:1-3; Psalms 139:21-22; Ecclesiastes 3:8; Numbers 31:1-18. In Titus 1:10-11, Paul says, "For there are many rebellious men, empty talkers and deceivers, especially those of the circumcision, **who must be silenced because ..." This clearly breaks the spirit of "love your enemy" and the truth that the heavenly Father is kind and gracious towards all people, even those who hate Him. Perfect Beings don't change so the belief that God commanded all the behavior of harming one's enemies as is presented in the Hebrew scriptures, is not from God, but rather from the men who wrote it and who used God to justify their selfishness or aggression.*

(6:1) "Beware of practicing your righteousness (*things you do to please your heavenly Father*) before men to be noticed by them; otherwise you have no reward with your Father who is in heaven.** (2) **"So when you give to the poor, do not let people know you are doing so, as the hypocrites (*a person who says what others ought to do or not do, but does not do so themselves*) do in the religious buildings and in public, so that they may be honored by men. Truly I say to you, they have their reward in full.** (3) **"But when you give to the poor, do not let your left hand know what your right hand is doing, (4) so that your giving will be in secret; and your Father who sees what is done in secret will reward you.**

(5) **"When you pray, you are not to be like the hypocrites; for they love to stand and pray in the religious buildings and in public so that they may be seen by men. Truly I say to you, they have their reward in full.** (6) **"But you, when you pray, go into your bedroom closet, close your door and pray to your Father who is in secret, and your Father who sees what is done in secret will reward you.***9 (7) **"And when you are praying, do not use meaningless repetition** (*repeat words that are not from your heart*) **as those with no knowledge about my Father do, for they suppose that they will be heard for their many words.** (8) **"So do not be like them; for your Father knows what you need before you ask him.**

*9 *This command of Joshua is nullified by Paul with these teachings – 1 Cor. 14:15, 1 Tim. 2:8. James 5:14 also seems to do so. It was a common religious practice to pray in public, but Joshua makes it perfectly plain that his disciples **don't do that**. To pray in public means to audibly speak to God around people in a public place – please christians, don't deceive yourselves. Any instance in the gospels of Joshua praying "in public" is handled by the principle found in John 11:42. In short, as the Master, he had a right that his student's do not have, which right he needed to exercise in order to teach prayer to his students.*

(9) "Pray, then, in this way: 'Our Father who is in heaven, Hallowed (*set apart from sinful men*) be Your name. (10) 'Your kingdom come. Your will be done, on earth as it is in heaven. (11) 'Give us this day our daily bread. (12) 'And forgive us our debts, as we also have forgiven our debtors. (13) 'And do not lead us to be tested (*a situation in which we can easily do something bad*), but deliver us from evil. (14) "For if you forgive others for their transgressions (*bad things said or done*), your heavenly Father will also forgive you. (15) "But if you do not forgive others, then your Father will not forgive your transgressions.

(16) "Whenever you fast (*choose to not eat*), do not put on a gloomy face as the hypocrites do, for they neglect their appearance so that they will be noticed by men when they are fasting. Truly I say to you, they have their reward in full. (17) "But you, when you fast, anoint (*put on your normal stuff*) your head and wash your face (18) so that your fasting will not be noticed by men, but by your Father who is in secret; and your Father who sees what is done in secret will reward you.

(22) "The eye is the lamp of the body; so then if your eye is clear, your whole body will be full of light. (23) "But if your eye is bad, your whole body will be full of darkness. If then the light that is in you is darkness, how great is the darkness!

(19) "Do not store up for yourselves treasures (*money and material things*) on earth, where moth and rust destroy, and where thieves break in and steal."[10] (20) "But store up for yourselves treasures in heaven, where neither moth nor rust destroys, and where thieves do not break in or steal; (21) for where your treasure is, there your heart will be also. (24) "No one can serve two masters; for either he will hate the one and love the other, or he will be devoted to one and despise the other. You cannot serve God and

wealth. (25) "For this reason I say to you, do not be worried about your life, as to what you will eat or what you will drink; nor for your body, as to what you will put on. Is not life more than food, and the body more than clothing? (26) "Look at the birds of the air, that they do not plant, nor harvest nor gather into barns, and yet your heavenly Father feeds them. Are you not worth much more than they?[*11]

[*10] *The teaching of Paul in Philip 4:12 is used to nullify Joshua's teaching on sharing, giving, striving for material simplicity and living a non-material oriented life.*

[*11] *Joshua teaches that humans are more valuable to God than animals. This does not mean we should be cruel to animals or that they don't have value. A compassionate person will treat animals with compassion, as they are creatures created by the Creator with some ability to sense and feel and know.*

(27) "And who of you by being worried can add a single hour to his life? (28) "And why are you worried about clothing? Observe how the flowers of the field grow; they do not work hard nor do they create their 'cloths', (29) yet I say to you that not even Solomon in all his glory clothed himself like one of these. (30) "But if God so clothes the grass of the field, which is alive today and tomorrow is thrown into the furnace, will he not much more clothe you? You of little faith! (31) "Do not worry then, saying, 'What will we eat?' or 'What will we drink?' or 'What will we wear for clothing?' (32) "For those who have no knowledge of my Father eagerly seek all these things; yet your heavenly Father knows that you need all these things. (33) "But seek first His kingdom and His righteousness, and all these things will be added to you. (34) "So do not worry about tomorrow; for tomorrow will care for itself. Each day has enough trouble of its own.

(7:1) "Do not judge (*condemn them as hopeless in some area*) **so that you will not be judged. (2) "For in the way you judge, you will be judged; and by your standard of measure, it will be measured to you.***12 (3) **"Why do you look at the speck that is in your brother's eye, but do not notice the log that is in your own eye? (4) "Or how can you say to your brother, 'Let me take the speck out of your eye,' and behold, the log is in your own eye? (5) "You hypocrite (***a person who says what others ought to do or not do, but does not do so themselves***), first take the log out of your own eye, and then you will see clearly to take the speck out of your brother's eye. (6) "Do not give what is holy (***set apart by God***) to dogs, and do not throw your pearls before swine (***pigs***), or they will trample them under their feet, and turn and tear you to pieces.**

*12 *Paul's teaching in 1 Cor. 2:15 – "the spiritual man judges all things" – is used to nullify this very important teaching of Joshua. While disciples are slow to judge individual persons, we are diligent to judge if a concept, teaching or belief is right or wrong, true or false as compared to Joshua's teachings. If we don't do this, we will be deceived, something he warned us not to be.*

(7) **"Ask, and it will be given to you; seek, and you will find; knock, and it will be opened to you. (8) "For everyone who asks receives, and he who seeks finds, and to him who knocks it will be opened. (9) "Or what man is there among you who, when his son asks for a loaf (***of bread***), will give him a stone? (10) "Or if he asks for a fish, he will not give him a snake, will he? (11) "If you then, being evil, know how to give good gifts to your children, how much more will your Father who is in heaven give what is good to those who ask him!***13 (12) **"In everything, therefore, treat people the same way you want them to treat you, for this is the law and the prophets (***God's truths contained in some passages in the Jewish scripture***).***14

*13 *Joshua's teaching on human nature – to be 'evil' is to be less than morally and spiritually perfect.*

*14 *Joshua the promised Jewish Messiah (and greater still, the Son of Mankind), says that God's message that He tried to get through the individuals who wrote the Hebrew scriptures, is all summed up on this one saying. Stated another way, if you do this, then you are morally perfect and you have no need of all of the law's humans (including Moses or Paul, etc.) create.*

(13) **"Enter through the narrow gate; for the gate is wide and the way is broad that leads to destruction, and there are many who enter through it.** (14) **"For the gate is small and the way is narrow** (*or difficult*) **that leads to life, and there are few who find it.***15 (15) **"Beware of the false prophets** (*those who claim to speak for God, but don't*)**, who come to you in sheep's clothing** (*accepted religious garb saying they are here to help you*)**, but inwardly are ravenous wolves** (*seeking to destroy you by making themselves your leader*)**. (16) "You will know them by their fruits. Grapes are not gathered from thorn bushes nor plums from weeds, are they? (17) "So every good tree bears good fruit, but the bad tree bears bad fruit. (18) "A good tree cannot produce bad fruit, nor can a bad tree produce good fruit. (19) "Every tree that does not bear good fruit is cut down and thrown into the fire. (20) "So then, you will know them by their fruits. (21) "Not everyone who says to me, 'Lord, Lord,' will enter the kingdom of heaven, but he who does the will of my Father who is in heaven will enter. (22) "Many will say to me on that day** (*the day of judgment, see Matt. 25:31-33*)**, 'Lord, Lord, did we not prophesy** (*speak God's truths*) **in your name, and in your name cast out demons** (*bad angels*)**, and in your name perform many miracles?' (23) "And then I will declare to them, 'I never knew you; Depart From Me, You Who Practice Lawlessness** (*those who say Joshua is their Lord, but don't do what HE says*)**.'**

This saying of Joshua runs completely against the current popular religious belief of the people of the U.S. The people have come to believe the way to life is easy (by grace and no effort), entertaining and comfortable, and most people will enter. What is the cause of the rejection of Joshua's saying? Joshua provides a primary cause in verse 15 – the people looking to others (e.g. Paul or their religious leaders) instead of to Joshua and thus believing wrong things.

(24) **"Therefore everyone who hears these words of mine and acts on them, may be compared to a wise man who built his house on the rock.** (25) **"And the rain fell, and the floods came, and the winds blew and slammed against that house; and yet it did not fall, for it had been founded on the rock.** (26) **"Everyone who hears these words of mine and does not act on them, will be like a foolish man who built his house on the sand.** (27) **"The rain fell, and the floods came, and the winds blew and slammed against that house; and it fell--and great was its fall."** (28) When Joshua had finished these words, the crowds were amazed at his teaching; (29) for he was teaching them as one having authority, and not as their bible experts.

(8:1) When Joshua came down from the mountain, large crowds followed him. (2) And a leper (*person with a very bad skin disease*) came to him and bowed down before him, and said, "Lord, if you are willing, you can heal me." (3) Joshua stretched out his hand and touched him, saying, "**I am willing; be healed.**" And immediately his leprosy was healed. (4) And Joshua said to him, "**See that you tell no one; but go, show yourself to the priest and present the offering that Moses commanded**[*16], **as a testimony to them.**"

[*16] *"Moses commanded", not 'my Father' or God. Many people believe Paul – who says all the teachings and commandments in the bible are God's – instead of believing Joshua and the simple truth given here. The only way a person can know for sure if a teachings or command in the Jewish scripture came from God, is if it matches Joshua's teachings or Joshua validates it by his own words.*

(5) And when Joshua entered Capernaum, a centurion (*roman officer/soldier*) came to him, imploring him, (6) and saying, "Lord, my servant is lying paralyzed at home, fearfully tormented (*in great pain*)." (7) Joshua said to him, "**I will come and heal him.**" (8) But the centurion said, "Lord, I am not worthy for you to come under my roof, but just say the word, and my servant will be healed. (9) "For I also am a man under authority, with soldiers under me; and I say to this one, 'Go!' and he goes, and to another, 'Come!' and he comes, and to my servant, 'Do this!' and he does it." (10) Now when Joshua heard this, he marveled and said to those who were following, "**Truly I say to you, I have not found such great faith with anyone in Israel. (11) "I say to you that many will come from east and west, and sit at the table with Abraham, Isaac and Jacob in the kingdom of heaven; (12) but the sons of the kingdom** (*those physical descendants of Jacob who have no faith*) **will be cast out into the outer darkness; in that place there will be weeping and gnashing of teeth** (*great anger*)." (13) And Joshua said to the centurion, "**Go; it shall be done for you as you have believed.**" And the servant was healed that very moment.

(14) When Joshua came into Peter's home, he saw his mother-in-law lying sick in bed with a fever. (15) He touched her hand, and the fever left her; and she got up and waited on him. (16) When evening came, they brought to him many who were demon-possessed; and he cast out the spirits with a word, and healed all who were ill. (17) This was to fulfill what was spoken through Isaiah the prophet (*a person who speaks God's truths*): "He Himself Took Our Infirmities (*physical weaknesses*) And Carried Away Our Diseases."

(18) Now when Joshua saw a crowd around him, he gave orders to depart to the other side of the sea. (19) Then a bible expert came and said to him, "Teacher, I will follow you wherever you go." (20) Joshua said to him, "**The foxes have holes and the birds of the air have nests, but the Son of Man** (*Joshua's favorite title for himself – it conveys both empathy with men as well as his being The Model for mankind*) **has nowhere to lay His head.**"[*17] (21) Another of the disciples said to him, "Lord, permit me first to go and bury my father." (22) But Joshua said to him, "**Follow me, and allow the** (*spiritually*) **dead to bury their own** (*physical*) **dead.**"[*18]

[*17]   *This saying hardly fits in with the religious leaders who teach that God wants his children to be materially wealthy. Joshua teaches his followers should lead materially simple and selfless lives just as he did and thus they should not store up treasure on earth, where rust and moth destroy.*

[*18]   *Joshua teaches in several places that those who follow him will have to leave their natural or legal families to do so – see Matt. 10. This is a normal part of the difficult way, not some exceptional thing that only happens in certain times, cultures or circumstances.*

(23) When he got into the boat, his disciples followed him. (24) And behold, there arose a great storm on the sea, so that the boat was being covered with the waves; but Joshua himself was asleep. (25) And they came to him and woke him, saying, "Save us, Lord; we are perishing!" (26) He said to them, "**Why are you afraid,**

you men of little faith?" Then he got up and rebuked the winds and the sea, and it became perfectly calm. (27) The men were amazed, and said, 'What kind of a man is this, that even the winds and the sea obey him?'

(28) When he came to the other side into the country of the Gadarenes, two men who were demon-possessed met him as they were coming out of the tombs. They were so extremely violent that no one could pass by that way. (29) And they cried out, saying, "What business do we have with each other, Son of God? Have you come here to torment us before the time?" (30) Now there was a herd of many swine (*pigs*) feeding at a distance from them. (31) The demons (*bad angels*) began to plead with him, saying, "If you are going to cast us out, send us into the herd of swine." (32) And he said to them, "**Go!**" And they came out and went into the swine, and the whole herd rushed down the steep bank into the sea and drowned in the waters. (33) The herdsmen ran away, and went to the city and reported everything, including what had happened to the demon possessed men. (34) And behold, practically the whole city came out to meet Joshua; and when they saw him, they implored him to leave their region.

(9:1) Getting into a boat, Joshua crossed over the sea and came to his own city. (2) And they brought to him a paralytic (*a person whose legs don't work*) lying on a bed. Seeing their faith, Joshua said to the paralytic, "**Take courage, son; your sins are forgiven.**" (3) And some of the bible experts said to themselves, "This fellow blasphemes (*speaks things against God*)." (4) And Joshua knowing their thoughts said, "**Why are you thinking evil in your hearts? (5) "Which is easier, to say, 'Your sins are forgiven,' or to say, 'Get up, and walk'? (6) "But so that you may know that the Son of Man** (*Joshua's favorite title for himself*) **has authority on earth to forgive sins**"--then he said to the paralytic, "**Get up, pick up your bed and go home.**" (7) And he got up and went home. (8) But when the crowds saw this, they were awestruck, and glorified God, who had given such authority to a man.

(9) As Joshua went on from there, he saw a man called Matthew, sitting in the tax collector's booth; and he said to him, "**Follow me!**" And he got up and followed him. (10) Then it happened that as Joshua was sitting at the table in the house, behold, many tax collectors and sinners (*those considered failures or 'losers' by moral people*) came and were dining with Joshua and his disciples. (11) When the religious leaders saw this, they said to his disciples, "Why is your Teacher eating with the traitors and bad people?" (12) But when Joshua heard this, he said, "**It is not those who are healthy who need a doctor, but those who are sick. (13) "But go and learn what this means: 'I Desire Compassion, And <u>Not Sacrifice</u>,' for I did not come to call the righteous, but sinners.**"

(14) Then the disciples of John (*the baptist*) came to him, asking, "Why do we and the religious leaders fast, but your disciples do not fast?" (15) And Joshua said to them, "**The friends of the bridegroom** (*the man getting married*) **cannot be sad as long as the bridegroom is with them, can they? But the days will come when the bridegroom is taken away from them, and then they will fast** (*not eat*). (16) "**But no one puts a**

patch of unshrunk cloth on an old garment; for the patch pulls away from the garment and a worse tear results. (17) **"Nor do people put new wine into old wineskins** (*animal skin containers*)**; otherwise the wineskins burst, and the wine pours out and the wineskins are ruined; but they put new wine into fresh wineskins, and both are preserved."** *19

*19   *A simple contrast between those who listen to Moses and the Jewish scripture versus those who listen to Joshua. A person cannot have two conflicting standards of truth – if they try, both will be torn apart and ruined.*

(18) While he was saying these things to them, a religious leader came and bowed down before him, and said, "My daughter has just died; but come and lay your hand on her, and she will live." (19) Joshua got up and began to follow him, and so did his disciples. (20) And a woman who had been suffering from a hemorrhage (*regular unhealthy bleeding*) for twelve years, came up behind him and touched the fringe of his cloak; (21) for she was saying to herself, "If I only touch his clothing, I will get well." (22) But Joshua turning and seeing her said, **"Daughter, take courage; your faith has made you well."** At once the woman was made well.

(23) When Joshua came into the official's house, and saw the flute-players and the crowd in noisy disorder, (24) he said, **"Leave; for the girl has not died, but is asleep."** And they began laughing at him. (25) But when the crowd had been sent out, he entered and took her by the hand, and the girl got up. (26) This news spread throughout all that land.

(27) As Joshua went on from there, two blind men followed him, crying out, "Have mercy on us, Son of David!" (28) When he entered the house, the blind men came up to him, and Joshua said to them, **"Do you believe that I am able to do this?"** They said to him, "Yes, Lord." (29) Then he touched their eyes, saying, **"It shall be done to you according to your faith."** (30) And their eyes were opened. And Joshua sternly warned them: **"See that no**

one knows about this!" (31) But they went out and spread the news about him throughout all that land.

(32) As they were going out, a mute (*unable to speak*), demon-possessed man was brought to him. (33) After the demon was cast out, the mute man spoke; and the crowds were amazed, and were saying, "Nothing like this has ever been seen in Israel." (34) But the religious leaders were saying, "He casts out the demons by the ruler of the demons."

(35) Joshua was going through all the cities and villages, teaching in their religious buildings and proclaiming the gospel of the kingdom, and healing every kind of disease and every kind of sickness. (36) Seeing the people, he felt compassion for them, because they were distressed and discouraged like sheep without a shepherd. (37) Then he said to his disciples, "**The harvest is plentiful, but the workers are few. (38) "Therefore beseech** (*diligently call upon*) **the Lord of the harvest to send out workers into His harvest.**"

(10:1) Joshua summoned his twelve disciples and gave them authority over unclean spirits, to cast them out, and to heal every kind of disease and every kind of sickness. (2) Now the names of the twelve sent ones (apostles) are these: The first, Simon, who is called Peter, and Andrew his brother; and James the son of Zebedee, and John his brother; (3) Philip and Bartholomew; Thomas and Matthew the tax collector; James the son of Alphaeus, and Thaddaeus; (4) Simon the Zealot, and Judas Iscariot, the one who betrayed him. (5) These twelve Joshua sent out after instructing them: **"Do not go in the place of the people with no knowledge of my Father, and do not enter any city of the Samaritans; (6) but rather go to the lost sheep of the house of Israel. (7) "And as you go, preach, saying, 'The kingdom of heaven is at hand.' (8) "Heal the sick, raise the dead, cleanse** (*heal*) **the lepers, cast out demons. Freely you received, freely give.**[20] (9) **"Do not acquire gold, or silver, or copper for your money belts, (10) or a bag for your journey, or even two coats, or sandals, or a staff; for the worker is worthy of his support. (11) "And whatever city or village you enter, ask who is worthy in it, and stay at his house until you leave that city. (12) "As you enter the house, give it your greeting. (13) "If the house is worthy, give it your blessing of peace. But if it is not worthy, take back your blessing of peace. (14) "Whoever does not receive you, nor heed your words, as you go out of that house or that city, shake the dust off your feet. (15) "Truly I say to you, it will be more tolerable for the land of Sodom and Gomorrah in the day of judgment than for that city.**

[20] *This principle is timeless. Disciples of Joshua do not compel others to pay for the work we do for the King. Nor do we sell things that turn people to our Father or Joshua. As we do the King's work, we can receive help and support. We give what we have freely received – we never insist on being paid for the message or help we bring.*

(16) "Behold, I send you out as sheep in the midst of wolves; so be shrewd as serpents and innocent as doves. (17) "So beware of men, for they will hand you over to the courts and scourge (*whip*) you in their religious buildings; (18) and you will even be brought before governors, kings and presidents for my sake, as a testimony to them and to the non-Jews. (19) "But when they hand you over, do not worry about how or what you are to say; for it will be given you in that hour what you are to say. (20) "For it is not you who speak, but it is the Spirit of your Father who speaks in you.

(21) "Brother will betray brother to death, and a father his child; and children will rise up against parents and cause them to be put to death. (22) "You will be hated by all because of my name, but it is the one who has endured (*lasted*) to the end who will be saved."[*21]

[*21] *A clear picture of part of the difficult way of following Joshua. The disciples of Joshua will be hated by others for our faith, for speaking our Master's words and doing what he says. We are not to give up for if we lose our life in this world, we will gain Life everlasting.*

(23) "But whenever they persecute (*harm you or your property*) you in one city, flee to the next; for truly I say to you, you will not finish going through the cities of Israel until the Son of Man (*Joshua's favorite title for himself*) comes. (24) "A disciple is not above his teacher, nor a servant above his master. (25) "It is enough for the disciple that he becomes like his teacher and the servant like his master. If they have called the head of the house Beelzebub (*the devil*), how much more will they malign (*say bad things about*) the members of his household! (26) "Therefore do not fear them, for there is nothing concealed that will not be revealed, or hidden that will not be known. (27) "What I tell you in the darkness, speak in the light; and what you hear whispered in your ear,

proclaim publicly. (28) "Do not fear those who kill the body but are unable to kill the soul; but rather fear him who is able to destroy both soul and body in hell.*22 (29) "Are not two sparrows sold for a cent? And yet not one of them will fall to the ground apart from your Father. (30) "But the very hairs of your head are all numbered. (31) "So do not fear; you are more valuable than many sparrows.

*22 This saying is the only time Joshua uses fear as a motivator for his followers. Since it is clear that love for our Father and Master is supposed to be our primary motivation for doing what Joshua says, Joshua here provides a secondary motivation if the primary motivation (love) fails. It is better to be temporarily constrained out of fear, than to sin due to our love failing. Please note that Joshua does not say that his Father will destroy a person in hell, but rather He is capable of it. The truth is that people send themselves to destruction against the Father's desire.

(32) "Therefore everyone who speaks of me to people, I will also speak favorably about him before my Father who is in heaven. (33) "But whoever ignores me before men, I will also ignore him before my Father who is in heaven. (34) "Do not think that I came to bring peace on the earth; I did not come to bring peace, but a sword (divide people). (35) "For I came to Set A Man Against His Father, And A Daughter Against Her Mother, And A Daughter-In-Law Against Her Mother-In-Law; (36) And A Man's Enemies Will Be The Members Of His Household. (37) "He who loves father or mother more than me is not worthy of me; and he who loves son or daughter more than me is not worthy of me. (38) "And he who does not take his cross and follow after me is not worthy of me.*23

*23 When a person follows' Joshua, it will divide the natural family. This is not some saying that only applies in certain special times or circumstances or between "christians" and "non-christians". Rather, it is a NORMAL part of the difficult way of following Joshua. Do not deceive yourself and play the coward and not speak and live out Joshua's truths amidst your natural family. If we ignore Joshua before our relatives, then we are not worthy to name him as our Master, and he will ignore us before his Father in heaven.

(39) **"He who has found his life** (*in this world; who becomes successful in the world*) **will lose it** (*all when they die*), **and he who has lost his life** (*in the world*) **for my sake will find it** (*Life Everlasting*).**[24]**

[24]   *A foundational teaching of Joshua on what is required to be his follower. We need to reflect on this saying and look at our life and ask how this is coming to pass. Are we actually losing our life in this world? What have we given up or what are we giving up that the world considers valuable and why? What are we truly living for?*

(40) **"He who receives you receives me, and he who receives me receives him who sent me.** (41) **"He who receives a prophet** (*a person who speaks God's truths*) **in the name of a prophet shall receive a prophet's reward; and he who receives a righteous man** (*a person who does right*) **in the name of a righteous man shall receive a righteous man's reward.** (42) **"And whoever in the name of a disciple gives to one of these little ones even a cup of cold water to drink, truly I say to you, he shall not lose his reward."**

(11:1) When Joshua had finished giving instructions to his twelve disciples, he left from there to teach and preach in their cities. (2) Now when John (*the baptist*), while imprisoned, heard of the works of Joshua, he sent word by his disciples (3) and asked him, "Are You the Expected One, or shall we look for someone else?" (4) Joshua answered and said to them, "**Go and report to John what you hear and see:** (5) **the Blind Receive Sight and the lame walk, the lepers are cleansed and the deaf hear, the dead are raised up, and the Poor Have The Gospel** (*Good News*) **Preached To Them.** (6) **"And blessed is he who is not offended by me or my words."**

(7) As these men were going away, Joshua began to speak to the crowds about John, **"What did you go out into the wilderness to see? A reed shaken by the wind? (8) "But what did you go out to see? A man dressed in soft clothing? Those who wear soft clothing are in kings' palaces! (9) "But what did you go out to see? A prophet** (*a person who speaks God's truths*)**? Yes, I tell you, and one who is more than a prophet. (10) "This is the one about whom it is written, *'behold, I send my messenger ahead of you, who will prepare your way before you.'* (11) "Truly I say to you, among those born of women there has not arisen anyone greater than John the Baptist! Yet the one who is least in the kingdom of heaven is greater than he. (12) "From the days of John the Baptist until now the kingdom of heaven suffers violence, and violent men seek to take it by force. (13) "For all the prophets and the law prophesied until John.**[*25] (14) **"And if you are willing to accept it, John himself is Elijah who was to come. (15) "He who has ears to hear, let him hear.**

[*25] *This saying of Joshua is also captured in Luke 16:16. The meaning is clear – there were two messages preached. The first – up until John - was the message of the Jewish law and prophets. The second, that John started, was the message of the kingdom of heaven of which Joshua is the King – the message to **all mankind**. Therefore the NEW way of the kingdom of heaven has been given by*

*the King and the old way is to be forsaken in favor of the new and superior way –
"the one who is least in the kingdom of heaven is greater than the greatest
prophet of the law and prophets", John the Baptist.*

(16) **"But to what shall I compare this generation** (*the
"generation" is the people alive between Joshua's first coming and
his second*)**? It is like children sitting in the market places,
who call out to the other children,** (17) **and say, 'We played
the flute for you, and you did not dance; we sang a sad
song, and you did not mourn.'** (18) **"For John came
neither eating nor drinking, and they say, 'he has a
demon!'** (19) **"The Son of Man came eating and drinking,
and they say, 'Behold, a man who eats too much and a
drunkard, a friend of traitors and bad people!' Yet wisdom
is proved by her deeds."**

(20) Then Joshua began to denounce (*judge as guilty*) the cities in
which most of his miracles were done, because they did not repent
(*feel truly sorry about your bad behavior and words, and change*).
(21) **"Woe to you, Chorazin! Woe to you, Bethsaida! For if
the miracles had occurred in Tyre and Sidon which
occurred in you, they would have repented long ago and
showed it by their actions.** (22) **"Nevertheless I say to you,
it will be more tolerable for Tyre and Sidon in the day of
judgment than for you.** (23) **"And you, Capernaum, will
not be exalted to heaven, will you? You will descend to
hell; for if the miracles had occurred in Sodom which
occurred in you, it would have remained to this day.** (24)
**"Nevertheless I say to you that it will be more tolerable for
the land of Sodom in the day of judgment, than for you."***26

---

*26 *Joshua teaches that the trunk of the fruit tree (faith in God) is greater than
the fruit of the tree (moral behavior). Those who behaved better (the people of
Capernaum) will have a worse judgment than those who behaved worse (the
immoral people of Sodom). Those who have much shown to them are more
accountable than those who are shown less. The standard and its creator is more
important than execution of that standard. The fact that God exists and has given*

mankind a standard (Joshua) against which they will be held accountable is more important than an individual(s) keeping the standard. Without the right standard, mankind will slide into destruction.

(25) At that time Joshua said, **"I praise You, Father, Lord of heaven and earth, that You have hidden these things from the smart and intelligent and have revealed them to little children.** (26) **"Yes, Father, for this way was well-pleasing in your sight.**[*27]

[*27] *A key principle of Joshua, repeated elsewhere in the form of "unless you change and become like little children, you will not enter the kingdom of God". This principle is a direct rebuke to all the theological and belief rubbish of so-called 'learned' men and their institutions. No books or degrees or religious 'anointing' or deep understanding is necessary to grasp the simple teachings of the Light – rather, a good heart and simple child-like faith are required. Stated another way, education the world's way – especially the religious world – will hinders one's ability to hear the Light.*

(27) **"All things have been handed over to me by my Father; and no one knows the Son except the Father; nor does anyone know the Father except the Son, and anyone to whom the Son wills to reveal him.** (28) **"Come to me, all who are weary and feeling burdened, and I will give you rest.** (29) **"Take my yoke** (*my authority*) **upon you and learn from me, for I am gentle and humble in heart, and You Will Find Rest For Your Souls.** (30) **"For my yoke is easy and my burden is light."**

(12:1) At that time Joshua went through the grain fields on the Sabbath (*the Jew's holy day, which the religious people believed no work at all should be done on*), and his disciples became hungry and began to pick the heads of grain and eat. (2) But when the religious leaders saw this, they said to him, "Look, your disciple's do what is not lawful to do on a Sabbath." (3) But he said to them, **"Have you not read what David did when he became hungry, he and his companions,** (4) **how he entered the house of God, and they ate the consecrated bread** (*special bread intended for a religious ritual*), **which was not lawful for him to eat nor for those with him, but for the priests alone?** (5) **"Or have you not read in the law, that on the Sabbath the priests in the temple break the Sabbath and are innocent?** (6) **"But I say to you that something greater than the temple is here.** (7) **"But if you had known what this means, 'I Desire Compassion, And <u>Not A Sacrifice</u>,' you would not have condemned the innocent.**[*28] (8) **"For the Son of Man is Lord of the Sabbath."**

[*28] *Joshua repeats a plain rebuke to the entire sacrificial religious system of the Jews or any other people group – a rebuke that came from God through men who lived among a people who wrongly relied upon their religious system, just like today. God desires compassion among humans, NOT religion, and especially not men's primitive sacrificial religion, including the 'christ died as a sacrifice' falsehood. Joshua was not a 'sacrifice' to appease his Father – a primitive and base concept created on a concept of a blood-thirsty god. See note 33 in the book of Mark.*

(9) Departing from there, he went into their religious building. (10) And a man was there whose hand was crippled. And they questioned Joshua, asking, "Is it lawful to heal on the Sabbath?"--so that they might trap him. (11) And he said to them, **"What man is there among you who has a sheep, and if it falls into a hole on the Sabbath, will he not take hold of it and lift it out?** (12) **"How much more valuable than is a man than a sheep!**[*29] **So then, it is lawful to do good on the Sabbath."** (13) Then he said to the man, **"Stretch out your hand!"** he

stretched it out, and it was restored to normal, like the other. (14) But the religious leaders went out and conspired against him, as to how they might destroy him.

*29 *Joshua teaches that humans are more valuable to God than animals. This does not give men license to abuse or mistreat animals, but it does rebuke the insanity of treating animals like humans or thinking that animals are intrinsically as valuable as humans. Yes, some humans act worse than animals, yet a human's intrinsic value is still greater than the best animal.*

(15) But Joshua, aware of this, withdrew from there. Many followed him, and he healed them all, (16) and warned them not to tell who he was. (17) This was to fulfill what was spoken through Isaiah the prophet: (18) "Behold, My Servant Whom I Have Chosen; My Beloved In Whom My Soul Is Well-Pleased; I Will Put My Spirit Upon Him, And He Shall Proclaim Justice To The Gentiles (*non-Jew or people with no knowledge of Joshua's Father*). (19) "He Will Not Argue, Nor Cry Out; Nor Will Anyone Hear His Voice In The Streets. (20) "A Battered Reed He Will Not Break Off, And A Smoldering Wick He Will Not Put Out, Until He Leads Justice To Victory. (21) "And In His Name The Gentiles (*non-Jew or people with no knowledge of Joshua's Father*) Will Hope." (22) Then a demon-possessed man who was blind and mute was brought to Joshua, and he healed him, so that the mute man spoke and saw. (23) All the crowds were amazed, and were saying, "This man cannot be the Son of David, can he?" (24) But when the religious leaders heard this, they said, "This man casts out demons only by Beelzebul (*Satan*) the ruler of the demons." (25) And knowing their thoughts Joshua said to them, **"Any kingdom divided against itself fails; and any city or house divided against itself will not stand.***30 (26) **"If Satan casts out Satan, he is divided against himself; how then will his kingdom stand? (27) "If I by Beelzebul cast out demons, by whom do your sons cast them out? For this reason they will be your judges. (28) "But if I cast out demons by the Spirit of God, then the kingdom of God has come upon you. (29) "Or how can anyone enter the strong man's house and carry**

off his property, unless he first ties up the strong man? And then he will take his stuff.

30 The religious system or kingdoms of men – with all the division of sects and denominations, etc. – are divided and thus do not stand. Christendom is an empty pretense whose hypocrisy is increasingly clear to those with eyes to see. Please consider joining with the King - see verse 30 below.

(30) "He who is not with me is against me; and he who does not gather with me scatters. (31) "Therefore I say to you, any sin and blasphemy (*bad things spoken*) **shall be forgiven people, but blasphemy against the Spirit shall not be forgiven. (32) "Whoever speaks a word against the Son of Man, it shall be forgiven him; but whoever speaks against the Holy Spirit, it shall not be forgiven him, either in this age or in the age to come.** (*See Mark 3:30 for understanding*)

(33) "Either make the tree good and its fruit good, or make the tree bad and its fruit bad; for the tree is known by its fruit. (34) "You brood of vipers, how can you, being evil, speak what is good? For the mouth speaks out of that which fills the heart. (35) "The good man brings out of his good treasure what is good; and the evil man brings out of his evil treasure what is evil. (36) "But I tell you that every careless word that people speak, they shall give an accounting for it in the day of judgment. (37) "For by your words you will be justified (*found innocent and gain freedom*)**, and by your words you will be condemned** (*found guilty and experience punishment*)**."** *31

31 Those who ignore Joshua and don't speak of him as their Master – and yet hear or read his words regularly – shall be condemned by their words, or lack thereof. A person does not have to say bad things about Joshua in order to condemn themselves. Rather, they just need to know about him and not make him their Master, and thus their words will be all about the world they love instead of about the Father and Master they claim to love.

(38) Then some of the bible experts and religious leaders said to him, "Teacher, we want to see a sign from you." (39) But he answered and said to them, **"An evil and adulterous generation**[*32] **desires a sign; and yet no sign will be given to it but the sign of Jonah the prophet** (*a person who speaks God's truths*); (40) **for just as Jonah Was Three Days And Three Nights In The Belly Of The Sea Creature, so will the Son of Man be three days and three nights in the heart of the earth** (*grave*). (41) **"The men of Nineveh will stand up with this generation at the judgment, and will condemn it because they repented at the preaching of Jonah; and behold, something greater than Jonah is here.** (42) **"The Queen of the South will rise up with this generation at the judgment and will condemn it, because she came from the ends of the earth to hear the wisdom of Solomon; and behold, something greater than Solomon is here.**

[*32] *"Generation" - those alive between Joshua's first coming and his second. The sign has been given – his defeating or overcoming physical death or resurrection.*

(43) **"Now when the unclean spirit goes out of a man, it passes through waterless places seeking rest, and does not find it.** (44) **"Then it says, 'I will return to my house from which I came'; and when it comes, it finds it unoccupied** (*the Spirit of God is not there*), **swept, and put in order** (*the person found religious morality*).[*33] (45) **"Then it goes and takes along with it seven other spirits more wicked than itself, and they go in and live there; and the last state of that man** (*religious*) **becomes worse than the first** (*struggling with outward sin*). **That is the way it will also be with this evil generation."**

[*33] *"Don't smoke, don't drink, don't to drugs" religious morality can never substitute for the life-changing power His Spirit brings – true love, peace, compassion, righteousness, etc. - real, lasting, meaningful change to the human heart and thus the human condition.*

(46) While he was still speaking to the crowds, behold, his mother and brothers were standing outside, seeking to speak to him. (47) Someone said to him, "Behold, your mother and your brothers are standing outside seeking to speak to you." (48) But Joshua answered the one who was telling him and said, **"Who is my mother and who are my brothers?"** (49) And stretching out his hand toward his disciples, he said, **"Behold my mother and my brothers!** (50) **"For whoever does the will of my Father who is in heaven, he is my brother and sister and mother."** *34

*34 *Clear words from the Master but only for those with ears to hear. Another clear teaching that says the natural family is secondary in the Kingdom of God. Who is your family, truly? Who do you spend your time with? Who do you want to spend your time with? Who do you share your daily life with? That is your family. And what is the bond for that family? Is it really Joshua of Nazareth and his Father? "Many will come in my name and deceive many".*

(13:1) That day Joshua went out of the house and was sitting by the sea. (2) And large crowds gathered to him, so he got into a boat and sat down, and the whole crowd was standing on the beach. (3) And he spoke many things to them in parables (*stories with hidden meanings*), saying, **"Behold, the farmer went out to plant seed; (4) and as he planted, some seeds fell beside the road, and the birds came and ate them up. (5) "Others fell on the rocky places, where they did not have much soil; and immediately they sprang up, though they had no depth of soil. (6) "But when the sun had risen, they were scorched; and because they had no root, they withered away. (7) "Others fell among the thorns, and the thorns came up and choked them out. (8) "Still others fell on the good soil and yielded a crop, some a hundredfold, some sixty, and some thirty. (9) "He who has ears, let him hear."**

(10) And the disciples came and said to him, "Why do you speak to them in parables?" (11) Joshua answered them, **"To you it has been granted to know the mysteries of the kingdom of heaven, but to them it has not been granted. (12) "For whoever has, to him more shall be given, and he will have an abundance; but whoever does not have, even what he has shall be taken away from him. (13) "Therefore I speak to them in parables; because while seeing they do not see, and while hearing they do not hear, nor do they understand. (14) "In their case the prophecy of Isaiah is being fulfilled, which says, *'You Will Keep On Hearing, But Will Not Understand; You Will Keep On Seeing, But Will Not Perceive; (15) For The Heart Of This People Has Become Dull, With Their Ears They Scarcely Hear, And They Have Closed Their Eyes, Otherwise They Would See With Their Eyes, Hear With Their Ears, And Understand With Their Heart And Return, And I Would Heal Them.'***

(16) **"But blessed are your eyes, because they see; and your ears, because they hear. (17) "For truly I say to you that**

many prophets (*a person who speaks God's truths*) **and righteous men desired to see what you see, and did not see it, and to hear what you hear, and did not hear it.** (18) **"Hear then the parable of the sower.** (19) **"When anyone hears the word of the kingdom and does not understand it, the evil one comes and snatches away what has been planted in his heart. This is the one on whom seed fell beside the road.** (20) **"The one on whom seed was thrown on the rocky places, this is the person who hears the word and immediately receives it with joy;** (21) **yet he has no firm root in himself, but is only temporary, and when trouble or hardship arises because of the word, immediately he falls away.** (22) **"And the one on whom seed was sown among the thorns, this is the person who hears the word, and the worry of the world and the deceitfulness of wealth choke the word, and it becomes unfruitful.** (23) **"And the one on whom seed was sown on the good soil, this is the man who hears the word and understands it; who indeed bears fruit and brings forth, some a hundredfold, some sixty, and some thirty."**

(24) Joshua presented another parable to them, saying, **"The kingdom of heaven may be compared to a man who planted good seed in his field.** (25) **"But while his men were sleeping, his enemy came and planted tares** (*weeds that look like wheat*) **among the wheat, and went away.** (26) **"But when the wheat sprouted and bore grain, then the tares became evident also.** (27) **"The servants of the landowner came and said to him, 'Sir, did you not plant good seed in your field? How then does it have tares?'** (28) **"And he said to them, 'An enemy has done this!' The servants said to him, 'Do you want us, then, to go and gather them up?'** (29) **"But he said, 'No; for while you are gathering up the tares, you may uproot the wheat with them.** (30) **'Allow both to grow together until the harvest; and in the time of the harvest I will say to the reapers** (*those who gather the wheat*)**, "First gather up the tares and**

bind them in bundles to burn them up; but gather the wheat into my barn."

(31) He presented another parable to them, saying, "**The kingdom of heaven is like a mustard seed, which a man took and planted in his field;** (32) **and this is smaller than all other seeds, but when it is full grown, it is larger than the garden plants and becomes a tree, so that the birds of the air come and nest in its branches.**"

(33) He spoke another parable to them, "**The kingdom of heaven is like leaven** (*yeast*)**, which a woman took and hid in three pints of flour until it was all leavened.**" (34) All these things Joshua spoke to the crowds in parables, and he did not speak to them without a parable. (35) This was to fulfill what was spoken through the prophet: "I Will Open My Mouth In Parables; I Will Utter Things Hidden Since The Foundation Of The World."

(36) Then he left the crowds and went into the house. And his disciples came to him and said, "Explain to us the parable of the tares of the field." (37) And he said, "**The one who plants the good seed is the Son of Man,** (38) **and the field is the world; and as for the good seed, these are the sons of the kingdom; and the tares are the sons of the evil one;** (39) **and the enemy who sowed them is the devil, and the harvest is the end of the age; and the reapers are angels.** (40) **"So just as the tares are gathered up and burned with fire, so shall it be at the end of the age.** (41) **"The Son of Man will send forth His angels, and they will gather out of His kingdom all stumbling blocks** (*people who cause others to sin*)**, and those who commit lawlessness** (*don't obey his commands nor keep his teachings*)**,** (42) **and will throw them into the furnace of fire; in that place there will be weeping and great anger.** (43) **"Then The Righteous Will Shine Forth As The Sun in the kingdom of their Father. He who has ears, let him hear!**

(44) **"The kingdom of heaven is like a treasure hidden in the field, which a man found and hid again; and from joy over it he goes and sells all that he has and buys that field.**

(45) **"Again, the kingdom of heaven is like a jewelry store owner seeking fine pearls, (46) and upon finding one pearl of great value, he went and sold all that he had and bought it.**

(47) **"Again, the kingdom of heaven is like a drag-net cast into the sea, and gathering fish of every kind; (48) and when it was filled, they drew it up on the beach; and they sat down and gathered the good fish into containers, but the bad fish they threw away. (49) "So it will be at the end of the age; the angels will come forth and take out the wicked from among the righteous, (50) and will throw them into the furnace of fire; in that place there will be weeping and great anger. (51) "Have you understood all these things?"** They said to him, "Yes." (52) And Joshua said to them, **"Therefore every writer who has become a disciple of the kingdom of heaven is like a head of a household, who brings out of his treasure things new and old."**

(53) When Joshua had finished these parables, he departed from there. (54) He came to his hometown and began teaching them in their religious building, so that they were astonished, and said, "Where did this man get this wisdom and these miraculous powers? (55) "Is not this the carpenter's son? Is not his mother called Mary, and His brothers, James and Joseph and Simon and Judas? (56) "And his sisters, are they not all with us? Where then did this man get all these things?" (57) And they took offense at him. But Joshua said to them, **"A prophet** (*a person who speaks God's truths*) **is not without honor except in his hometown and in his own household."** *35 (58) And he did not do many miracles there because of their unbelief.

*35 *A man or woman who meets Joshua and becomes his disciple and thus starts living differently and speaking differently and gives Joshua the credit will be an offense to their natural family. See Matt. 10:33-38 and Matt. 12:46-50.*

(14:1) At that time Herod the tetrarch (*Roman ruler of that area*) heard the news about Joshua, (2) and said to his servants, "This is John the Baptist; he has risen from the dead, and that is why miraculous powers are at work in him." (3) For when Herod had John arrested, he bound him and put him in prison because of Herodias, the wife of his brother Philip. (4) For John had been saying to him, "It is not lawful for you to have her." (5) Although Herod wanted to put him to death, he feared the crowd, because they regarded John as a prophet. (6) But when Herod's birthday came, the daughter of Herodias danced before them and pleased Herod, (7) so much that he promised with an oath to give her whatever she asked. (8) Having been prompted by her mother, she said, "Give me here on a platter the head of John the Baptist." (9) Although he was grieved, the king commanded it to be given because of his oaths, and because of his dinner guests. (10) He sent and had John beheaded in the prison. (11) And his head was brought on a platter and given to the girl, and she brought it to her mother. (12) His disciples came and took away the body and buried it; and they went and reported to Joshua.

(13) Now when Joshua heard about John, he withdrew from there in a boat to a secluded place by himself; and when the people heard of this, they followed him on foot from the cities. (14) When he went ashore, he saw a large crowd, and felt compassion for them and healed their sick. (15) When it was evening, the disciples came to him and said, "This place is remote and the hour is already late; so send the crowds away, that they may go into the villages and buy food for themselves." (16) But Joshua said to them, "**They do not need to go away; you give them something to eat!**" (17) They said to him, "We have here only five loaves and two fish." (18) And he said, "**Bring them here to me**." (19) Ordering the people to sit down on the grass, he took the five loaves and the two fish, and looking up toward heaven, he blessed the food, and breaking the loaves he gave them to the disciples, and the disciples gave them to the crowds, (20) and they all ate and were satisfied. They picked up what was left over of the broken pieces, twelve full baskets. (21)

There were about five thousand men who ate, besides women and children.

(22) Immediately he made the disciples get into the boat and go ahead of him to the other side, while he sent the crowds away. (23) After he had sent the crowds away, he went up on the mountain by himself to pray; and when it was evening, he was there alone. (24) But the boat was already a long distance from the land, battered by the waves; for the wind was strong. (25) And in the fourth watch of the night Joshua came to them, walking on the sea. (26) When the disciples saw him walking on the sea, they were terrified, and said, "It is a ghost!" And they cried out in fear. (27) But immediately Joshua spoke to them, saying, "**Take courage, it is I; do not be afraid**." (28) Peter said to him, "Lord, if it is you, command me to come to you on the water." (29) And he said, "**Come!**" And Peter got out of the boat, and walked on the water and came toward Joshua. (30) But seeing the wind, he became frightened, and beginning to sink, he cried out, "Lord, save me!" (31) Immediately Joshua reached out his hand and took hold of him, and said to him, "**You of little faith, why did you doubt?**" (32) When they got into the boat, the wind stopped. (33) And those who were in the boat bowed before him, saying, "You are certainly God's Son!"

(34) When they had crossed over, they came to land at Gennesaret. (35) And when the men of that place recognized him, they sent word into all that surrounding district and brought to him all who were sick; (36) and they implored him that they might just touch the fringe of his clothes; and as many as touched it were cured.

(15:1) Then some religious leaders and bible experts came to Joshua from Jerusalem and said, (2) "Why do your disciples break our religious traditions? For they do not wash their hands when they eat bread." (3) And he answered and said to them, "**Why do you yourselves break the commandment of God for the sake of your tradition?** (4) "**For** (*you believe*) **God said, 'Honor Your Father and Mother,' And, 'He Who Speaks Evil Of Father Or Mother Is To Be Put To Death.'** (5) "**But then you say, 'Whoever says to his father or mother, "Whatever** (*material things*) **I have that would help you has been given to God,"** (6) **he is not to honor his father or his mother.' And by this you make of no effect** (*nullify or cancel*) **the word of God for the sake of your tradition.** (7) "**You hypocrites** (*a person who says what others ought to do or not do, but does not do so themselves*), **rightly did Isaiah prophesy of you:** (8) '**This People Honors Me With Their Lips, But Their Heart Is Far Away From Me.** (9) '**But In Vain** (*useless manner*) **Do They Worship Me, Teaching As Doctrines** (*needed beliefs*) **The Precepts** (*teachings*) **Of Men.**'" *36

*36 *This teaching about how people cancel out or nullify the desires of God as captured by those who spoke His desires, has not slowed down one bit over the centuries. Part of the purpose of the bible-religious system is to drown out Joshua's voice so that their bible doctrine and theology will nullify Joshua's teachings. For example, Paul says 'fight in nations wars if the government says you have to' (Rom. 13), whereas Jesus teaches, "love your enemies".*

(10) After Joshua called the crowd to him, he said to them, "**Hear and understand.** (11) "**It is not what enters into the mouth** (*food*) **that makes a man dirty before God, but what proceeds out of the mouth, this makes the man dirty before God.**" (12) Then the disciples came and said to him, "Do you know that the religious leaders were offended when they heard this statement?" (13) But he answered and said, "**Every plant which my heavenly Father did not plant shall be uprooted.** (14) "**Let them alone; they are blind guides of the blind.**

And if a blind man guides a blind man, both will fall into a pit." *37

*37 *Religious leaders are blind guides. A religious leader is simply someone who says, acts or implies that you need them in order to know God and what God wants for your life. What don't you understand about "Let them alone"? The average religious person will say, 'oh, my pastor/priest/minister etc. is not blind' and thus deceive themselves for Joshua says they are.*

(15) Peter said to him, "Explain the parable to us." (16) Joshua said, "**Are you still lacking in understanding also?** (17) "**Do you not understand that everything that goes into the mouth passes into the stomach, and is eliminated?** (18) "**But the things that proceed out of the mouth come from the heart, and those make a man dirty before God.** (19) "**For out of the heart come evil thoughts, murders, adulteries** (*a married person having sex with someone other than their spouse*), **fornications** (*touching another person in a sexual way before marriage*), **thefts, false witness** (*lying*), **slanders** (*saying false things about someone*). (20) "**These are the things which make a man's heart dirty; but to eat with unwashed hands does not make a man dirty before God.**" *38

*38 *A perfect example of a tradition of men (Moses' rule) nullifying Joshua's teachings. Joshua plainly says it is not what a person eats that make them displeasing (unclean) to God, rather it is the sins which come out of the heart. And yet there are millions of people who say they 'believe in christ' who won't eat things believing that what they eat will make them unclean!*

(21) Joshua went away from there, and withdrew into the district of Tyre and Sidon. (22) And a Canaanite woman from that region came out and began to cry out, saying, "Have mercy on me, Lord, Son of David; my daughter is cruelly demon-possessed." (23) But he did not answer her a word. And his disciples came and implored him, saying, "Send her away, because she keeps shouting after us." (24) But he answered and said to her, "**I was sent only to the**

lost sheep of the house of Israel." (25) But she came and began to bow down before him, saying, "Lord, help me!" (26) And he answered and said, "**It is not good to take the children's bread and throw it to the little dogs**." (27) But she said, "Yes, Lord; but even the dogs feed on the crumbs which fall from their masters' table." (28) Then Joshua said to her, "**O woman, your faith is great; it shall be done for you as you wish**." And her daughter was healed at once.

(29) Departing from there, Joshua went along by the Sea of Galilee, and having gone up on the mountain, he was sitting there. (30) And large crowds came to him, bringing with them those who were lame (*could not walk*), crippled, blind, mute (*could not speak*), and many others, and they laid them down at his feet; and he healed them. (31) So the crowd marveled as they saw the mute speaking, the crippled restored, and the lame walking, and the blind seeing; and they glorified the God of Israel. (32) And Joshua called his disciples to him, and said, "**I feel compassion for the people, because they have remained with me now three days and have nothing to eat; and I do not want to send them away hungry, for they might faint on the way**." (33) The disciples said to him, "Where would we get so many loaves in this desolate place to satisfy such a large crowd?" (34) And Joshua said to them, "**How many loaves do you have?**" And they said, "Seven, and a few small fish." (35) And he directed the people to sit down on the ground; (36) and he took the seven loaves and the fish; and giving thanks, he broke them and started giving them to the disciples, and the disciples gave them to the people. (37) And they all ate and were satisfied, and they picked up what was left over of the broken pieces, seven large baskets full. (38) And those who ate were four thousand men, besides women and children. (39) And sending away the crowds, Joshua got into the boat and came to the region of Magadan.

(16:1) The religious leaders came up, and testing Joshua, they asked him to show them a sign from heaven. (2) But he replied to them, **"When it is evening, you say, 'It will be fair weather, for the sky is red.'** (3) **"And in the morning, 'There will be a storm today, for the sky is red and threatening.' Do you know how to tell the appearance of the sky, but cannot tell the signs of the times?** (4) **"An evil and adulterous** (*unfaithful*) **generation seeks after a sign; and a sign will not be given it, except the sign of Jonah** (*Jonah was contained-inactive for three days*)." And he left them and went away.

(5) And the disciples came to the other side of the sea, but they had forgotten to bring any bread. (6) And Joshua said to them, **"Watch out and beware of the leaven** (*yeast*) **of the religious leaders."** (7) They began to discuss this among themselves, saying, "He said that because we did not bring any bread." (8) But Joshua, aware of this, said, **"You men of little faith, why do you discuss among yourselves that you have no bread?** (9) **"Do you not yet understand or remember the five loaves of the five thousand, and how many baskets full you picked up?** (10) **"Or the seven loaves of the four thousand, and how many large baskets full you picked up?** (11) **"How is it that you do not understand that I did not speak to you concerning bread? But beware of the leaven** (*teachings*) **of the religious leaders."** *39 (12) Then they understood that he did not say to beware of the leaven of bread, but of the teachings of the religious leaders.

*39 *Nothing has changed. Beware of the teachings of the religious leaders who nullify both Joshua's teachings and his leadership with their actions and with their many words, and thus substitute themselves as your leader and teacher. Dear reader, this is not referring to flagrant deceivers, but rather the average bible teacher and pastor/minister...religious leaders.*

(13) Now when Joshua came into the district of Caesarea Philippi, he was asking His disciples, **"Who do people say that the Son of Man is** (*or, I am*)**?"** (14) And they said, "Some say John the

Baptist; and others, Elijah; but still others, Jeremiah, or one of the prophets." (15) He said to them, "**But who do you say that I am?**" (16) Simon Peter answered, "**You are the Messiah, the Son of the living God.**" (17) And Joshua said to him, "**Blessed are you, Simon Barjona, because flesh and blood did not reveal this to you, but my Father who is in heaven. (18) "I also say to you that you are Peter, and upon this rock** (*possibly pointing to the earth*) **I will build my church** (*my Family of people called out of the world*)**; and the gates of Hades will not overpower it. (19) "I will give you the keys of the kingdom of heaven; and whatever you bind on earth shall have been bound in heaven, and whatever you loose on earth shall have been loosed in heaven.**"*40 (20) Then he warned the disciples that they should tell no one that he was the Messiah.

*40   *Many religious people and their leaders use this passage to say that Joshua made Peter his sole leader or representative on earth. This view is wrong for the following reasons. First, Joshua says that binding and loosing is available to all his disciples in Matt. 18:18-19. Second, Joshua says that only he is to be the leader of his followers (Matt. 23:8-12). Third, Peter failed to do what he ought to have done several times – denying Joshua for example. Peter is not the sinless Son of Man, and thus is an inadequate leader for men's souls as is any man or woman. Only the Good Shepherd is worthy to be the leader of our souls and only he is he represents the owner of the sheep.*

(21) From that time Joshua began to show his disciples that he must go to Jerusalem, and suffer many things from the leaders of Israel (*religious and political*), and be killed, and be raised up on the third day. (22) Peter took him aside and began to rebuke him, saying, "God forbid it, Lord! This shall never happen to you." (23) But he turned and said to Peter, "**Get behind me, Satan! You are a stumbling block to me; for you are not setting your mind on God's interests, but man's.**" (24) Then Joshua said to his disciples, "**If anyone wishes to come after me, he must deny himself, and take up his cross and follow me. (25) "For whoever wishes to save his life will lose it; but**

whoever loses his life for my sake will find it. (26) "For what will it profit a man if he gains the whole world and forfeits (*loses or gives away*) his soul? Or what will a man give in exchange for his soul? *⁴¹ (27) "For the Son of Man is going to come in the glory of his Father with his angels, and Will Then Repay Every Man According To His Deeds (*what he has done*). (28) "Truly I say to you, there are some of those who are standing here who will not taste death until they see the Son of Man (*Joshua's favorite title for himself*) coming in his kingdom (*see the following verses*)."

*⁴¹ *Sadly, people don't value their souls because they have been deceived into thinking they don't have one. All of the wealth and material things on the earth will be of no comfort to a person after a person leaves their body and they see what they threw away (Life Everlasting) in exchange for what they love in the world...a few years of pleasure, material comfort or money etc.*

(17:1) Six days later (*after the saying of Joshua regarding seeing the Son of Man coming in his kingdom*) Joshua took with him Peter and James and John his brother, and led them up on a high mountain by themselves. (2) And he was transfigured (*he changed appearance*) before them; and His face shone like the sun, and His garments became as white as light (*perhaps the preview of his coming in his kingdom*). (3) And behold, Moses and Elijah appeared to them, talking with him. (4) Peter said to Joshua, "Lord, it is good for us to be here; if you wish, I will make three tabernacles (*small shelters*) here, one for you, and one for Moses, and one for Elijah."

(5) While he (*Peter*) was still speaking, a bright cloud overshadowed them, and behold, a voice out of the cloud said, **"This is My beloved Son, with whom I am well-pleased; listen to <u>HIM</u>!** *42 (6) When the disciples heard this, they fell face down to the ground and were terrified. (7) And Joshua came to them and touched them and said, **"Get up, and do not be afraid."** (8) And lifting up their eyes, they saw no one except Joshua himself alone. (9) As they were coming down from the mountain, Joshua commanded them, saying, **"Tell the vision to no one until the Son of Man has risen from the dead."** (10) And his disciples asked him, "Why then do the bible experts say that Elijah must come first?" (11) And he answered and said, **"Elijah is coming and will restore all things; (12) but I say to you that Elijah already came, and they did not recognize him, but did to him whatever they wished. So also the Son of Man is going to suffer at their hands."** (13) Then the disciples understood that he had spoken to them about John the Baptist.

*42 *The great error of mankind. The Creator Himself spoke and said, "Listen to my Son". And yet humanity goes on its own way, rejecting that plea of our Designer, and substituting just about anything or anyone – a book, the bible; Moses; Paul, pastor so-and-so, etc. – for the one true leader appointed by the Creator, the Light of the world. "And this is the condemnation, that human's love the darkness rather than the Light" – see John 3:19.*

(14) When they came to the crowd, a man came up to Joshua, falling on his knees before him and saying, (15) "Lord, have mercy on my son, for he acts crazy and is very ill; for he often falls into the fire and often into the water. (16) "I brought him to your disciples, and they could not cure him." (17) And Joshua answered and said, **"You unbelieving and corrupted generation, how long shall I be with you? How long shall I put up with you? Bring him here to me**." (18) And Joshua rebuked him, and the demon came out of him, and the boy was cured at once. (19) Then the disciples came to Joshua privately and said, "Why could we not drive it out?" (20) And he said to them, **"Because of the littleness of your faith; for truly I say to you, if you have faith the size of a** (*small*) **mustard seed, you will say to this mountain, 'Move from here to there,' and it will move; and nothing will be impossible to you**".

(22) And while they were gathering together in Galilee, Joshua said to them, **"The Son of Man is going to be delivered into the hands of men; (23) and they will kill him, and he will be raised on the third day**." And they were deeply grieved.

(24) When they came to Capernaum, those who collected the fifty dollar tax came to Peter and said, "Does your teacher not pay the tax?" (25) He said, "Yes." And when he came into the house, Joshua spoke to him first, saying, **"What do you think, Simon? From whom do the rulers of the world collect tolls or taxes - from their sons or from strangers?"** (26) When Peter said, "From strangers," Joshua said to him, **"Then the sons are exempt. (27) "However, so that we do not give them cause to arrest us, go to the sea and throw in a hook, and take the first fish that comes up; and when you open its mouth, you will find a gold coin. Take that and give it to them for you and me."**

(18:1) At that time the disciples came to Joshua and said, "Who then is greatest in the kingdom of heaven?" (2) And he called a child to himself and set him before them, (3) and said, "**Truly I say to you, unless you are converted** (*changed*) **and become like children, you will not enter the kingdom of heaven.** (4) "**Whoever then humbles** (*does not think himself important*) **himself as this child, he is the greatest in the kingdom of heaven.** (5) "**And whoever receives one such child in my name receives me;** (6) **but whoever causes one of these little ones who believe in me to stumble** (*or sin*), **it would be better for him to have a heavy millstone** (*huge donut shaped rock*) **hung around his neck, and to be drowned in the depth of the sea.** (7) "**Woe to the world because of its stumbling blocks** (*sinful ways*)! **For it is inevitable that stumbling blocks come; but woe to that man through whom the stumbling block comes!** (8) "**If your hand or your foot causes you to stumble** (*sin*), **cut it off and throw it from you; it is better for you to enter life crippled or lame, than to have two hands or two feet and be cast into the eternal fire.** (9) "**If your eye causes you to stumble, pluck it out and throw it from you. It is better for you to enter life with one eye, than to have two eyes and be cast into the fiery hell.** (10) "**See that you do not despise one of these little ones, for I say to you that their angels in heaven continually see the face of my Father who is in heaven.**"*43

---

*43 *This whole passage from verse 1 is in the context of children. First, we must become as a simple, humble child in order to enter the kingdom of heaven – it is not some complex, intellectual, theological exercise – rather it is a simple thing of the heart called faith. Second, if adults sin against children, those adults will be held accountable and their judgment will be harsh.*

(12) "**What do you think? If any man has a hundred sheep, and one of them has gone astray, does he not leave the ninety-nine on the mountains and go and search for the one that is straying?** (13) "**If it turns out that he finds it, truly I say to you, he rejoices over it more than over the**

ninety-nine which have not gone astray. (14) "So it is not the will of your Father who is in heaven that one of these little ones perish.

(15) "If your brother sins, go and show him his fault in private; if he listens to you, you have won your brother. (16) "But if he does not listen to you, take one or two more with you, so that By The Mouth Of Two Or Three Witnesses Every Fact May Be Confirmed. (17) "If he refuses to listen to them, tell it to the church (*spiritual Family of called out one's*); and if he refuses to listen even to the church (*spiritual Family*), let him be to you as a person who has no knowledge about my Father and a traitor. (18) "Truly I say to you, whatever you bind on earth shall have been bound in heaven; and whatever you loose on earth shall have been loosed in heaven. (19) "Again I say to you, that if two of you agree on earth about anything that they may ask, it shall be done for them by my Father who is in heaven. (20) "For where two or three have gathered together in my name, I am there with them." *44

*44 *Here Joshua lays out a critical dynamic of family life. The family are the called out ones (the 'church') living together as a family as love would dictate; not as acquaintances who are part of the same religious organization. When a person sins and will not express remorse, the escalation pattern is laid out with the final step being the family removes trust from the individual.*

(21) Then Peter came and said to him, "Lord, how often shall my brother sin against me and I forgive him? Up to seven times?" (22) Joshua said to him, "**I do not say to you, up to seven times, but up to seventy times seven. (23) "For this reason the kingdom of heaven may be compared to a king who wished to settle accounts with his servants. (24) "When he had begun to settle them, one who owed him one-hundred thousand dollars was brought to him. (25) "But since he did not have the means to repay, his lord commanded him to be sold, along with his wife and children and all that he**

had, and repayment to be made. (26) "So the servant fell to the ground and lay on his face before him, saying, 'Have patience with me and I will repay you everything.' (27) "And the lord of that servant felt compassion and released him and forgave him the debt.

(28) "But that servant went out and found one of his fellow servants who owed him fifty dollars; and he grabbed him and began to choke him, saying, 'Pay back what you owe.' (29) "So his fellow servant fell to the ground and began to plead with him, saying, 'Have patience with me and I will repay you.' (30) "But he was unwilling and went and threw him in prison until he should pay back what was owed. (31) "So when his fellow servants saw what had happened, they were deeply grieved and came and reported to their lord all that had happened. (32) "Then summoning him, his lord said to him, 'You wicked servant, I forgave you all that debt because you pleaded with me. (33) 'Should you not also have had mercy on your fellow servant, in the same way that I had mercy on you?' (34) "And his lord, moved with anger, handed him over to the cruel jailers until he should repay all that was owed him. (35) "My heavenly Father will also do the same to you, if each of you does not forgive his brother from your heart."

(19:1) When Joshua had finished these words, he departed from Galilee and came into the region of Judea beyond the Jordan; (2) and large crowds followed him, and he healed them there. (3) Some religious leaders came to Joshua, testing him and asking, "Is it lawful for a man to divorce his wife for any reason at all?" (4) And he answered and said, "**Have you not read that He who created them from the beginning Made Them Male And Female, (5) and said, 'For This Reason A Man Shall Leave His Father And Mother And Be Joined To His Wife, And The Two Shall Become One Flesh'? (6) "So they are no longer two, but one flesh. What therefore God has joined together, let no man separate.**" *45 (7) They said to him, "Why then did Moses command to Give Her A Certificate Of Divorce And Send Her Away?" (8) He said to them, "**Because of your hardness of heart Moses** (not God) **permitted you to divorce your wives; but from the beginning it has not been this way. (9) "And I say to you, whoever divorces his wife, except for her sexual impurity before marriage, and marries another woman commits adultery** (*"adultery" is a married person having sex with someone other than their spouse*)." (10) The disciples said to him, "If the relationship of the man with his wife is like this, it is better not to marry." (11) But he said to them, "**Not all men can accept this statement, but only those to whom it has been given. (12) "For there are eunuchs** (*men without testicles*) **who were born that way from their mother's womb; and there are eunuchs who were made eunuchs by men; and there are also eunuchs who made themselves eunuchs for the sake of the kingdom of heaven.** *46 **He who is able to accept this, let him accept it.**"

---

*45   *Here, Joshua validates two important things. First, that God is the Creator of the genders - the One who created sexual reproduction. Second, that 'marriage' (the joining of two people) consists of a "Man" and his "Wife", and no other alternatives. The following teachings make it clear that this joining of a husband and a wife is to be permanent; that divorce is the result of "a hard heart(s)"; that to divorce a spouse wrongly and to take another spouse is to commit adultery.*

After the teachings on the importance of faithfulness to one's spouse, Joshua provides another way for a person to live other than marriage – abstain from sexual expression. So, only two options are given. Be faithful to your husband or wife for the duration of your life, or abstain from sexual relations (eunuch). Joshua's other teachings on sexual immorality fit perfectly with the teaching that only a "husband and wife" comprise the one-flesh union in which sexual expression is blessed by the heavenly Father. All expressions of a sexual nature outside of the "husband and wife" relationship make us unclean, according to Joshua.

(13) Then some children were brought to him so that he might lay his hands on them and pray; and the disciples rebuked them. (14) But Joshua said, "**Let the children alone, and do not hinder them from coming to me; for the kingdom of heaven belongs to such as these.**" (15) After laying His hands on them, he departed from there.

(16) And someone came to him and said, "Teacher, what good thing shall I do that I may obtain eternal life?" (17) And he said to him, "**Why are you asking me about what is good? There is only One who is good; but if you wish to enter into Life, keep the commandments.**" (18) Then he said to him, "Which ones?" And Joshua said, "**You Shall Not Commit Murder; You Shall Not Commit Adultery** (*"adultery" is a married person having sex with someone other than their spouse*)**; You Shall Not Steal; You Shall Not Bear False Witness** (*lie for self-gain or to avoid justice*)**; (19) Honor Your Father And Mother; And You Shall Love Your Neighbor As Yourself.**" (20) The young man said to him, "All these things I have kept; what am I still lacking?" (21) Joshua said to him, "**If you wish to be complete, go and sell your possessions and give to the poor, and you will have treasure in heaven; and come, follow me.**" (22) But when the young man heard this statement, he went away very sad; for he was one who owned much property. (23) And Joshua said to his disciples, "**Truly I say to you, it is hard for a rich man to enter the kingdom of heaven. (24) "Again I say to you, it is**

easier for a camel to go through the eye of a needle, than for a rich man to enter the kingdom of God." *47 (25) When the disciples heard this, they were very surprised and said, "Then who can be saved?" (26) And looking at them Joshua said to them, **"With people this is impossible** (*to save one's self apart from God*), **but with God all things are possible** (*for He made the sure Way, follow Joshua*)."

*47   *This teaching is merely an example of Joshua's basic teaching on being his follower – we must lose our life in this world in order to find Life everlasting. We cannot live for money or material things – a common way of seeking to keep our lives in this world - and also enter the kingdom of God.*

(27) Then Peter said to him, "Behold, we have left everything and followed you; what then will there be for us?" (28) And Joshua said to them, **"Truly I say to you, that you who have followed me, in the New Age when the Son of Man will sit on his glorious throne, you also shall sit upon twelve thrones, judging the twelve tribes of Israel.** (29) **"And everyone who has left houses or brothers or sisters or father or mother or children or farms for my name's sake, will receive many times as much, and will inherit eternal life.** (30) **"But many who are first will be last; and the last, first.***48

*48   *Those who have forsaken what the people of the world say is valuable – material things, religion, careers, blood and legal relatives, etc. - in order to follow Joshua, will both inherit eternal life, as well as be counted as "last" or "poor" or "foolish" or "crazy" by the people who love the world and are thus unwilling to put their faith in Joshua and his Father.*

(20:1) "For the kingdom of heaven is like a landowner who went out early in the morning to hire workers for his vineyard. (2) "When he had agreed with the workers for twenty dollars for the day, he sent them into his vineyard. (3) "And he went out about nine o'clock and saw others standing around in the market place; (4) and to those he said, 'You also go into the vineyard, and whatever is right I will give you.' And so they went. (5) "Again he went out about the twelve o'clock and three o'clock, and did the same thing. (6) "And about five o'clock he went out and found others standing around; and he said to them, 'Why have you been standing here doing nothing all day long?' (7) "They said to him, 'Because no one hired us.' He said to them, 'You go into the vineyard too.'

(8) "When evening came, the owner of the vineyard said to his foreman, 'Call the workers and pay them their wages, beginning with the last group to the first.' (9) "When those hired about five o'clock came, each one received twenty dollars. (10) "When those hired first came, they thought that they would receive more; but each of them also received twenty dollars. (11) "When they received it, they grumbled at the landowner, (12) saying, 'These last men have worked only one hour, and you have made them equal to us who have borne the burden and the scorching heat of the day.' (13) "But he answered and said to one of them, 'Friend, I am doing you no wrong; did you not agree to work for twenty dollars? (14) 'Take what is yours and go, but I wish to give to this last man the same as to you. (15) 'Is it not lawful for me to do what I wish with what is my own? Or is your eye envious because I am generous?' (16) "So the last shall be first, and the first last."

(17) As Joshua was about to go up to Jerusalem, he took the twelve disciples aside by themselves, and on the way he said to them, (18) **"Behold, we are going up to Jerusalem; and the Son of Man will be delivered to the religious leaders and**

politicians and lawyers, and they will condemn him to
death, (19) and will hand him over to the gentiles to mock
and scourge (*beat with a whip*) and crucify him (*nail him to
some wood*), and on the third day he will be raised up."

(20) Then the mother of the sons of Zebedee came to Joshua with
her sons, bowing down and making a request of him. (21) And he
said to her, "What do you wish?" She said to him, "Command that in
your kingdom these two sons of mine may sit one on your right and
one on your left." (22) But Joshua answered, "**You do not know
what you are asking. Are you able to endure that which I
am about to endure?**" They said to him, "We are able." (23) He
said to them, "**My suffering you shall endure; but to sit on
my right and on my left, this is not mine to give, but it is
for those for whom it has been prepared by my Father.**" [*49]
(24) And hearing this, the other ten sent ones (*apostles*) became
mad with the two brothers. (25) But Joshua called them to himself
and said, "**You know that the rulers of these who have no
knowledge of my Father lord it over them, and their great
men exercise authority over them. (26) "It is not this way
among you, but whoever wishes to become great among
you shall be your servant, (27) and whoever wishes to be
first among you shall be your servant;**[*50] (28) **just as the
Son of Man did not come to be served, but to serve, and to
give his life a ransom for many.**" [*51]

[*49] *Another clear contradiction to the trinity doctrine – obviously "my Father" is
not 'myself'!*

[*50] *This teaching of the Light, along with Matt. 23:8-12, leave no doubt that
disciples of the Light have no leaders other than the Master himself. Sadly, Paul
in Eph. 4:11, as well as Heb. 13:17 and some other passages, are direct
contradictions to these plain teachings, and thus are used to nullify the Light.*

[*51] *Joshua here tells us the meaning of his death, or the purpose behind his dying.
Please note, he himself plainly says his death will serve as "**a ransom**", **NOT a
sacrifice**! A ransom to pay an evil third party (Satan) so that captives (people*

who understand they are captives) can be set free. Joshua never said his death will be some kind of a sacrifice to appease his Father – that is just human religion which has NO BASIS in Joshua's teachings or life events.

(29) As they were leaving Jericho, a large crowd followed him. (30) And two blind men sitting by the road, hearing that Joshua was passing by, cried out, "Lord, have mercy on us, Son of David!" (31) The crowd sternly told them to be quiet, but they cried out all the more, "Lord, Son of David, have mercy on us!" (32) And Joshua stopped and called them, and said, "**What do you want me to do for you?**" (33) They said to him, "Lord, we want our eyes to be opened." (34) Moved with compassion, Joshua touched their eyes; and immediately they regained their sight and followed him.

(21:1) When they had approached Jerusalem and had come to Bethphage, at the Mount of Olives, then Joshua sent two disciples, (2) saying to them, "**Go into the village opposite you, and immediately you will find a donkey tied there and colt (***a young horse***) with her; untie them and bring them to me.** (3) **"If anyone says anything to you, you shall say, 'The Lord has need of them,' and immediately he will send them**." (4) This took place to fulfill what was spoken through the prophet: (5) "Say To The Daughter Of Zion, 'Behold Your King Is Coming To You, Gentle, And Mounted On A Donkey, Even On A Colt, The Foal Of A Beast Of Burden.'" (6) The disciples went and did just as Joshua had instructed them, (7) and brought the donkey and the colt, and laid their coats on them; and he sat on the coats.

(8) Most of the crowd spread their coats in the road, and others were cutting branches from the trees and spreading them in the road. (9) The crowds going ahead of him, and those who followed, were shouting, "Hosanna to the Son of David; Blessed Is He Who Comes In The Name Of The Lord; Hosanna in the highest!" (10) When he had entered Jerusalem, all the city was stirred, saying, "Who is this?" (11) And the crowds were saying, "This is the prophet Joshua, from Nazareth in Galilee." (12) And Joshua entered the temple and drove out all those who were buying and selling in the temple, and overturned the tables of the money changers and the seats of those who were selling doves. (13) And he said to them, "**It is written in your bible, 'My House Shall Be Called A House Of Prayer'; but you are making it a Robbers' Den**." (14) And the blind and the lame came to him in the temple, and he healed them. (15) But when the religious leaders and the bible experts saw the wonderful things that he had done, and the children who were shouting in the temple, "Hosanna to the Son of David," they became indignant (16) and said to him, "Do you hear what these children are saying?" And Joshua said to them, "**Yes; have you never read, 'Out Of The Mouth Of Infants And Nursing Babies You Have Prepared Praise For Yourself'?**" (17) And he left them and went out of the city to Bethany, and spent the night there.

(18) Now in the morning, when he was returning to the city, he became hungry. (19) Seeing a lone fig tree by the road, he came to it and found nothing on it except leaves only; and he said to it, "**No longer shall there ever be any fruit from you.**" And at once the fig tree withered. (20) Seeing this, the disciples were amazed and asked, "How did the fig tree wither all at once?" (21) And Joshua answered and said to them, "**Truly I say to you, if you have faith and do not doubt, you will not only do what was done to the fig tree, but even if you say to this mountain, 'Be taken up and cast into the sea,' it will happen.** (22) "**And all things you ask in prayer, believing, you will receive.**" *52

*52 *When Joshua supposedly says something that does not match reality – for example, people do not receive "all things" they ask for in prayer - we need to consider the possibilities. First, he did not actually say it; it was inaccurately recorded; or the text was modified by subsequent translators. Second, the saying only applied to the time Joshua was on the earth during his first coming. Third, it is a saying that requires faith to bring the saying to pass.*

(23) When he entered the temple, the chief religious leaders and the political leaders of the people came to him while he was teaching, and said, "**By what authority are you doing these things, and who gave you this authority?**" (24) Joshua said to them, "**I will also ask you one thing, which if you tell me, I will also tell you by what authority I do these things.** (25) "**The baptism of John was from what source, from heaven or from men?**" And they began reasoning among themselves, saying, "If we say, 'From heaven,' he will say to us, 'Then why did you not believe him?' (26) "But if we say, 'From men,' we fear the people; for they all regard John as a prophet." (27) And answering Joshua, they said, "We do not know." He also said to them, "**Neither will I tell you by what authority I do these things.**

(28) "**But what do you think? A man had two sons, and he came to the first and said, 'Son, go work today in the**

vineyard.' (29) "And he answered, 'I will not'; but afterward he regretted it and went. (30) "The man came to the second and said the same thing; and he answered, 'I will, sir'; but he did not go. (31) "Which of the two did the will of his father?" They said, "The first." Joshua said to them, "Truly I say to you that those you consider unpatriotic and prostitutes will get into the kingdom of God before you. (32) "For John came to you in the way of righteousness and you did not believe him; but the unpatriotic and prostitutes did believe him; and you, seeing this, did not even feel remorse afterward so as to believe him.

(33) "Listen to another parable. There was a landowner who Planted A Vineyard And Put A Wall Around It And Dug A Wine Press In It, And Built A Tower, and rented it out to vine-growers and went on a journey. (34) "When the harvest time approached, he sent his servants to the vine-growers to receive his produce. (35) "The vine-growers took his servants and beat one, and killed another, and threw stones at a third. (36) "Again he sent another group of servants larger than the first; and they did the same thing to them. (37) "But afterward he sent his son to them, saying, 'They will respect my son.' (38) "But when the vine-growers saw the son, they said among themselves, 'This is the heir; come, let us kill him and seize his inheritance.' (39) "They took him, and threw him out of the vineyard and killed him. (40) "Therefore when the owner of the vineyard comes, what will he do to those vine-growers?" (41) They said to him, "He will bring those wretches to a wretched end, and will rent out the vineyard to other vine-growers who will pay him the proceeds at the proper seasons." (42) Joshua said to them, "Did you never read in the scriptures, 'The Stone Which The Builders Rejected, This Became The Chief Corner stone; This Came About From The Lord, And It Is Marvelous In Our Eyes'? (43) "Therefore I say to you, the kingdom of God will be taken away from you and given to a people, producing the fruit

of it. (44) **"And he who falls on this stone will be broken to pieces; but on whomever it falls, it will scatter him like dust**." (45) When the religious leaders and bible experts heard his parables, they understood that he was speaking about them. (46) When they sought to seize him, they feared the people, because they considered him to be a prophet.

(22:1) Joshua spoke to them again in parables, saying, (2) **"The kingdom of heaven may be compared to a king who gave a wedding celebration for his son.** (3) **"And he sent out his servants to call those who had been invited to the wedding celebration, and they were unwilling to come.** (4) **"Again he sent out other servants saying, 'Tell those who have been invited, "Behold, I have prepared my dinner; my oxen and my fattened livestock are all butchered and everything is ready; come to the wedding feast."'** (5) **"But they paid no attention and went their way, one to his own farm, another to his business,** (6) **and the rest seized his servants and mistreated them and killed them.** (7) **"But the king was enraged, and he sent his armies and destroyed those murderers and set their city on fire.** (8) **"Then he said to his servants, 'The wedding is ready, but those who were invited were not worthy.** (9) **'Go therefore to the streets, and as many as you find there, invite to the wedding feast.'** (10) **"Those servants went out into the streets and gathered together all they found, both evil and good; and the wedding hall was filled with dinner guests.** (11) **"But when the king came in to look over the dinner guests, he saw a man there who was not dressed in wedding clothes** (*did not seek to honor the king*), (12) **and he said to him, 'Sir, how did you come in here without wedding clothes?' And the man was speechless.** (13) **"Then the king said to the servants, 'Bind him hand and foot, and throw him into the outer darkness; in that place there will be weeping and gnashing of teeth** (*great anger*).**'** (14) **"For many are called, but few are chosen."**

(15) Then the religious leaders went and plotted together how they might trap Joshua in what he said. (16) And they sent their disciples to him, along with those from another religious sect, saying, "Teacher, we know that you are truthful and teach the way of God in truth, and don't look to others for answers; for you are not partial to anyone. (17) "Tell us then, what do you think? Is it lawful to give a poll-tax to Caesar, or not?" (18) But Joshua perceived

their mean intention, and said, "**Why are you testing me, you hypocrites** (*a person who says what others ought to do or not do, but does not do so themselves*)? (19) **"Show me the coin used for the poll-tax**." And they brought him a dollar coin. (20) And he said to them, "**Whose likeness and inscription is this?**" (21) They said to him, "Caesar's." Then he said to them, "**Then render** (*give*) **to Caesar the things that are Caesar's; and to God the things that are God's**." (22) And hearing this, they were amazed, and leaving him, they went away.

(23) On that day some men from another religious sect (*who say there is no resurrection*) came to Joshua and questioned him, (24) asking, "Teacher, Moses said, 'If A Man Dies Having No Children, His Brother As Next Of Kin Shall Marry His Wife, And Raise Up Children For His Brother.' (25) "Now there were seven brothers with us; and the first married and died, and having no children left his wife to his brother; (26) so also the second, and the third, down to the seventh. (27) "Last of all, the woman died. (28) "In the resurrection, therefore, whose wife of the seven will she be? For they all had married her." (29) But Joshua answered and said to them, "**You are mistaken, not understanding the scriptures nor the power of God.** (30) **"For in the resurrection they neither marry nor are given in marriage, but are like angels in heaven.** (31) **"But regarding the resurrection of the dead, have you not read what was spoken to you by God:** (32) **'I Am** (*present tense statement "I am" made long after Abraham, Isaac and Jacob had died*) **The God Of Abraham, And The God Of Isaac, And The God Of Jacob'? He is not the God of the dead but of the living**." (33) When the crowds heard this, they were astonished at his teaching.

(34) But when the religious leaders heard that Joshua had silenced their religious competitors, they gathered themselves together. (35) One of them, a lawyer, asked him a question, testing him, (36) "Teacher, which is the great commandment in the Law?" (37) And he said to him, " **'You Shall Love The Lord Your God With All Your Heart, And With All Your Soul, And With All Your**

Mind.' (38) **"This is the great and most important commandment. (39) "The second is like it, 'You Shall Love Your Neighbor As Yourself.'** (40) **"On these two commandments depend the whole law and the prophets**."

(41) Now while the religious leaders were gathered together, Joshua asked them a question: (42) **"What do you think about the Messiah, whose son is he?"** They said to him, "The son of David." (43) He said to them, **"Then how does David in the Spirit call him 'Lord,' saying, (44) 'The Lord Said To My Lord, "Sit At My Right Hand, Until I Put Your Enemies Beneath Your Feet"'? (45) "If David then calls him 'Lord,' how is he his son?"** (46) No one was able to answer him a word, nor did anyone dare from that day on to ask him another question.

(23:1) Then Joshua spoke to the crowds and to his disciples, (2) saying: "**The judges, lawyers and the religious leaders have seated themselves in the chair of Moses** (*in the position of authority*); (3) **therefore all that they tell you, do and observe, but do not do as they do; for they say things and do not do them.** (4) "**They tie up heavy burdens and lay them on men's shoulders, but they themselves are unwilling to move them with so much as a finger.** (5) "**But they do all their deeds to be noticed by men; for they put on expensive suits and some put on special religious clothing.** (6) "**They love the place of honor at celebrations and the best seats in the religious meetings,** (7) **and respectful greetings in the market places, and being called 'teacher' by men.** (8) "**But do not be called a spiritual 'teacher'; for One is your Teacher, and you are all brothers.** (9) "**Do not call anyone on earth your father; for One is your Father, he who is in heaven.** (10) "**Do not be called leaders; for One is your Leader, that is, Messiah.** (11) "**But the greatest among you shall be your servant.** (12) "**Whoever exalts himself shall be humbled; and whoever humbles himself shall be exalted.**"[53]

[53] *This teaching of the Light, along with Matt. 20:25-27, leave no doubt that disciples of the Light have no leaders other than the Master himself. Sadly, Paul in Eph. 4:11, as well as Heb. 13:17 and some other passages directly contradict these plain teachings, and thus are used to nullify perhaps one of the most important teachings of the Light – that he is the only leader of his followers, "for One is...".*

(13) "**But woe to you** (*throwing away eternal Life*), **bible experts and religious leaders, hypocrites** (*a person who says what others ought to do or not do, but does not do so themselves*), **because you shut off the kingdom of heaven from people; for you do not enter in yourselves, nor do you allow those who are entering to go in.**"[54] (14) "**Woe to you, bible experts and religious leaders, hypocrites** (*a person who says what others ought to do or not do, but does not do so themselves*),

because you devour (*take*) **widows' houses, and for a
pretense** (*put on a show for people*) **you make long prayers**
(*see Matt. 6:6*); **therefore you will receive greater
condemnation.**

*53 Sadly, the very work of the religious leaders is to prevent those who seek to
enter the kingdom of heaven from doing so. They do this by creating a substitute
(or counterfeit) to Joshua and his Way. This commentator does not believe that
they do this consciously, but rather are deceived themselves and thus deceive
others –the blind lead the blind into a pit.*

(15) **"Woe to you, bible experts and religious leaders,
hypocrites, because you travel around on sea and land to
make one proselyte** (*person who has the same religion,
doctrine-beliefs*); **and when he becomes one, you make him
twice as much a son of hell as yourselves.**

(16) **"Woe to you, blind guides, who say, 'Whoever swears
by the religious building, that is nothing; but whoever
swears by the expensive decorations is obligated.'** (17)
**"You foolish and blind men! Which is more important, the
expensive decorations or the building that you believe
makes the decorations special?** (18) **"And, 'Whoever
swears by the altar** (*a religious table for sacrifices*), **that is
nothing, but whoever swears an oath by the offering** (*the
animal killed*) **on it, he must keep his oath.'** (19) **"You blind
men, which is more important, the offering, or the altar
you believe sanctifies** (*cleans*) **the offering?** (20)
"Therefore, whoever swears (*makes a promise*) **by the altar,
swears both by the altar and by everything on it.** (21) **"And
whoever swears by the temple, swears both by the temple
and by him who dwells within it.** (22) **"And whoever
swears by heaven, swears both by the throne of God and
by him who sits upon it.**

(23) **"Woe to you, bible experts and religious leaders,
hypocrites! For you give ten percent of your *gross* income,**

and have neglected the weightier provisions of the law: justice and mercy and faithfulness; but these are the things you should have done without neglecting the others. (24) "You blind guides, who strain out a gnat (*keep religious rules*) and swallow a camel (*don't live by justice, mercy or faithfulness*)!

(25) "Woe to you, bible experts and religious leaders, hypocrites! For you clean the outside of the cup and of the dish, but inside they are full of robbery and self-pleasing. (26) "You blind religious leader, first clean the inside of the cup and of the dish, so that the outside of it may become clean also. (27) "Woe to you, bible experts and religious leaders, hypocrites! For you are like nicely painted graves which on the outside appear beautiful, but inside they are full of dead men's bones and all things you consider filthy. (28) "So you, too, outwardly appear righteous to men, but inwardly you are full of hypocrisy (*two-facedness*) and lawlessness (*not obeying the spirit of the law*).[*54]

[*54] *Is there a more accurate description of the average religious leader, politician or lawyer? The fancy clothes and proper behavior, but only seeing others faults and not their own and breaking the rules and bending the laws for their own benefit.*

(29) "Woe to you, bible experts and religious leaders, hypocrites! For you build the tombs of the those who spoke God's words and adorn the monuments of the righteous, (30) and say, 'If we had been living in the days of our fathers, we would not have been partners with them in shedding the blood of the prophets (*people who spoke God's truths*).' (31) "So you testify against yourselves, that you are sons of those who murdered the prophets. (32) "Fill up, then, the measure of the guilt of your fathers. (33) "You serpents, you brood of vipers, how will you escape the sentence of hell?

(34) "Therefore, behold, I am sending you prophets (*people who speak the Truth's Words*) and wise men and writers; some of them you will kill and crucify, and some of them you will whip in your religious buildings, and persecute from city to city, (35) so that upon you may fall the guilt of all the righteous bloodshed on earth, from the blood of righteous Abel to the blood of Zechariah, the son of Berechiah, whom you murdered between the temple and the altar. (36) "Truly I say to you, all these things will come upon this generation.

(37) "Jerusalem, Jerusalem, who kills the prophets (*people who speak God's truths*) and stones those who are sent to her! How often I wanted to gather your children together, the way a hen gathers her chicks under her wings, and you were unwilling. (38) "Behold, your house is being left to you desolate! (*Completely empty*) (39) "For I say to you, from now on you will not see me until you say, 'Blessed Is He Who Comes In The Name Of The Lord!'"

(24:1) Joshua came out from the temple and was going away when his disciples came up to point out the temple buildings to him. (2) And he said to them, "**Do you see all these buildings? Truly I say to you, not one stone here will be left upon another, which will not be torn down.**" (3) As he was sitting on the Mount of Olives, the disciples came to him privately, saying, "Tell us, when will these things happen, and what will be the sign of your coming, and of the end of the age?" (4) And Joshua answered and said to them, "**See to it that no one misleads you.** (5) "**For many will come in my name, saying, 'I am God's appointed one', and will mislead many.** (6) "**You will be hearing of wars and rumors of wars. See that you are not frightened, for those things must take place, but that is not yet the end.** (7) "**For nation will rise against nation, and kingdom against kingdom, and in various places there will be famines and earthquakes.** (8) "**But all these things are merely <u>the beginning</u> of birth pains.** (9) "**Then they will deliver you to tribulation** (*trouble, namely mean and harmful treatment*)**, and will kill you, and you will be hated by all nations because of my name.** (10) "**At that time many will fall away and will betray one another and hate one another.** (11) "**Many false prophets** (*people who claim to speak for God but don't*) **will arise and will mislead many.** (12) "**Because lawlessness** (*obeying no rules except those from which they perceive they will benefit from*) **is increased, most people's love will grow cold.** (13) "**But the one who endures to the end, he will be saved.** (14) "**This gospel of the kingdom shall be preached in the whole world as a testimony to all the nations, and then the end will come.**

(In this commentator's opinion, the following is specifically for his disciples in Israel and could well have happened in 70AD when the Roman general Titus destroyed Jerusalem and the Jewish nation.)

(15) "**Therefore when you see the Abomination Of Desolation which was spoken of through Daniel the prophet** (*a person who spoke God's truths*)**, standing in the**

holy place (*the most special place in the Jew's temple*) **(let the reader understand), (16) then those who are in Judea must flee to the mountains. (17) "Whoever is on the housetop must not go down to get the things out that are in his house. (18) "Whoever is in the field must not turn back to get his clothes. (19) "But woe to those who are pregnant and to those who are nursing babies in those days! (20) "But pray that your flight will not be in the winter, or on a sabbath.**

(In this commentator's opinion, Joshua resumes with an 'all human history' global view.)

(21) "For then there will be a great tribulation (*harsh trouble*)**, such as has not occurred since the beginning of the world until now, nor ever will. (22) "Unless those days had been cut short, no life would have been saved; but for the sake of the elect** (*chosen ones*) **those days will be cut short. (23) "Then if anyone says to you, 'Behold, here is the Messiah,' or 'There he is,' do not believe him. (24) "For false spiritual leaders and false prophets** (*people who claim to speak for God but don't*) **will arise and will show great signs and wonders, so as to mislead, if possible, even the chosen ones.**[*55] **(25) "Behold, I have told you in advance. (26) "So if they say to you, 'Behold, he is in the wilderness,' do not go out, or, 'Behold, he is in the inner rooms,' do not believe them. (27) "For just as the lightning comes from the east and flashes even to the west** (*unmistakable physical event people will see*)**, so will the coming of the Son of Man be. (28) "Wherever the corpse is, there the vultures will gather.**

[*55] *This is the third warning about being deceived or misled in this section of teachings about future events – see also verses 5 & 11. Yet, how many people are truly concerned about being deceived by people saying they represent God or Joshua? Sadly, very few, and thus you have masses of people being misled by the religious leaders who say they represent God.*

(29) "But immediately after the tribulation (*harsh trouble*) of those days The Sun Will Be Darkened, And The Moon Will Not Give Its Light, And The Stars Will Fall from the sky, and the powers of the heavens (*celestial bodies like planets, stars or asteroids*) will be shaken. (30) "And then the sign of the Son of Man will appear in the sky, and then all the people of the earth will mourn, and they will see the Son Of Man Coming On The Clouds Of The Sky with power and great glory. (31) "And he will send forth his angels with A Great Trumpet and They Will Gather Together His elect (*chosen ones*) from the four winds, from one end of the sky to the other.

(32) "Now learn the parable from the fig tree: when its branch has already become tender and puts forth its leaves, you know that summer is near; (33) so, you too, when you see all these things, recognize that he is near, right at the door. (34) "Truly I say to you, this generation (*people living between Joshua's first coming and his second*) will not pass away until all these things take place.

(35) "Heaven and earth will pass away, but my words (*not the bibles' or the scripture*) will not pass away.

(36) "But of that day and hour no one knows, not even the angels of heaven, nor the Son, but the Father alone.[*56] (37) "For the coming of the Son of Man will be just like the days of Noah. (38) "For as in those days before the flood they were eating and drinking, marrying and giving in marriage, until the day that Noah entered the ark, (39) and they did not understand until the flood came and took them all away; so will the coming of the Son of Man be. (40) "Then there will be two men in the field; one will be taken and one will be left. (41) "Two women will be grinding at the mill; one will be taken and one will be left. (42) "Therefore be on the alert, for you do not know which

day your Lord is coming. (43) "But be sure of this, that if the head of the house had known at what time of the night the thief was coming, he would have been on the alert and would not have allowed his house to be broken into. (44) "For this reason you also must be ready; for the Son of Man is coming at an hour when you do not think he will.

*56   *Another saying which contradicts the trinity doctrine.*

(45) "Who then is the faithful and sensible servant whom his master put in charge of his household to give them their food at the proper time? (46) "Blessed is that servant whom his master finds so doing when he comes. (47) "Truly I say to you that he will put him in charge of all his possessions. (48) "But if that evil servant says in his heart, 'My master is not coming for a long time,' (49) and begins to beat his fellow servants and eat and drink with drunkards; (50) the master of that servant will come on a day when he does not expect him and at a time which he does not know, (51) and will cut him in pieces and assign him a place with the hypocrites (*a person who says what others ought to do or not do, but does not do so themselves*); in that place there will be weeping and great anger.

(25:1) "Then the kingdom of heaven will be comparable to ten virgins (*a woman who kept herself pure and thus never had sex*), who took their lamps and went out to meet the bridegroom (*husband to be*). (2) "Five of them were foolish, and five were wise. (3) "For when the foolish took their lamps, they took no oil (*fuel*) with them, (4) but the wise took oil in containers along with their lamps. (5) "Now while the bridegroom was delayed, they all got drowsy and began to sleep. (6) "But at midnight there was a shout, 'Behold, the bridegroom! Come out to meet him.' (7) "Then all those virgins jumped up and adjusted their lamps. (8) "The foolish said to the wise, 'Give us some of your oil, for our lamps are going out.' (9) "But the wise answered, 'No, there will not be enough for us and you too; go instead to the sellers and buy some for yourselves.' (10) "And while they were going away to make the purchase, the bridegroom came, and those who were ready went in with him to the wedding celebration; and the door was shut. (11) "Later the other virgins also came, saying, 'Lord, lord, open up for us.' (12) "But he answered, 'Truly I say to you, I do not know you.' (13) "Be on the alert then, for you do not know the day nor the hour.

(14) "For it is just like a man about to go on a journey, who called his own servants (*employees*) and entrusted his possessions to them. (15) "To one he gave five thousand dollars, to another, two, and to another, one, each according to his own ability; and he went on his journey. (16) "Immediately the one who had received the five thousand went and traded with it, and gained five more thousand. (17) "In the same manner the one who had received the two thousand gained two more. (18) "But he who received the one thousand went away, and dug a hole in the ground and hid his master's money.

(19) "Now after a long time the master of those servants came and settled accounts with them. (20) "The one who had received the five thousand came up and brought five more thousand, saying, 'Master, you entrusted five thousand to me. See, I have gained five more thousand.' (21) "His master said to him smiling warmly, 'Well done, good and faithful servant. You were faithful with a few things, I will put you in charge of many things; enter into the joy of your master.' (22) "Also the servant who had received the two thousand came up and said, 'Master, you entrusted two thousand to me. See, I have gained two more thousand.' (23) "His master said to him smiling warmly, 'Well done, good and faithful servant. You were faithful with a few things, I will put you in charge of many things; enter into the joy of your master.' (24) "And the one who had received the one thousand came up and said, 'Master, I knew you to be a hard man, reaping where you did not sow and gathering where you scattered no seed – taking from others unjustly. (25) 'And I was afraid, and went away and hid your thousand in the ground. See, you have what is yours.' (26) "But his master answered and said to him, 'You wicked, lazy servant, you knew that I reap where I did not sow and gather where I scattered no seed. (27) 'Then you ought to have put my money in the bank, and on my arrival I would have received my money back with interest. (28) 'Therefore take away the thousand from him, and give it to the one who has the ten thousand.' (29) "For to everyone who has, more shall be given, and he will have an abundance; but from the one who does not have, even what he does have shall be taken away. (30) "Throw out the worthless servant into the outer darkness; in that place there will be weeping and great anger.

(31) "But when the Son of Man comes in his glory, and all the angels with him, then he will sit on his glorious throne. (32) "All the nations will be gathered before him;

and he will separate the people from one another, as the shepherd separates the sheep (*viewed as good*) from the goats (*viewed as bad*); (33) and he will put the sheep on his right, and the goats on the left. (34) "Then the King will say to those on his right, 'Come, you who are blessed of my Father, inherit the kingdom prepared for you from the foundation of the world. (35) 'For I was hungry, and you gave me something to eat; I was thirsty, and you gave me something to drink; I was a stranger, and you invited me in; (36) I was naked, and you clothed me; I was sick, and you visited me; I was in prison, and you came to me.' (37) "Then the righteous will answer him, 'Lord, when did we see you hungry, and feed you, or thirsty, and give you something to drink? (38) 'And when did we see you a stranger, and invite you in, or naked, and clothe you? (39) 'When did we see you sick, or in prison, and come to you?' (40) "The King will answer and say to them, 'Truly I say to you, to the extent that you did it to one of these <u>brothers of mine</u>, even the one considered the least important, you did it to me.' [*57]

[*57] *The scene is the judgment of all people by the King. The King puts himself in the shoes of his followers by saying, "I was hungry, thirsty, naked, in prison". Why were his followers' hungry, thirsty, naked, in prison? Persecution and rejection are the normal experience in all times and in all cultures for those who faithfully follow Joshua – do not be deceived. A difficult life in the world **caused by faith and faithfulness** (example: being in prison due to one's faith) – not due to normal human suffering that all might experience - will result in inheriting the kingdom prepared by God for those who love Him. Many christians use this passage to justify 'prison ministries', but as Joshua says, it is we his followers who are in prison due to our doing what he says, not because we committed crimes worthy of punishment.*

(41) "Then he will also say to those on his left, 'Depart from me, accursed ones, into the eternal fire which has been prepared for the devil and his angels[*58]; (42) for I was hungry, and you gave me nothing to eat; I was thirsty,

and you gave me nothing to drink; (43) I was a stranger, and you did not invite me in; naked, and you did not clothe me; sick, and in prison, and you did not visit me.' (44) "Then they themselves also will answer, 'Lord, when did we see you hungry, or thirsty, or a stranger, or naked, or sick, or in prison, and did not take care of you?' (45) "Then he will answer them, 'Truly I say to you, to the extent that you did not do it to one of the least important of these (*the sheep on his right hand*), you did not do it to me.' (46) "These will go away into the eternal punishment (*or 'eternal fire' see verse 41 – meaning a just punishment followed by destruction in the eternal fire*), but the righteous into eternal life." *59

*58   *Please note that the "eternal fire" was not prepared for people, but for the devil and his angels – it was not the Father's intent to create that for people, but sadly people choose to send themselves there.*

*59   *This is the only saying of Joshua that could be construed to support the concept of everlasting punishment. This commentator rejects that concept based on the many teachings of Joshua regarding his Father's mercy and compassion. The Father cannot grant mercy to those who are not looking for mercy (unbelieving, proud, stubborn, fearful, selfish, hard hearted, etc.); and He will not force people to be in His realm or presence (the kingdom) who do not want to be. Thus, he created a process of administering justice (for those who reject his mercy) and a place of destruction for those who send themselves there through their un-faith and non-love. The fire or means of destruction is eternal, not the state of the soul who chooses justice instead of mercy. Eternal punishment is unjust, for there is no sin identified by Joshua as meriting eternal punishment. There is an unforgivable sin (see Mark 3:30) – meaning a person who commits it cannot make it into the kingdom - but not a sin meriting eternal punishment.*

(26:1) When Joshua had finished all these words, he said to his disciples, (2) **"You know that after two days the Passover** (*religious holiday important to the Jews*) **is coming, and the Son of Man is to be handed over for crucifixion** (*a cruel means of punishing and killing someone*)." (3) Then the religious leaders and the elders of the people were gathered together in the court of the main religious leader, named Caiaphas; (4) and they plotted together to seize Joshua secretly and kill him. (5) But they were saying, "Not during the festival, otherwise a riot might occur among the people."

(6) Now when Joshua was in Bethany, at the home of Simon the leper, (7) a woman came to him with an alabaster container of very costly perfume, and she poured it on his head as he reclined at the table. (8) But the disciples were mad when they saw this, and said, "Why this waste? (9) "For this perfume might have been sold for a high price and the money given to the poor." (10) But Joshua, aware of this, said to them, **"Why do you bother this woman? For she has done a good deed to me. (11) "For you always have the poor with you; but you do not always have me. (12) "For when she poured this perfume on my body, she did it to prepare me for burial. (13) "Truly I say to you, wherever this gospel is preached in the whole world, what this woman has done will also be spoken of in memory of her."**

(14) Then one of the twelve, named Judas Iscariot, went to the religious leaders (15) and said, "What are you willing to give me to betray him to you?" And they weighed out thirty pieces of silver to him. (16) From then on he began looking for a good opportunity to betray Joshua.

(17) Now on the first day of Unleavened Bread (*a Jewish feast-holiday*) the disciples came to Joshua and asked, "Where do you want us to prepare for you to eat the Passover?" (18) And he said, **"Go into the city to a certain man, and say to him, 'The Teacher says, "My time is near; I am to keep the passover**

at your house with my disciples."'" (19) The disciples did as Joshua had directed them; and they prepared the Passover. (20) Now when evening came, Joshua was reclining at the table with the twelve disciples. (21) As they were eating, he said, "**Truly I say to you that one of you will betray me.**" (22) Being deeply grieved, they each one began to say to him, "Surely not I, Lord?" (23) And he answered, "**He who dipped his hand with me in the bowl is the one who will betray me. (24) "The Son of Man is to go, just as it is written of him; but woe to that man by whom the Son of Man is betrayed! It would have been good for that man if he had not been born.**" (25) And Judas, who was betraying him, said, "Surely it is not I, Rabbi?" Joshua said to him, "**You have said it yourself.**"

(26) While they were eating, Joshua took some bread, and after a blessing, he broke it and gave it to the disciples, and said, "**Take, eat; this is as my body.**" (27) And when he had taken a cup and given thanks, he gave it to them, saying, "**Drink from it, all of you; (28) for this is as my blood of the covenant** (*promise*)**, which is poured out for many for forgiveness of sins** (*see "ransom" in Matt. 20:28*). (29) "**But I say to you, I will not drink of this fruit of the vine** (*the wine he just gave them in the cup*) **from now on until that day when I drink it new with you in my Father's kingdom.**" *60 (30) After singing a song, they went out to the Mount of Olives.

*60 *Please note there is no call by Joshua to make some ritual out of the meaning of his metaphors that evening. He used appropriate metaphors to teach his disciples about the events about to unfold.*

(31) Then Joshua said to them, "**You will all fall away because of me this night, for it is written, 'I Will Strike Down The Shepherd, And The Sheep Of The Flock Shall Be Scattered.' (32) "But after I have been raised, I will go ahead of you to Galilee.**" (33) But Peter said to him, "Even though all may fall away because of you, I will never fall away." (34) Joshua said to him, "**Truly I say to you that this very night,**

before a rooster crows, you will deny me three times." (35) Peter said to him, "Even if I have to die with you, I will not deny you." All the disciples said the same thing too.

(36) Then Joshua came with them to a place called Gethsemane, and said to His disciples, "**Sit here while I go over there and pray.**" (37) And he took with him Peter and the two sons of Zebedee (*James and John*), and began to be grieved and distressed. (38) Then he said to them, "**My soul is deeply grieved, to the point of death; remain here and keep watch with me.**" (39) And he went a little beyond them, and fell on his face and prayed, saying, "**My Father, if it is possible, let this cup** (*upcoming suffering*) **pass from me; yet not as I will, but as You will.**" (40) And he came to the disciples and found them sleeping, and said to Peter, "**So, you men could not keep watch with me for one hour?** (41) "**Keep watching and praying that you may not enter into temptation; the spirit is willing, but the flesh is weak.**" (42) He went away again a second time and prayed, saying, "**My Father, if this cannot pass away unless I drink it, Your will be done.**" (43) Again he came and found them sleeping, for their eyes were heavy. (44) And he left them again, and went away and prayed a third time, saying the same thing once more. (45) Then he came to the disciples and said to them, "**Are you still sleeping and resting? Behold, the hour is at hand and the Son of Man is being betrayed into the hands of sinners** (*people not seeing their faults and thus not seeing their need for forgiveness and change*)**.** (46) "**Get up, let us be going; behold, the one who betrays me is at hand!**"

(47) While he was still speaking, behold, Judas, one of the twelve, came up accompanied by a large crowd with swords and clubs, who came from the religious leaders and elders of the people. (48) Now he who was betraying him gave them a sign, saying, "Whomever I kiss, he is the one; seize him." (49) Immediately Judas went to Joshua and said, "**Hail, Rabbi!**" and kissed him. (50) And Joshua said to him, "**Friend, do what you have come for.**" Then they came and laid hands on Joshua and seized him. (51) And behold,

one of those who were with Joshua reached and drew out his sword, and struck the servant of the chief religious leader and cut off his ear. (52) Then Joshua said to him, **"Put your sword back into its place; for all those who take up the sword shall die by the sword. (53) "Or do you think that I cannot appeal to my Father, and he will at once put at my disposal more than twelve legions** (*thousands*) **of angels? (54) "How then will the scriptures be fulfilled, which say that it must happen this way?"** (55) At that time Joshua said to the crowds, **"Have you come out with swords and clubs to arrest me as you would against a robber? Every day I used to sit in the temple teaching and you did not seize me. (56) "But all this has taken place to fulfill the scriptures of the prophets.**" Then all the disciples left him and ran away.

(57) Those who had seized Joshua led him away to Caiaphas, the chief religious leader, where the bible experts and the elders were gathered together. (58) But Peter was following Joshua at a distance as far as the courtyard of the chief religious leader, and entered in, and sat down with the officers to see the outcome.

(59) Now the religious leaders and the whole leadership council kept trying to obtain false testimony against Joshua, so that they might put him to death. (60) They did not find any, even though many false witnesses came forward. But later on two came forward, (61) and said, "This man stated, 'I am able to destroy the temple of God and to rebuild it in three days.'" (62) The chief religious leader stood up and said to him, "Do you not answer? What is it that these men are testifying against you?" (63) But Joshua kept silent. And the chief religious leader said to him, "I adjure (*compel*) you by the living God, that you tell us whether you are the Messiah, the Son of God." (64) Joshua said to him, **"You have said it yourself; nevertheless I tell you, hereafter you will see The Son Of Man Sitting At The Right Hand Of Power, and Coming On The Clouds Of Heaven**." (65) Then the chief religious leader tore his robes and said, "He has blasphemed! What further need do we have of witnesses? Behold, you have now heard the blasphemy

(*speaking against God*); (66) what do you think?" They answered, "He deserves death!" (67) Then they spat in his face and beat him with their fists; and others slapped him, (68) and said, "Prophesy to us, you Messiah; who is the one who hit you?"

(69) Now Peter was sitting outside in the courtyard, and a servant-girl came to him and said, "You too were with Joshua the Galilean." (70) But he denied it before them all, saying, "**I do not know what you are talking about**." (71) When he had gone out to the gateway, another servant-girl saw him and said to those who were there, "This man was with Joshua of Nazareth." (72) And again he denied it with an oath, "**I do not know the man**." (73) A little later the bystanders came up and said to Peter, "Surely you too are one of them; for even the way you talk gives you away." (74) Then he began to curse and swear, "**I do not know the man!**" And immediately a rooster crowed. (75) And Peter remembered the word which Joshua had said, "**Before a rooster crows, you will deny me three times**." And he went out and wept bitterly.

(27:1) Now when morning came, all the religious, legal and political leaders of the people conferred together against Joshua to put him to death; (2) and they bound him, and led him away and delivered him to Pilate the Roman governor. (3) Then when Judas, who had betrayed him, saw that Joshua had been condemned, he felt remorse and returned the thirty pieces of silver to the religious and political leaders, (4) saying, "I have sinned by betraying innocent blood." But they said, "What is that to us? See to that yourself!" (5) And he threw the pieces of silver into the temple sanctuary and departed; and he went away and hanged himself. (6) The religious leaders took the pieces of silver and said, "It is not lawful to put them into the temple treasury, since it is the price of blood." (7) And they conferred together and with the money bought the Potter's Field as a burial place for strangers. (8) For this reason that field has been called the Field of Blood to this day. (9) Then that which was spoken through Jeremiah the prophet was fulfilled: "And They Took The Thirty Pieces Of Silver, The Price Of The One Whose Price Had Been Set by the sons of Israel; (10) And They Gave Them For The Potter's Field, As The Lord Directed Me."

(11) Now Joshua stood before the governor, and the governor questioned him, saying, "Are you the King of the Jews?" And Joshua said to him, "**It is as you say.**" (12) And while he was being accused by the religious and political leaders, he did not answer. (13) Then Pilate said to him, "Do you not hear how many things they say against you?" (14) And he did not answer him with regard to even a single charge, so the governor was quite amazed.

(15) Now at the feast the governor was accustomed to release for the people any one prisoner whom they wanted. (16) At that time they were holding a notorious prisoner, called Barabbas. (17) So when the people gathered together, Pilate said to them, "Whom do you want me to release for you? Barabbas, or Joshua who is called Messiah?" (18) For he knew that because of envy they had handed him over. (19) While he was sitting on the judgment seat, his wife sent him a message, saying, "Have nothing to do with that righteous man (*Joshua*); for last night I suffered greatly in a dream because of

him." (20) But the religious and political leaders persuaded the crowds to ask for Barabbas and to put Joshua to death. (21) But the governor said to them, "Which of the two do you want me to release for you?" And they said, "Barabbas." (22) Pilate said to them, "Then what shall I do with Joshua who is called Messiah?" They all said, "Crucify him!" (23) And he said, "Why, what evil has he done?" But they kept shouting all the more, saying, "Crucify him!" (24) When Pilate saw that he was accomplishing nothing, but rather that a riot was starting, he took water and washed his hands in front of the crowd, saying, "I am innocent of this man's blood; see to that yourselves." (25) And all the people said, "His blood shall be on us and on our children!" (26) Then he released Barabbas for them; but after having Joshua whipped, he handed him over to be crucified (*a brutal punishment causing death*).

(27) Then the soldiers of the governor took Joshua into the Praetorium and gathered the whole Roman guard around him. (28) They stripped him and put a scarlet robe on him. (29) And after twisting together a crown of thorns, they put it on his head, and a reed in his right hand; and they knelt down before him and mocked him, saying, "Hail, King of the Jews!" (30) They spat on him, and took the reed and began to beat him on the head. (31) After they had mocked him, they took the scarlet robe off him and put his own garments back on him, and led him away to crucify him. (32) As they were coming out, they found a man of Cyrene named Simon, whom they forced to carry his cross. (33) And when they came to a place called Golgotha, which means Place of a Skull, (34) they gave him wine to drink mixed with gall (*a kind of pain dulling medicine*); and after tasting it, he was unwilling to drink. (35) And when they had crucified (*drove spikes through his arms and legs*) him, they divided up his garments (*clothes*) among themselves by casting lots. (36) And sitting down, they began to keep watch over him there. (37) And above his head they put up the charge against him which read, "THIS IS JOSHUA THE KING OF THE JEWS."

(38) At that time two robbers were crucified with him, one on the right and one on the left. (39) And those passing by were yelling

abuse at him, scornfully shaking their heads (40) and saying, "You who are going to destroy the temple and rebuild it in three days, save yourself! If you are the Son of God, come down from the cross." (41) In the same way the religious leaders also, along with the bible experts and political leaders, were mocking him and saying, (42) "He saved others; he cannot save himself. He is the King of Israel; let him now come down from the cross, and we will believe in him. (43) "He Trusts In God; Let God Rescue him now, If He Delights In Him; for he said, 'I am the Son of God.'" (44) The robbers who had been crucified with him were also insulting him with the same words.

(45) Now from the sixth hour darkness fell upon all the land until the ninth hour. (46) About the ninth hour Joshua cried out with a loud voice, saying, **"Eli, Eli, Lama Sabachthani?" that is, "My God, My God, Why Have You Forsaken Me?"** (47) And some of those who were standing there, when they heard it, began saying, "This man is calling for Elijah." (48) Immediately one of them ran, and taking a sponge, he filled it with sour wine and put it on a reed, and gave him a drink. (49) But the rest of them said, "Let us see whether Elijah will come to save him." (50) And Joshua cried out again with a loud voice, and yielded up his spirit. (51) And behold, the veil of the temple (*a large cloth separating wall*) was torn in two from top to bottom; and the earth shook and the rocks were split. (52) The tombs were opened, and many bodies of the saints who had fallen asleep were raised; (53) and coming out of the tombs after his resurrection they entered the holy city and appeared to many.

(54) Now the centurion, and those who were with him keeping guard over Joshua, when they saw the earthquake and the things that were happening, became very frightened and said, "Truly this was the Son of God!" (55) Many women were there looking on from a distance, who had followed Joshua from Galilee while ministering to him. (56) Among them was Mary Magdalene, and Mary the mother of James and Joseph, and the mother of the sons of Zebedee. (57) When it was evening, there came a rich man from

Arimathea, named Joseph, who himself had also become a disciple of Joshua. (58) This man went to Pilate and asked for the body of Joshua. Then Pilate ordered it to be given to him. (59) And Joseph took the body and wrapped it in a clean linen cloth, (60) and laid it in his own new tomb, which he had hewn out in the rock; and he rolled a large stone against the entrance of the tomb and went away. (61) And Mary Magdalene was there, and the other Mary, sitting opposite the grave.

(62) Now on the next day, the day after the preparation, the religious leaders and the bible experts gathered together with Pilate, (63) and said, "Sir, we remember that when he was still alive that deceiver said, 'After three days I am to rise again.' (64) "Therefore, give orders for the grave to be made secure until the third day, otherwise his disciples may come and steal him away and say to the people, 'he has risen from the dead,' and the last deception will be worse than the first." (65) Pilate said to them, "You have a guard; go, make it as secure as you know how." (66) And they went and made the grave secure, and along with the guard they set a seal on the stone.

(28:1) Now after the Sabbath, as it began to dawn toward the first day of the week, Mary Magdalene and the other Mary came to look at the grave. (2) And behold, a severe earthquake had occurred, for an angel of the Lord descended from heaven and came and rolled away the stone and sat upon it. (3) And his appearance was like lightning and his clothing as white as snow. (4) The guards shook for fear of him and became like dead men. (5) The angel said to the women, "Do not be afraid; for I know that you are looking for Joshua who has been crucified. (6) "He is not here, for he has risen, just as he said. Come, see the place where he was lying. (7) "Go quickly and tell his disciples that he has risen from the dead; and behold, he is going ahead of you into Galilee, there you will see him; behold, I have told you." (8) And they left the tomb quickly with fear and great joy and ran to report it to his disciples. (9) And behold, Joshua met them and greeted them. And they came up and took hold of his feet and bowed before him. (10) Then Joshua said to them, **"Do not be afraid; go and take word to my brothers and sisters to leave for Galilee, and there they will see me."**

(11) Now while they were on their way, some of the guard came into the city and reported to the religious leaders all that had happened. (12) And when they had assembled with the political leaders and consulted together, they gave a large sum of money to the soldiers, (13) and said, "You are to say, 'His disciples came by night and stole him away while we were asleep.' (14) "And if this should come to the Roman governor's ears, we will win him over and keep you out of trouble." (15) And they took the money and did as they had been instructed; and this story was widely spread among the Jews, and is to this day.

(16) But the eleven disciples proceeded to Galilee, to the mountain which Joshua had designated. (17) When they saw him, they bowed in reverence before him; but some were doubtful. (18) And Joshua came up and spoke to them, saying, **"All authority has been given to me in heaven and on earth. (19) "Go therefore and make disciples of all the nations,**[*61] (20) **teaching them to observe all that I commanded you; and**

take comfort, for I am with you always, even to the end of the age."

*61 *Most bible versions have the following phrase inserted in the latter part of verse 19: "baptizing them in the name of the Father and the Son and the Holy Spirit", however, this is unlikely from Joshua, but rather and most likely added later by the religious leaders who gain much power over the people with this ritual. Many sects teach that a ritual of water baptism is necessary to gain entry into heaven and that only their 'ordained' leaders can perform this heaven-gaining ritual. This is a totally foreign concept to Joshua and is in fact contradicted by a number of his teachings on what a person needs to gain Eternal Life. In all his many teachings, Joshua never taught – except in this alleged instance - that his disciples needed to be water baptized in order to 'gain salvation'. (The only exception to that would be Mark 16:16, which saying is found in a section of text at the end of Mark that is highly questionable [including such sayings as, "these signs will accompany those who believe...that they will pick up snakes, and drink deadly poison and will not be hurt] and not included in most manuscript copies.)*

Joshua teaches elsewhere what makes his disciples spiritually "clean" and it is not physical water, but rather "his words" (see John 15:3). John, in chapter 4 verse 2 of his book, explicitly states that Joshua did not baptize people. Also, in all of Joshua's teachings, he never mentioned the "name" of his Father, nor the "name" of the Holy Spirit. He apparently didn't think the name of his Father was important for his disciples to know, and the Holy Spirit has no name, for he is the Father's Spirit somehow apportioned to the individual. To add this ritual at the very end of his instructions before he left this world - and in the midst of the most important departing instruction - seems very odd indeed. Finally, if you read the passage without the "baptize" phrase, it reads very well...in fact, this author believes it reads more naturally than with the inserted baptize phrase. "Making disciples" has everything to do with "teaching them to observe everything all that I commanded you" and nothing to do with a water ritual.

End of the four gospel's accounts.

Summary of Joshua's Truths:

Here is a summary of the simple truths that Joshua taught and that you just read:

- God exists...He is the Designer and Creator of the human race.
- God communicated to mankind through one perfect messenger, his beloved Son, Joshua of Nazareth.
- Not only was Joshua of Nazareth God's messenger, but also His model for what a human being should be like.
- Not only was Joshua of Nazareth God's messenger and model, but also His appointed leader for mankind. The vast majority of people on the earth and through history will ignore him and not submit to him, but those who truly follow him, will have him and him alone as their sole/soul Life leader.
- To hear and believe the Creator and His Son, we must have faith. To know what they want, we must have faith in the correct thing, which is the Father/Creator and His Son, Joshua of Nazareth – NOT the bible or 'the scripture' or the religious systems of men and their teachings which wrongly claim to represent him.
- Joshua of Nazareth taught that God wants people to love, and care for, each other...to treat one another rightly, with kindness, compassion, fairness, goodness and graciousness. He wants us to share what we have with one another, and to build things that help people and advance His primary purpose which is that people are loved/cared for/helped with our weaknesses and infirmities and difficulties. Those who live this way and love him and His Life are of the Light.
- All wrong doing, fear and hatred, harming others, selfish behavior, self-pride and the conflict it brings – in short, living for anything other than love and truth and rightness -

is against the revealed will (Joshua's teachings) of the Creator.

- All conflict that harms people and that has self-pride or fear or selfishness as its motivation is against the Creator's will...there is no justified aggression against others before God. All conflict caused by pride, fear or selfishness is wrongful conflict. All who practice initiating - or support by participating in - such wrongful conflict, cannot enter into eternal life in that state. All who bring wrongful conflict are of the darkness and condemn themselves.

- God wants people to live or exist forever, and the way to attain to that Eternal Life is to admit that our self-pride, fear or selfishness has kept us away from our Father/Creator. We then need to have remorse for that life of pride, fear and selfishness and to change and get to know God through His Son - to listen to His Son and do what His Son says which is essentially to love others, care about what is true, and do what he says is right.

- Those who hear accurately of the Son and his teachings and who refuse to submit to the Son and thus God's Way of Love, Rightness and Peace are of the darkness and will **send themselves** to just consequences and destruction at the end of their physical lives...they reject Life Everlasting for the things they valued in this life above their Father and His love for them and His desire for love, rightness, faith, peace, selflessness, etc.

- Those who don't hear accurately of the Son will have their conscience as their guide, and those who listen to their conscience and practice love, compassion, rightness, forgiveness, graciousness; those who don't cause wrongful conflict and who seek to help others; these will also preserve their soul after death and enter into Eternal Life.

Two Basic and Clear Options

So, if you have made it through the four gospels, you have been exposed to the person and claims of the one who called himself among other things "The Light of the World", the Judge of every human being, and the Freedom Giver to every human being. You now must **do something** with that person and his claims.

You only have two options.

The first is to reject his person and his claims. This is the normal response.

Of course, most people will not say outright, "I reject Jesus of Nazareth and his claims about himself". Rather, they will reject the "Jesus Christ" of Christian religion or the claims of the real Jesus they dislike, and merely pay lip service to him and stuff about him they do like. For example, they might say things like, 'he was a great teacher and leader' (non-religious response); or, 'I believe he was God incarnate' (religious response), even while they have **no sincere intention to place their faith in him and his Father nor study his teachings nor order their life by his teachings**. These are they that hear or read with their mind only, and his truths and message never penetrate their heart or soul – who they truly are. These are those where the seed falls on the bad soil, whose hearts are not good.

Another very popular version of rejecting him is to believe or say something like, 'we just can't know if those writings accurately recorded Jesus' story and teachings'. Sadly this response if very common among Christians - on the one hand, they say they "believe in the Lord Jesus Christ" and on the other, they say, "well, we can't really know if those gospels are accurate". This is very dishonest and what they are really saying is, "I want to make up a 'Lord Jesus Christ' that fits my life..." or, 'I really don't have faith but I'm afraid to express that'.

Another very common way to reject the real Jesus of Nazareth who reveals himself through his own words in the four 'gospel' is to believe or say something like, 'oh, well, that is a matter of

348

interpretation'. What is often being conveyed with that statement is, 'well, I disagree with that saying of Jesus and don't want to do that or live that way'. Or so say something like, 'oh, well, that only applied to the people in that culture at that time...that doesn't apply to us today'.

There are MANY ways to reject the historical and real Joshua of Nazareth and his teachings for mankind without just plainly saying, 'I reject his person and/or his teachings'. Or, said another way, there are many ways to select the first option.

The second option is *to **simply believe him** – not stuff **about** him, but rather believe what he says about himself, about God and about human life.*

Suggested Test:

If you have read Joshua of Nazareth's teachings with a sincere desire to understand what he teaches, you should be able to understand and correctly define the concepts he addressed. Here is a test to see if you have really thought about what he said and thus have listened well.

1. What is love?

2. What is faith?

3. What is truth?

4. What is the church?

5. What is the bible?

6. What is the scripture?

7. What is religion?

8. What is a Christian?

9. What is Christianity?

10. What is a Master?

11. How many spiritual leaders does a follower of Joshua have?

12. What is the world?

13. Who or what defines what is true or false in regard to spiritual or moral issues for a follower of Joshua?

14. What is the difference between the terms "shepherd" and "pastor"?

15. Who is God?

16. Is Joshua also the Father?

17. If we love our Master, will we speak of him to others?

18. Is it easy to be a follower of Joshua?

19. What is the new command of Joshua?

20. What is the primary purpose of the Holy Spirit?

21. What is eternal life?

22. How does one enter into the state of eternal life?

23. How does one remain in the state of eternal life?

24. What is "the gospel" according to Joshua?

25. What does it mean to hunger and thirst for righteousness?

26. Who in history and in an authentic way, defeated or overcame death?

27. Is there a teaching of Joshua that justifies aggression or violence against other people?

28. Is there a teaching(s) in the bible that justifies aggression or violence against other people?

29. Should a follower of Joshua stand by and watch; participate in; or do nothing about, people doing things that go against Joshua's teachings or encourage others to do the same?

30. Does getting a passing score in this quiz mean you are a follower of Joshua?

31. With what aspects of our nature and in what priority are we to love our Father back?

32. If we love our Father, will we speak of him to others?

33. Is God angry with people?

34. Is God in control?

35. Does God perform miracles today?

36. Does God love you more than other people?

37. Does God take side in men's conflicts?

38. Does God communicate directly with individuals outside of normal prayer as taught by Joshua?

39. Does God care about how you dress?

40. Does God care about your appearance?

41. Does God care about having water poured on you?

42. Does God care about one day more than another?

43. Does God stop bad things from happening in people's lives?

44. What is the primary purpose of prayer?

45. Does God have many names?

46. Is mankind basically good?

47. Does the book of revelation represent Joshua of Nazareth?

48. Are Christians in general obeying Joshua's teachings about unity in John 17?

49. Was there anyone else in history who was authentically resurrected from the dead?

50. Which of the hundreds of bible versions is correct?

51. Does Joshua teach that he will come back to earth someday?

52. Who was Paul of Tarsus?

53. If God is so loving why do bad things happen?

54. Where is God when the child is being beaten?

55. Is hell real?

56. Does God send people to hell?

57. Does God answer prayer?

58. What or who is the Holy Spirit?

59. Does God want people to have spiritual authority over other people?

60. Does the bible provide an accurate creation story?

Answers:

1. At its core, **love** is valuing another person and having compassion on others which leads to selfless behavior towards them. Associated aspects of love are a desire to care for and help someone, and to want to be with them and share life with them.

2. **Faith** is a simple trust or confidence in someone or something. Faith is not beliefs about something.

3. **Truth** is what is real...it is most often used to mean being in accord with fact or reality, or fidelity to an original or to a standard or ideal. Truth is the correct understanding of what is true and false, right or wrong in any realm. Joshua the messenger says he is the truth that matters about human life, human existence and the human soul or spirit. When he says, "I am the truth", that would be an exclusive claim in the realm of defining humans and human behavior that would stand against other such claims...in other words, if another person also claimed that they are the truth regarding defining human life and human behavior, they would contradict Joshua and one of them would be a false claim.

4. The '**church**' or ekklesia are the collective followers of Joshua who have been called out of the world and have responded. What the 'church' is not is buildings or programs or organization leadership or meetings.

5. The **bible** is a book the first of which was compiled by people in the 4th century; it is made up of smaller books written by different authors. The book contains histories of certain people groups, as well as the author's beliefs about God and what they believed God did. The life and teachings of Joshua of Nazareth are contained in four books that were also placed in the bible at the beginning of what is called the new testament.

6. In a christian context, the **scripture** is essentially synonymous with the bible.

7. **Religion** is the things that people believe and practice in regard to being accepted by God or a better afterlife, or their spiritual beliefs and associated practices, apart from what Joshua of Nazareth teaches.

8. A ***christian*** is a person who identifies with some sect or denomination of the bible based or christian religious system; or a person who has beliefs about 'christ', but which beliefs are generally not grounded in Joshua of Nazareth's teachings nor do those beliefs generally result in the practicing of some of the more important teachings of Joshua of Nazareth.

9. ***Christianity*** is a religious system made up of people who claim "Jesus Christ" as their figurehead or God. It is made up of material wealth including buildings and property; beliefs about God derived from the bible and thousands of other sources; leadership exercising power over people in a myriad of titles; practices including rituals, singing, gathering for meetings which typically involve some form of entertainment; and helping people deemed less fortunate usually through impersonal material means or their sect's doctrine.

10. A person's ***Master*** is someone a person looks to, and submits to, as the person with the best knowledge, understanding, skills, experience, wisdom in a particular life domain.

11. One, **Joshua only**.

12. The ***world*** is the people of the earth who reject Joshua of Nazareth as their leader or those who don't live by the light of their conscience.

13. **Joshua alone**.

14. **Nothing**. Here is the Wiki definition, "The word "pastor" derives from the Latin noun *pastor* which means "shepherd" and relates to the Latin verb *pascere* - "to lead to pasture, set to grazing, cause to eat".

15. God is the ***Designer and Creator*** of the life on the earth, and the Father of all human beings. God is spirit or metaphysical and thus not physical.

16. No, Joshua is the unique ***Son of God***, the perfect messenger of the Creator.

17. **Yes**. Our mouth will proclaim that which we love supremely, whether Joshua or other people or things.

18. **No**. Followers of Joshua will renounce what the world considers valuable; will love others when they are hated by them; will be alone due to rejection by people who reject

Joshua; are persecuted, slandered, mocked, derided, etc. by those who reject Joshua.

19. That his followers love one another – **have compassion on one another and act selflessly towards one another**; that we care for one another in this life and thus be together as a people – even as he loved his first disciples, for this manifestation of love for one another is the only way the people of the earth who don't believe Joshua, will know that we are his followers and that he exists and is relevant.

20. The primary purpose of the ***Holy Spirit*** is to enable people to receive the teachings of Joshua and to bear witness to Joshua as the truth that mankind needs.

21. **Eternal life** is to know our Father and Joshua, the one whom He sent.

22. One **enters into eternal life** by being born from above – which is to see ourselves as having been governed by pride, fear and selfishness and thus having hurt others; and who have ignored the Father who Created and loves both us and those we hurt, and can help us to be what we ought to be as human beings. This born from above process or event will cause an adult person to feel deep remorse for these things; to look for forgiveness from their Creator; and to place one's faith in our Father and His Son.

23. One **remains in the state of eternal life** by continuing to have faith in Joshua and his Father and by doing one's best to love them back and do what Joshua says which is to love others.

24. The good news is that the Creator **sent a Messenger and Leader** to reveal who the Creator is and what He is like; to set people free from their pride, fear and selfishness; to show people how human's ought to live once free; and to provide a sure way for people to return to their Maker/Father...to go Home to be with the One who loves them more than any other.

25. It means to **care** enough **about what is true or false, right or wrong** to say and do something about it. It requires courage and humility.

26. **Only Joshua of Nazareth.**

27. **No**. Other's looked to as major messengers of God – like Moses or Muhammad - do have teachings that advocate or justify aggression and/or violence towards others.
28. **Yes, hundreds**. There are many that are said to be given directly by God. For example, "Thus says the Lord of hosts, 'I will punish Amalek for what he did to Israel, how he set himself against him on the way while he was coming up from Egypt. Now go and strike Amalek and utterly destroy all that he has, and do not spare him; but put to death both man and woman, child and infant, ox and sheep, camel and donkey." 1 Sam. 15:2-3.
29. **No**.
30. **No, not necessarily**. It would mean, however, that you would be very accountable for your correct understanding.
31. **Heart** (will), soul (emotions), mind (intellect) and strength.
32. **Yes**.
33. **No**. The Father is disappointed in people's behavior, and the Father is sad over the pain people cause each other, but He is not angry or vengeful or spiteful towards those who bring the harm or conflict.
34. God is **not in control of the people of the earth nor of the natural events of the earth**. God is in control of the realm in which he exists and that does not include the physical realm of the earth.
35. **No**. The main purpose of miracles was to bear witness to who Joshua was. Miracles ceased after he left.
36. **No**, he loves all people the same. He might appreciate or be pleased with a person's heart or actions more than another person's but he values all people equally.
37. **No**. God is against all wrongful conflict and will never side with those engaged in wrongful conflict, even if they claim "Jesus Christ" and pray for God's help.
38. **No**. God does not provide individuals with 'revelations' or other special communications about himself or about events on the earth or in heaven. He spoke once and finally through His Son.
39. **No**, other than you don't dress in order to promote yourself sexually or to purposely offend another individual.
40. **No**, other than you make a reasonable effort at personal hygiene and grooming. He does not care about the color of

your skin or the shape of your flesh or how well you can speak or communicate or how "smart" you are. He only cares about what is inside you, your heart and soul, and thus **how you behave**.

41. **No**. All forms of water baptism are meaningless to God and do nothing for the person.

42. **No**. God exists outside of time and His Son makes it clear that God does not care about one day of the week more or less than another. God wants people to behave rightly during all their waking hours.

43. **No**. He does not intervene in the affairs of men nor the natural events of the earth.

44. The primary purpose of prayer is to help us **build our faith** in our Father and for us to learn to go to Him with the things we suffer or are concerned about.

45. **No**, the single being that is the Creator and Sustainer has one name, but it does not matter to Him what people call him. Rather what matters is that people listen to His Messenger, His Son.

46. **No**. It would depend upon your standard to judge that. According to Joshua of Nazareth, mankind has a predisposition towards evil, not good.

47. **No**. The book of revelation was written by a man who had a spiritual vision which vision provided the content of the book. The part that allegedly represents the words of Joshua of Nazareth has contradictions with the teachings of Joshua of Nazareth as recorded in the gospels. The book itself opens with a falsehood, saying that the things described in it will "soon come to pass", which promise was written some 2,000 years ago.

48. **No**, not with many thousands of divisions, with each division thinking their beliefs and practices are better than the other thousands of divisions, and with that separation preventing love.

49. **No**. Prove this out yourself.

50. Most of the more literal bible translations accurately convey the story, teachings and concepts of Joshua of Nazareth.

51. **Yes, he does**. He does not say when, and in his teachings he both implies it might be a long time as well as suggesting we be ready for it at any time. He also teaches that certain

signs will precede his second coming...signs that are earth wide, catastrophic, and unmistakable...signs which have not yet occurred. See Matt. 24.

52. Paul was the man who supposedly had a vision about Joshua, and **whose letters to other Christians provided the majority of what is called the new testament**. Paul ignored or contradicted (either by ignorance or knowingly) several of Joshua's most important teachings and thus serves as the model – and provides the teachings for - the religious leadership of Christendom that developed after Joshua went back to his Father.

53. If the playground monitor is so loving, why do children get hurt on it? 'If the parent loved the child, why did she allow her son to go parachuting in the first place?' The **Father's love is distinct from his willingness or ability to help people on this earth**. See the next question.

54. **God does not cause evil, nor does He prevent humans from perpetrating it**. Human suffering is caused by humans and natural earth events, not God. God is in control of the realm (or dimension) in which He exists – and force is not the way he governs. It is a common God-belief that God is all powerful including in the physical realm. This is a false belief. We all want the 'security blanket' so to speak, of a belief that God will save us in our dire need. The truth is we need faith to see that leaving this world and being with Him is better than anything this world can provide.

55. **Yes**. Joshua speaks of a place that God created in order to provide justice to Satan and his followers. He also teaches that people can and do send themselves there after they leave their bodies. He also teaches it is a place of suffering. He does not teach that his Father sends people there, but rather people send themselves there. Nor does he teach that people will suffer eternal torment there. Rather, he teaches that people who reject his Father and himself after having accurately heard about them; and those who do not live according to their conscience and thus cause unnecessary conflict and who harm others; send themselves there for just punishment and then destruction.

56. **No**, the Father does not send people to hell. Rather, people send themselves to judgment and destruction.
57. God hears our prayers and He empathizes with us and he has compassion on us, but **He does not intervene in our physical lives**.
58. It is **the Father's spirit somehow apportioned to those who have faith in Joshua**.
59. **No**. See Matt. 20:25-27 & 23:8-10
60. **No**, other than God, the Creator and Designer, did design and create biological life.

Falsehoods, Lies and Destiny

If you have understood Joshua well, you should be able to see at some level what religion is and how it is used to hide and destroy the heavenly Father's will as expressed through Joshua. **Religion is the things people believe and do in the name of God or 'the spiritual', which things have no basis in Joshua's teachings or which contradict or nullify what Joshua says**. Please read the previous sentence slowly and carefully and seek to understand what it means, for this is the very reason people hated and subsequently killed Joshua...because he exposed the falseness and loveless-ness and emptiness and wrongness of mankind's religions.

In the bible/Christian realm, their religion would include – but not be limited to – things like the following:

Religious Belief or Practice	Joshua's Teaching
Looking to "the bible as the word of God".	Joshua is the Word of God to man-kind.
Listening to the religious leaders to understand God and what God wants	Listen to Joshua to understand God and what God wants
Relying on the religious leaders to tell you what Joshua means	Have child-like faith and you will understand Joshua's teachings
'Going to church'	Be the called-out ones
Paying the religious leaders to substitute for Joshua	Follow Joshua
The rituals performed while 'at church'	Joshua does not ask for rituals, but rather for love
Paying a 'tithe' to support the religious organization	God doesn't need nor want money or material things
Substituting worship with singing	Worship in spirit and truth
Having prayer meetings with people praying out loud	When we pray, pray in private and in secret.
Paying to build a religious temple usually called 'the	Use the money to help others

church'	
Paying clergy to say words at weddings and funerals	Have people who actually knew the deceased speak from the heart

Perhaps one of the most powerful things used to control people is fear. Unfortunately, we humans are very susceptible to fear guiding our beliefs and behavior. In truth, we as human beings don't need to be guided by fear. However, we do need another motivation for us to do what is right if we don't have fear guiding us, and that other and higher motivation is **love**. Remember, **the core of God's love is selfless behavior motivated by compassion**. If all people were motivated by *that* love, this world would be a radically different and an infinitely better place.

Unfortunately, this is not so, so in place of the truest love, most have fear motivating them to avoid doing wrong things. In other words, fear would motivate me to do whatever it takes to avoid loss or damage to my person or life...to defend my life in this world. Selfishness motivates me to preserve or advance my own well-being in this world no matter how it might affect others. Fear is a powerful trap due to our selfish nature, **motivating us to protect our self-interests at all costs**. The examples at the beginning of this book in the "Human Beings Fundamental Problem: A Nature Ruled by Self-Pride, Fear and Selfishness" section, are examples of fear working in a selfish human being. Unfortunately, we are not naturally loving and selfless so our default motivation is fear and selfishness.

Political leaders use fear for their political ends when they say things like, 'that nation wants to harm us so we ought to do this...' or, 'those extremists are among us and must be rooted out'. Business leaders use fear when they say things like, 'this bad thing is probably going to happen so you need to buy our products or services to be ready...'; or, 'if you don't have this product or service, people won't like or accept you'; or, 'if we don't make our profit margins, we are all going to be out of jobs'.

Religious leaders use fear when they say things like, 'if you don't believe this, God will be mad at your'; or, 'if you don't do this or if you do that, God will condemn you to hell'. The threat of hell is a very powerful fear motivator, **perhaps the greatest ever created and used by people against others**. Hell, as defined by the religious leaders, is a place of eternal torment...where a person's soul will be tormented forever. Many people will reasonably do whatever they think is necessary to avoid everlasting torture! Thus, most religions, including bible/Christian religion, have been very effective, over the centuries, at controlling many people by fear.

Here is the ultimate fear trap explained in a bit more detail.

Belief 1: Part of God's character is that he is an angry, vengeful, wrathful being, who is eager to want to punish and destroy those people who fail to meet his perfect moral standard – the sinners and transgressors...see the Hebrew scripture to see this.

Belief 1 is false.

Belief 2: Due to that part of God's character of 'holiness', anger, vengeance and wrath, he created a place of eternal torture for those people who don't meet his perfect moral standards.

Belief 2 is false.

Belief 3: Therefore, those who don't meet God's perfect moral standards (*as given and explained by the religious leaders*) – will be sent to eternal torment by God.

Belief 3 is false.

In come the religious leaders with their self-serving religious system to allegedly try and help people avoid hell and instead enter into heaven. What is perhaps the most popular 'protestant' solution to the hell problem? It is something like, 'just believe God's grace and believe this stuff about Jesus and participate in our religious organizations (in reality, give money to us), and you will be heaven bound'.

An historical example of religious leaders using fear for money to enrich themselves is this - much of the billions of dollars of wealth that the leaders who make up and control the Roman Catholic religious system control, came from the fear concepts of purgatory and hell that they propagated and used for **many centuries** to take money from people.

In essence, religious leaders say that if you don't believe and do what "God wants", you are going to hell – a place where you will be tormented forever. In reality, if you don't believe and **do what the religious leaders want** (not God), then they tell you, you are going to hell. Tragically, the religious leaders do not represent Joshua's Father, the Creator...rather, Joshua represents God. As you have seen if you have read and understood his teachings well, Joshua says that he is to be people's life/spiritual leader, not anyone else. And Joshua wants people to actually love one another each day, and not play foolish, selfish, empty games based on men's religion. God does not exist in the little box called "religion" that people put Him in. Rather, He is the great Spirit which created our soul and spirit and He expects human beings to love each other all the time in all contexts of daily life...he expects us to do what is right, chiefly love one another.

The reality is that we ourselves set our after-physical-death-destiny by what we choose to do with the life we were given. **God condemns no one, nor does He send people to hell** – a real place of captivity, justice and destruction - not of eternal torment.

Joshua speaks for the Creator, God and he says:

> **"I did not come to destroy men's lives, but to save them".**

> **"For God so loved the people of the earth, that He gave His only begotten Son, that whoever puts their faith in him shall not destroy themselves, but rather have eternal life. For God did not send the Son into the world to judge the world, but that the world might be saved through Him."**

Most religious leaders teach that **what you *believe*** is what determines if God sends you to heaven or hell. There are two falsehoods and one truth in that statement. One falsehood is that what one believes is solely responsible for one's after-physical-death destiny. The other falsehood is that God determines a person's destiny. The truth is that a person's beliefs do play a role in determining one's destiny, but only a role, not the sole determining factor.

Finding Eternal Life Amidst the Darkness

Joshua teaches that ***our choices*** around **faith, beliefs and behavior** are what will determine where we end up after our body dies. We determine our after-physical-death destiny by our choices regarding these three things.

1. **Whether we choose to trust – which is to place our faith in - God**. An act of our heart or will illuminated by our soul.

Faith is required to enter into Life. It is best to place one's faith in the Creator Father revealed by the only person in history to defeat death to prove that all he said about God was true. In other words, we can place our faith in the right thing (the Father revealed by Joshua) or the wrong thing(s) (ourselves; money; a god of our own making or the making of religious leaders like the many 'jesus" of christianity; etc.). Faith is what causes us to be properly motivated to execute the third point below. If we place our faith in a god that we are confused about or wrong about, that will likely lead to wrong behavior and that will hinder us or prevent us from attaining the Life the Life offers.

2. **What we choose to believe ABOUT God (not whether he exists or not).** An intellectual act of the mind.

A person only has two choices regarding the things they believe about God. One is to believe Joshua of Nazareth, and thus believe right things about the Creator. Two, is to believe one or more of the many other voices – both dead voices still speaking from books, living people, or self – who claim to know God, what God is like and what God wants. Those who choose the former – those who listen only to Joshua of Nazareth to understand God – will have the best opportunity to **truly know the Living Creator God**. Please listen to the Light regarding the importance of knowing the true and living God...

..."and **this is eternal life, that you might know God** and the one whom He sent"...

Furthermore, to know God is to love Him and to love Him includes doing what He wants. Those who choose to listen to people other than Joshua of Nazareth (or in addition to Joshua of Nazareth), will at best be confused about God, and at worst, will be badly wrong about God. The people who make up the world's religions make this critical mistake – Muslim, Jew, Hindi, Christian, etc. To have wrong beliefs about God, His Person and His desire for human beings, will prevent us or hinder us from attaining the Life the Life offers.

3. **Whether we choose to DO what God says we ought to do**.

Finally, we should do what the true and living God says. Why? Because He created human beings and knows his intent for those created beings...He had a purpose for creating us, and His Messenger provided that purpose. His Son, the Messenger, Joshua of Nazareth, says that a primary way to manifest our love for our Father is to do what He says. Is that not true of parental human relationships? In other words, if our child loves us, won't they want to please us by doing what we ask? And what God wants us to do is not difficult at all...

The true and living God's top priority is that human beings love and thereby care for one another. Yes, it is that simple :)

Furthermore, our choice in making God's appointed Leader our Leader will cause us to be in unity, harmony, peace with other followers and cause a desire to help others through the things that we do. If we don't do that, then we fail at the primary purpose of the life we were given, and again, this will prevent us from attaining the Life the Life offers. We need to change into better human beings...real, measurable progress, for this is what proves we are doing what He says and thus actually improving as a human being.

In summary, it does matter what we believe about God and our existence. **But what matters equally as much is whether we actually place our faith in the correct God, and how we choose to live our lives each day.** In other words and for example, there are hundreds of millions of people who say something to the effect of, 'oh yes, I am a christian and I believe in the lord jesus christ', but then the next moment they will justify killing their enemies; or they will seldom or never speak his important truths to others; or they will not significantly share any of their material things with non-natural-family members; or they will deceive others to gain money; or they will very seldom treat others the way they want to be treated; or a many other things which contradict the Light's teachings! So, their stated beliefs will not help them...will not bring them into everlasting Life, but will only serve to bring greater self-condemnation upon themselves. The more we know, the more accountable we will be for acting upon what we say we know.

Many will respond to these truths by saying, 'well, you are right back to fear as the primary motivating for listening to God, because you are saying that if we don't listen to God, then we condemn ourselves to destruction'. That is a false or incorrect statement. God did not create fear nor does He use it to motivate or manipulate free-will human beings. Rather, people are trapped IN THEIR OWN FEAR, and this in spite of the true Creator's love and His reaching out to us in love. Self-condemnation is a consequence of our choices to enter into, and then remain in, the state of self-pride and fear and selfishness, and NO ONE has to choose to remain in that state of being. Joshua came and offers anyone who will listen to HIM the key to open our self-made jail cell and thus be truly free.

Humans are not neutral beings, meaning we are predisposed to a state of self-pride and fear and selfishness due to our nature. Our choice is simple to understand but difficult to make. Remain bound or guided by our nature of self-pride and fear and selfishness, or reach out past ourselves to the One who can set us free...the One who can lift us out of our self-made pit.

The correct question is not, 'how come God...', but rather, 'why don't I want to practice love as God defines that and asks of me'?

Why is it wrong for the Creator to have set it up that free-will beings would need to choose love (as HE defines that) in order to be rewarded with the Greater Life? Why would that be unjust?

God gave us our soul and gave us a free will to choose what to do with the life he gave us on this earth. You fault Him for giving you life? You would prefer to never have existed? What about, 'it is better to have loved and lost than to never have loved at all'? Do you believe that is a true saying? What it is saying is that love is perhaps the most important aspect of human existence and to not experience or practice love is to miss out on the most important aspect of human existence...to miss the purpose of why we were created to begin with. And that 'missing' was not God's fault, but ours.

Is that not also true about existence? In other words, it is better to have existed and been given the chance and opportunity to better ones self and preserve one's existence (through faith and love) than to have never existed at all. We don't have to choose to condemn and destroy ourselves by a life lived in bondage to self-pride, fear and selfishness and all the wrong behavior those things bring...there is a Way out of that darkness.

Primary Manifestations of Self-Pride and Fear and Selfishness for the Average Christian

Here are some examples of the Christian or biblian's response to the disciple of Joshua repeating Joshua's truths that the Christian does not agree with...

Example 1:

- 'You think you know more than leader /pastor /bishop /scholar /author so-and-so? Who do you think you are?'

    - This is an example of the logical fallacy of appeal to authority. It is a pride based objection not based on reason. The proper reaction to hearing something different would be, "Oh, that is a real and interesting difference...I need to check that out".

Example 2:

- 'I've read the bible many times, studied it for many years, and I know what it says and you are wrong.'

    - This is an example of the logical fallacy of appeal to expert opinion. It is a pride based objection not based on reason. The proper reaction would be to take one of the "truths" the disciple is stating, and provide reasons why it is wrong.

Example 3:

- 'Are you saying that all the leaders of Christian religion are wrong.'
    - This is an example of the logical fallacy of argument from incredulity. It is a pride based objection not based on reason. The proper reaction would be to consider what Joshua of Nazareth said, find the quote to validate it is accurate and in context, and evaluate the claim to see if it is true.

Two Enlightening Conversations

Following are two typical conversations this author has had with Christians of all stripes. DJ stands for Disciple of Joshua and AC stands for Average Christian.

The Christianity Conversation:

DJ	Did you know that Christianity - as represented by the leaders of all its divided organizations (what are often referred to as denominations or churches) - does not represent the person or teachings of Jesus of Nazareth accurately?
AC	I don't think I heard you right...could you please say that again?
DJ	Sure. Did you know that Christianity - as represented by the leaders of all its divided organizations (what are often referred to as denominations or churches) - do not represent the person or teachings of Jesus of Nazareth accurately?
AC	OK. I just wanted to be sure. So, you are saying that all those Christian leaders are wrong about the person they call Jesus Christ?
DJ	Well, they do have some facts about him correct, like he was a real person who lived some 2,000 years ago. But yes, in general, they have one thing in common...they disregard his most important teachings regarding what God wants for human beings and instead substitute their religion. That is why there is so much division and so little love among Christians.
AC	Wow. I don't even know how to process that. So, you think you know more than all those Th.D. and PhD theologians who spend their lives studying the bible and writing books about God? (*Logical fallacy, argument from incredulity.*)
DJ	Well, what I know is the person and teachings of Joshua of Nazareth since I am one of his followers. I don't claim anything regarding other people's knowledge. I just know what Joshua teaches...he alone is my standard of truth regarding God claims, and my Standard says they are, in general, fundamentally wrong.

AC	OK, so what is the main thing the hundreds of millions of people who identify with some Christian label have wrong about Jesus?
DJ	They don't listen to HIM and thus they don't love one another as he defines that...they treat each other just like any other people groups like Jews or French or agnostics or whatever...
AC	What do you mean they don't love one another? I don't hear about a lot of conflict among Christian denominations or sects?
DJ	Well, I guess northern Ireland between the Catholics and protestants doesn't count? However, that is not the main point. The main point is this - love is not about lack of conflict. Love is about sharing life together; caring for one another without asking for money to do so. Love draws people together to help one another...love makes a tight group of people sharing their lives together. This, the vast majority of Christians do not do.
AC	What do you mean? Christians go to church and have friends?
DJ	Yes, they do. And Muslims go to Mosque and have friends. And Jews go to synagogue and have friends, etc. That is not love as defined by Joshua of Nazareth. That is merely gathering in the same place due to a shared belief about God, and having friends like anyone else. Even evil people have friends, you know.
AC	OK, so what are you saying? That people ought to live together like some kind of commune or cult? (Logical fallacy, appeal to fear.)
DJ	Well, those are strong fear words-concepts you use in order to bias the truth I am trying to share with you. Whatever ideological baggage you associate with the term "commune" for example, is causing you to reject the simple truth I am sharing with you...that people who truly love each other are together, not apart.
AC	Listen, all I know is that it is not normal for people who are not related by blood or law to live together.
DJ	Perhaps what is "normal" in the world is loveless-ness? Perhaps you don't have true love for other people or others

	don't truly love you? Perhaps you are part of what is "normal" and thus part of the problem?
AC	Yeah, well, whatever...obviously the Christians have it right and you have it wrong.
DJ	Why? Because the Christians live no differently than any other people group and thus you are comfortable with them? They will not say you are wrong nor ask you to change nor ask you to do anything that you might think will put you at risk for what you want out of this life – thus, you like them.
AC	What is wrong with that? Live and let live. I don't need anyone and what I have I have worked for and deserve is mine to do what I want with.
DJ	Include not sharing your life or your material things with others, correct?
AC	I don't know what you are talking about with this 'sharing your life' stuff. And I am not obligated to share my stuff with anyone except maybe some of my family.
DJ	Perhaps your not knowing what I am talking about proves my point that Christians live a life bound by self-pride and fear and selfishness, just like the vast majority of the rest of the people on the planet.
AC	Yeah, well, you seem to be the only one saying God wants people to live like a cult.
DJ	So, you define people caring more about each other than about material things – which is what love causes people to do - a "cult"?
AC	All I know is that what you are saying goes against the bible and thus what you are saying is not true.
DJ	But doesn't your bible say in the second chapter of the book of Acts, "And all those who had believed were together and had all things in common; and they began selling their property and possessions and were sharing them with all, as anyone might have need."?
AC	Yeah, well our senior pastor is always warning us to be careful to understand the culture at the time things were written in the bible so we can have a proper understanding.
DJ	So, principles to live by given by Jesus of Nazareth – who said he speaks for the unchanging eternal God - regarding basic human relationships and behavior, can change

	depending upon the culture at the time?
AC	Yes.
DJ	So, then, doesn't that principle essentially nullify all objective concepts of truth in the bible? In other words, when, for example, Jesus says, "love your enemy", that all important principle may not mean what it says because Jesus said that in a different culture about 2,000 years ago?
AC	Well, yes, I suppose so, because no good American is going to love a Russian or North Korean, for example, because those people are evil.
DJ	Well, it appears you will only listen to what you want to hear, and that you will use religious relativism as taught by your religious leaders, to explain away those things that you are not willing to receive or do...like "love one another".
AC	Whatever. You have your interpretation and I have mine. Later, dude.

The Bible is Not God's Word Conversation

DJ	Did you know that the bible is not God's Word to mankind like most contemporary religious leaders teach?
AC	You must be kidding? Most Christians – and we are talking many millions of people over many centuries – have believed that the bible is God's Word and you are saying it is not? (False argument, appeal to popularity.)
DJ	Well, I'm not sure how you could objectively prove your contention that millions of people believed that the bible is God's Word over the past many centuries? But OK, if you want to believe that, that is fine. However, the number of people believing something is not a legitimate means to determine if something is true. At one point in history, most people believed the earth was flat.
AC	Well, the apostle Paul says that all scripture is inspired of God, so who are you to dispute Paul? (False argument, appeal to authority.)
DJ	Well, I am just a follower of the One who defeated death to prove what he taught was true. He is my standard for knowing what is true about God or not. And he never said that the Holy Spirit would guide a bunch of authors to write

373

	God's thoughts down and that those writings would be compiled into a book. Rather, Joshua said that HIS PERSON and HIS WORDS were revealing his Father and his Father's desire for mankind.
AC	But the scripture says that the bible is God's Word. (False argument, circular reasoning.)
DJ	Well, that is both a false statement as well as circular reasoning which also is a logical fallacy. The bible does not contain any statement that says, "the bible is God's Word".
AC	Yes it does, Paul says, "All Scripture is inspired by God".
DJ	Yes, Paul does say that, but Paul is not talking about "the bible" when he refers to "scripture". You have taken that out of context and have made a wrong assumption. In writing to Timothy, Paul says in the prior sentence, "and that from childhood you have known the sacred writings which are able to give you the wisdom that leads to salvation". He was talking to Timothy and refers to "the sacred writings" meaning "scripture", which Timothy had known "from childhood". So Paul was plainly talking about the Hebrew scripture that Timothy, a Jew, grew up hearing, NOT what would later be called "the new testament". So, when Paul said, "All scripture", he plainly was referring to what you call the old testament.
AC	Well, that is your interpretation.
DJ	Well, I don't see how "from childhood" is open to interpretation given what we know about when Paul's letter of second Timothy was written. Clearly the new testament was not written nor compiled when Timothy was a child nor even when Paul wrote that letter to Timothy...these are facts I encourage you to validate.
AC	Yeah, well you are a nutcase who rejects what everyone knows is true. (Logical fallacy, personal attack instead of arguing facts.)
DJ	In addition, the bible does identify the "Word of God", and it is Jesus of Nazareth, not a book people call 'the bible'. See John 1:1, Luke 1:2 and Rev. 19:13. Instead of listening to Paul's opinions about God and his Hebrew view of his Hebrew scripture, why don't you listen to the One who says, "You search the Scriptures because you think that **in them**

	you have eternal life; it is these that testify about **me**; and yet you are unwilling to come to **me** so that you may have life."
AC	I do listen to Jesus, but I also listen to the bible.
DJ	But he just said you should not look to the bible or the scriptures to have life. And he also says, "If you continue in **my word**, then you are truly disciples of mine; and you will know the truth, and the truth will make you free." Why do you continue to look to 'the bible' or 'the scripture', when he says don't do that and that freedom lies in his words/truths alone?
AC	Well, there are thousands of christian leaders who disagree with you. (False argument. Appeal to popularity or authority.)
DJ	In addition, how can you listen to Jesus who says, "love your enemies" while at the same time listen to the writers of the Hebrew scripture who say essentially, "hate and kill your enemies"?
AC	Well, God is both wrathful and loving...there is no contradiction.
DJ	Well, then you are not looking to Jesus to understand God, since Jesus never once said his Father was a Being of wrath and instead says his Father is a Being of compassion. In addition, if you would stop and think for a moment, what kind of a person/being could simultaneously be both motivated by anger, wrath and vengeance towards other people and at the same time love them? Or stated another way, how could a person/being have a nature of both eager to punish and destroy and at the same time be desiring to show mercy or love?
AC	All I know is that the bible is true and you are a fool for rejecting that simple truth. (Non-reasoned, defensive pride response.)
DJ	Well, a single book that contains contradictions regarding a single subject is not true, your non-reasoned, religious objection notwithstanding.
AC	The bible does not contain contradictions. (False statement)
DJ	So, in 1 Sam. 15, the Hebrew scripture has God ordering Saul to take vengeance on their enemies and kill thousands of women, children and even young infants. At the same time,

	God, who doesn't change, has His Son telling mankind, "Love your enemies".
AC	Like I said, God is both a God of wrath and a God of love.
DJ	Seems like those women, children and infants would have a hard time appreciating the "love of God". Perhaps the simple truth is that the god of the Hebrew scriptures is a different god than the God revealed by Jesus of Nazareth. At best, the Hebrew god is a schizophrenic, un-principled being who is mostly an angry, vengeful, wrathful being most of the time, desiring the killing of one's enemies; and a god of mercy some very little of the time. I would suggest you try and imagine a person who was like that and envision what they would be like. I think if you were honest, you would see they would likely be classified as at best, unstable or deranged or at worst, violently insane.
AC	God's ways are not our ways...God is God and can do what he likes.
DJ	True, but the same can be said of any tyrant or dictator. **The issue is one of character, not authority**. Any being who orders the slaughter of women, children and even infants is evil and not worthy to be listened to.
AC	But God could foresee that those women, children and infants of the Amalekite people would grow up to do evil.
DJ	OK, so let me get this right. God could foresee that all those thousands of women, children and infants would go on to live lives of evil, and so God had them all destroyed, correct?
AC	Yes.
DJ	So, why did god not kill all the Nazi's and their children? Or Pol Pot and his group's children? Or Genghis Khan and his group's children? I would suggest that there have been a whole lot more people in history, other than the perceived enemies of the descendants of Jacob at the time the book of 1 Samuel was written, who were evil. Usually, adult men like, say, Hitler or Stalin more recently, or some of the Caesars like Nero back in those days. Why did God, being God, not use surgical strikes to take them out? Would that not be the best way to handle that? Was he not able to foresee the evil of Hitler, for example? For that matter, I don't see many women leaders of evil in history...so, why kill all the infant

	girls?
AC	God does what God does and who are we to question him? (Implied threat of authority.)
DJ	We are beings that have the capacity to use reason to determine what is true and what is false. Again, yes, if the god you speak of existed, he could do what he wanted. But if he does evil – like kill infants - or 'speaks' falsehoods, he is not worthy of respect or of listening to. I can't speak for others, but I am a follower of the Light of the world and he doesn't ask me to check my mind in at the door when thinking about God things. Rather, he asks that I make good and right moral judgements and reason well. Furthermore, he tells me that God, his Father, does not kill people, nor want to kill people, nor does he want one group to kill another, nor does God order the killing of one people group by another. Why don't you try listening to the real Jesus of Nazareth instead of the one created by the religious leaders?
AC	Well I guess we have different Gods.
DJ	Yes, my God, the One who Jesus of Nazareth says is his and our Father, is a God of love...that is the defining aspect of His nature. Yes, He is also a perfect being who only expresses that which is true, and does not err nor does He ever do what is wrong. He hates violence among his created ones, human beings. For that matter, He is grieved at the lack of love among his created ones. Indeed, we do have different Gods. Why not switch to the true and living God of love and enter into Life?

Religious Fear and Pride: An Impenetrable Wall

How many people have been, are, and will be harmed due to the manifestations or behavior that are associated with religious fear and pride? Well, we can answer the "have been" as it has been many millions of people – probably hundreds of millions of people - and that is not counting the Nazi persecution of the Jews.

Here is an example of the religious fear and pride dynamic played out.
Person 1 says something about God that contradicts challenges or calls into question person 2's beliefs about God. Person 2 says to themselves some form of the statement, "Oh, if I am wrong about God, I might be rejected by God and perhaps sent to hell". That statement is a fear-based statement.

Person 2's next thought is something to the effect of, "Well, I have all these intelligent people I respect who gave me my beliefs about God (or 'I studied the scripture myself...') and they (or I) can't all be wrong, so I am correct and that other person is wrong." This is a statement of self-pride. Reason is not used to arrive at truth, rather, current beliefs are defended.

Person 2 then says to person 1, some form of the statement, 'Sorry, but you are wrong about God for this reason...' If person 1 does not 'admit' they were wrong, but rather uses reason well to try and show person 2 they are wrong, then the mixture of fear and self-pride will often turn into hatred. Hatred is a strong dislike of another person who one perceives as having wronged them in some way; or strong dislike by seeing a person as against them or somehow threatening them and thus worthless and worthy of punishment, harm or death.

This simple dynamic - while not comprehensive and while coming in slightly different forms - has played itself out probably trillions of times over the millennia among human beings. Sometimes it just leads to merely a disagreement between two people. Sometimes, it leads to war with countless thousands or millions killing each other in the name of God. One thing is certain, though, fear and pride are at the heart of it. Not necessary fear of the other person, but rather **fear of God due to ignorance**...fear of what God might do to me if I am wrong about who He is or what He wants of me. And of course, basic self-pride which says, 'I am not wrong'.

A disciple of Joshua will experience this dynamic regularly if they are faithful in speaking the Light's truths to people they encounter. Here is how it usually plays out. The disciple is talking to a religious person, and hears the religious person say something that is contrary to what the Light of the world teaches. The disciple will quote or convey the teaching or saying of Joshua that demonstrates the error in the religious person's belief about God. The religious person will oftentimes be offended to some degree and want to argue with the disciple.

The disciple might make some clarifications as to why the belief is wrong as the discussion progresses. If the religious person will not listen to the Light's teaching but instead will try and defend their error, the tone for the religious person will often demonstrate the self-pride or fear that is driving their effort to hold onto a wrong belief.

At some point - usually when the disciple uses reason well several times to try and show the person their error - the religious person will move from fear to self-pride and start making personal attacks on the disciple. Since the disciple is using reason well to demonstrate the other person's false beliefs; and the person with wrong beliefs is bound by self-pride or fear; the person with wrong beliefs will normally respond with personal attacks, and so they attack the messenger instead of humble themselves and receive truth.

What personal, fear-based attacks are most common? Some of the most popular attacks from biblians and christians are calling the disciple a "heretic" or "a cult leader" or "part of a cult". The biblian or christian who has failed in their argument(s) has two choices - be humble and accept the truth the disciple is trying to convey, or let fear and self-pride drive them to attack the messenger. Sadly, the latter is the most common response.

So, what exactly is a "heretic" or a "heresy"? Merriam-Webster says "heresy" is "adherence to a religious opinion contrary to church dogma"; "an opinion, doctrine, or practice contrary to the truth or to generally accepted beliefs or standards". Thus a "heretic" is a person who holds an opinion or doctrine or belief that is contrary to "church dogma" or "generally accepted beliefs or standards".

So, the question is, who determines the correct "church dogma" or "generally accepted beliefs or standards"? The roman catholic people and the protestant people cannot even agree on what books to include in their 'sacred scripture' or bible and has called the 'other side' heretics - and killed them - for centuries! In fact, the biblian/christian religious system is made up of thousands of divisions, which divisions are caused by one sects/denominations religious opinions or dogma differing from the others!

The biblians and christians seem to thrive on excommunicating one another - by some estimates, there are tens of thousands of divisions - and often in their forming a new sect/division, the reason they give was that their previous sect was starting to "adopt heresy" or that 'God has given this guy/gal some new important revelation'. Ironically, the new teaching that causes the division is often offered by some charismatic individual who says some version of "god says listen to me". Why is this ironic? See the definition of "cult" below!

How about the "cult" accusation and attack? Merriam-Webster defines "cult" as, "a small religious group that is not part of a larger and more accepted religion and that has beliefs regarded by many people as extreme or dangerous"; or, "great devotion to a person, idea, object, movement, or work."

Here is Wiki's shot at "cult" - "In the sociological classifications of religious movements in English, a cult is a religious or social group with socially deviant or novel beliefs and practices. However, whether any particular group's beliefs and practices are sufficiently deviant or novel is often unclear, thus making a precise definition problematic. In the English speaking world, the word often carries derogatory connotations, but in other European languages, it is used as English-speakers use the word "religion", sometimes causing confusion for English-speakers reading material translated from other languages. The word "cult" has always been controversial because it is (in a pejorative sense) considered a subjective term, used as an ad hominem attack against groups with differing doctrines or practices, which lacks a clear or consistent definition."

Wiki's description hits the nail on the head in two respects. First, they recognize the lack of authoritative standard to judge "whether any particular group's beliefs and practices are sufficiently deviant or novel". Which of the thousands of sects which have divide from, or excommunicated each other makes that judgment?! Second, the term is often used as an ad hominem attack (personal attack) against a person or other group who does not tow the party line of the religious person (or their sect or division or denomination) who is leveling the accusation.

I find the accusation of "cult" by biblians and christians against disciples of Joshua like myself as particularly ironic and irrational. Here are two reasons that show the accusation is based on fear and/or self-pride and not on reason or the teachings of Joshua of Nazareth.

1. We disciples have "Jesus Christ" (specifically, the words of the historical Jesus or Joshua of Nazareth as recorded in the four gospel books) as our ONLY Standard for knowing God just as he says we ought! Odd that that would be such a problem or offense for those who claim "Jesus Christ" as their God!

2. Those who define "cult" as more of this - "great devotion to a person" - seem to be quite blind to the fact that many of their religious leaders are venerated and 'followed' by their congregations, thus fulfilling the definition of "cult"!

Ironically, we as disciples of Joshua seek to follow ONLY the historical Joshua of Nazareth revealed by his own words in the four gospel books! In other words, we disciples seek very hard to NOT receive the adoration of other people towards us since our Master says "do not call another person a spiritual leader or teacher"...rather, we point people towards the Light instead of ourselves and we do NOT take authority over others.

381

In contrast, the religious world (just like the other world realms, like entertainment, for example) is filled with men and women who clearly have many followers who are devoted to THEM to some degree, and those religious leaders eagerly encourage this adoration since they like the power and influence over of those people. In fact, the number of devoted followers is a big part of how those religious leaders claim their 'ministry' is a success. In short, many christian leaders and sects fit the world's definition of "cult leaders" and "cult"!

In truth, any God-belief that varies from a religious person's beliefs - and whatever sect they are a part of - if spoken with conviction and shown plainly to contradict what the religious person considers their core or foundational beliefs or 'church doctrine' - will likely be judged as 'heresy' or 'cultic' and thus those who hold it a 'heretic' or part of a 'cult'.

In truth, throwing "heretic" or "cult leader" at someone is done so by a person who is losing or has lost the 'truth' battle and is operating in their own insecurity and through fear and/or self-pride and thus attacking the messenger. Those who resort to name calling are insecure in their own beliefs and cannot use reason to defend their beliefs well.

In times past and in certain places, that could get a person burned at the stake. In many nations still today, you might well be killed for expressing a God-belief that goes against the ruling or majority groups 'accepted orthodoxy'. In the U.S., you are shunned, cast out, slandered as a 'heretic' or 'cult' by the religious people...and no doubt in some areas, killed.

In conclusion, religious fear and pride cause a huge amount of conflict in the world - it always has and it always will. Human's 'operating system', as given by their Creator, includes a conscience which knows at some level that having a proper understanding of one's existence and what to do with that existence/life - and the likely Cause of one's existence - is very important. Thus God-beliefs are a very sensitive issue for many billions of people...and that sensitivity is caused by fear of the Unknown God. Whether Christian or Muslim or Jew, etc. - they all have the same scary, vengeful, wrathful god who, they have been taught, sends many to hell - one of the **great lies that the religious people of the world create and believe in order to stay away from** the Creator and His Light/Messenger.

The good news is that you don't have to be afraid of your Creator...you don't have to be ruled or controlled or heavily influenced by fear. Nor do you have to put yourself in a cage of ignorance created by your self-pride. All you need to do is to care about what is true and right no matter where that leads you, and if you do, you will find the Life He so much wants you to enter into!

The Great Religious Delusion

Here is Merriam-Webster's definition of "Delusion":

"A persistent false psychotic belief regarding the self or persons or objects outside the self that is maintained despite indisputable evidence to the contrary."

Surely most religious people are in fact, delusional. However, just because the average religious person has false beliefs about God does not mean that God does not exist. It simply means they are wrong about some or many aspects of God...wrong about His character, nature or abilities.

Some of the more prominent and ubiquitous beliefs that most mono-theistic religious people hold about God that are clearly delusional are the beliefs that God is all-powerful (Omnipotent), all-knowing/seeing (Omniscient), all-places-at-once (Omnipresent) and loving/merciful. Together these beliefs form a very clear and plain logical fallacy.

For people/beings who truly love another person/being and who have the ability to save/prevent/protect that other person/being will surely intervene to do so. It is one of the most basic characteristics of true love...to sacrifice one's self to help another.

And here is the undeniable logic showing the error of the biblian/religious people's beliefs...therefore, God who is both all-powerful in all realms as well as loving/merciful would surely help the person experiencing wrongful harm. Surely if God is both all-powerful in all realms as well as having love for all people, then He would, for example, not let the 5 year old girl suffer horrible, damaging abuse. God not helping the innocent having evil perpetrated on them is no different than the scenario of a two-hundred and fifty pound strong man seeing a sniveling pervert abusing a young child and doing NOTHING about it.

The simple truth is that people make up gods to help assuage, alleviate or quell their fear. Everyone wants a 'superman' to be 'watching their back'. One of the most popular beliefs among the monotheistic religions is that God is all powerful, and thus, he can protect me in this scary place people call the world. However, having false or delusional beliefs to handle fear is not a good solution to the problem! False beliefs about God does nothing but help people who don't believe He exists justify their unbelief.

It is really very simple IF you are going to allow truth to shape your beliefs...IF God is all powerful in this realm people call the world; AND he loves me/'his people' ('especially me since I belong to the right religion'); THEN God will not let harm come to me, since people/beings who love don't allow harm to come to those they love if they can prevent it. Is this not the thinking of religious people? And don't the facts of daily life on this earth scream of the falsehood of that belief?

I encourage the reader to reject or not adopt false beliefs about anything, including God. If the reader is a Christian or biblian, I exhort you to come out from the Great Delusion that is your religion.

There is much we cannot verify about the One the Light called "my Father in heaven". But equally true, is there is much we can verify regarding claims about God that either do or do not stand the test of reason and logic. Which leads to the final section of this book.

Perhaps Life's Most Important Question:
Am I Part of the Problem or Part of the Solution?

These statements are true of you and me...

We are either part of the problem or part of the solution. We are either actively being and bringing the Solution, or we are not, and thus we are part of the problem.

We must be free ourselves before we can effectively help others find freedom.

Sound reason – which leads to truth - will lead me to the One who can help me.

Without practicing and experiencing true love with others, we are missing the primary purpose of our existence, and we are not fulfilling the desire of our Creator Father.

We are either part of the problem of human conflict, or we are part of the solution by being peacemakers bringing the Leader, the Prince of Peace, people need. Not the 'christ' of Christianity, but the real, actual Light of the world who can only be properly known by his own words as captured and preserved in the four 'gospel' books.

We either care about what is true and right regarding human life, relationships and God, or we don't. That is, we either lend our voice and efforts in the fight for what is true and right, or we don't and sit silently in our selfish bubble and like billions of others, live a largely loveless and/or wasted existence and neglect, harm or destroy ourselves and one another.

What kind of person are you? Are YOU part of the problem or part of the solution? Do YOU know the Leader and are YOU bringing that leader to others? While a moral standard is good, it is NOT the solution since people need a reason to hold to a moral standard. While being a 'kind' person is good, it is NOT the solution, since kindness is not love and for that matter, people need a reason to be kind. No, the solution is a Leader who can both provide the 'rules' for human life as well as motivate us to want to hold to them.

If you are confused about that, then let me state the question in a different way. Are YOU listening to the Light of the world and both practicing and proclaiming his truths, or not? It is a simple question that deserves a simple and true answer.

Please don't deceive yourself if you are a Christian, thinking that because you are a Christian, you are part of the solution; or because you hold to some moral standard you are part of the solution; or that you don't harm others you are part of the solution. Sadly, Christians are not only not part of the problem, but their religion nullifies and/or hides the True Solution and makes it difficult for people to find him. To sit in your buildings you call 'the church' and to sing songs about God-stuff and do your little rituals, is offensive to the One you call your God...and since you claim you can see, your self-condemnation will remain.

Are you one of those who are aware in your soul how your own life has not been going well and who, due to Joshua's teachings, now see how far short you fall of God's intention for a human being? Do you see you are not practicing love as Joshua defines love? I hope this describes you, dear reader. If this is you, do what Joshua says. Deeply regret your own failed leadership of your life – or choosing the wrong people to trust or to lead you - and how you have hurt other people with your pride, fear or selfishness and the wrong that flows from those things. Deeply regret how you have ignored your heavenly Father and His love for you, and how you have not made **any significant effort to love Him back** or the many people around you. And then, fall before the King asking for forgiveness, and he will lift you up, and he will say with compassion, "I forgive you", and, "come, follow me" :)

For a fuller explanation or elaboration of the above concepts, please see our web site at www.thepeacefulrevolution.info

www.ingramcontent.com/pod-product-compliance
Lightning Source LLC
Chambersburg PA
CBHW070118100426
42744CB00010B/1852